ASSESSING THE PUBLIC LIBRARY PLANNING PROCESS

Information Management, Policy, and Services
Peter Hernon, Editor

Technology and Library Information Services
  Carol Anderson and Robert Hauptman
Information Policies
  Robert H. Burger
Organizational Decision Making and Information Use
  Mairéad Browne
Library Performance Accountability and Responsiveness: Essays in Honor of Ernest R. DeProspo
  Charles C. Curran and F. William Summers
Gatekeepers in Ethnolinguistic Communities
  Cheryl Metoyer-Duran
Curriculum Initiative: An Agenda and Strategy for Library Media Programs
  Michael B. Eisenberg and Robert E. Berkowitz
Resource Companion to Curriculum Initiative: An Agenda and Strategy for Library Media Programs
  Michael B. Eisenberg and Robert E. Berkowitz
Information Problem-Solving: The Big Six Skills Approach to Library & Information Skills Instruction
  Michael B. Eisenberg and Robert E. Berkowitz
Research for School Library Media Specialists
  Kent R. Gustafson and Jane Bandy Smith
The Role and Importance of Managing Information for Competitive Positions in Economic Development
  Keith Harman
A Practical Guide to Managing Information for Competitive Positioning in Economic Development
  Keith Harman
Librarianship: The Erosion of a Woman's Profession
  Roma Harris
Microcomputer Software for Performing Statistical Analysis: A Handbook for Supporting Library Decision Making
  Peter Hernon and John V. Richardson (Editors)
Public Access to Government Information, Second Edition
  Peter Hernon and Charles R. McClure
Statistics for Library Decision Making: A Handbook
  Peter Hernon, et al.
Libraries: Partners in Adult Literacy
  Deborah Johnson, Jane Robbins, and Douglas L. Zweizig
Information Seeking as a Process of Construction
  Carol Kuhlthau
Library and Information Science Research: Perspective and Strategies for Improvement
  Charles R. McClure and Peter Hernon (Editors)
U.S. Government Information Policies: Views and Perspectives
  Charles R. McClure, Peter Hernon, and Harold C. Relyea
U.S. Scientific and Technical Information Policies: Views and Perspectives
  Charles C. McClure and Peter Hernon
Assessing the Public Library Planning Process
  Annabel K. Stephens

For Information Specialists
  Howard White, Marcia Bates, and Patrick Wilson
Public Library Youth Services: A Public Policy Approach
  Holly G. Willett

In Preparation:
Meaning and Method in Information Studies
  Ian Cornelius
Service Quality in Academic Libraries
  Peter Hernon and Ellen Altman
Women in the History of American Librarianship
  Suzanne Hildenbrand (Editor)
Knowledge Diffusion in the U.S. Aerospace Industry
  Thomas E. Pinelli et al.

ASSESSING THE PUBLIC LIBRARY PLANNING PROCESS

Annabel K. Stephens
University of Alabama

Ablex Publishing Corporation
Norwood, New Jersey

Copyright © 1995 by Ablex Publishing Corporation

All rights reserved. No part of this publication may be reproduced, stored in a retrieval system, or transmitted, in any form or by any means, electronic, mechanical, photocopying, microfilming, recording, or otherwise, without permission of the publisher.

Printed in the United States of America.

Library of Congress Cataloging-in-Publication Data
Stephens, Annabel.
    Assessing the public library planning process / Annabel K. Stephens.
    p. cm.
    ISBN 1-56750-186-9 (cloth : alk. paper). — ISBN 1-56750-187-7 (pbk. : alk. paper)
    1. Public libraries—Planning. 2. Public libraries—United States—Planning. I. Title
Z678.S72 1995
027.4—dc20   95-31310
                                                                                              CIP

Ablex Publishing Corporation
355 Chestnut Street
Norwood, NJ 07648

Contents

List of Figures/Tables	ix
Acknowledgments	xi
Preface	xiii
1 Comprehensive Planning and the Public Library Planning Process	
Comprehensive Planning for Libraries	2
Description of *A Planning Process for Public Libraries*	10
Libraries' Experiences with *A Planning Process for Public Libraries*	12
Summary	23
2 Lessons Learned From Libraries' Experiences with *A Planning Process for Public Libraries*	25
Author's Conclusions Based on Three Southern Libraries' Experiences	26
Recommendations of Librarians and Others Who Used and Studied *A Planning Process for Public Libraries*	46
Lessons Learned and Recommendations for Revising the 1980 Planning Manual	53
Summary	57
3 The Revised Planning Manual: *Planning and Role Setting for Public Libraries: A Manual of Options and Procedures*	59
Introducing *Planning and Role Setting for Public Libraries*	60
Description of *Planning and Role Setting for Public Libraries*	62
How Does *Planning and Role Setting* Differ From *A Planning Process*?	64
Extent of Libraries' Use of *Planning and Role Setting for Public Libraries*	68
Published Reports, Studies and Critiques of Libraries' Use of *Planning and Role Setting for Public Libraries*	71

Results of Author's Study of the Use of *Planning and Role Setting*	76
Summary	85

4 The Impact of *Planning and Role Setting for Public Libraries* on Its Users — 87

Impacts Reported in the Literature	88
Process' Impact As Reported to Researcher	89
Negative Comments	108
Summary	112

5 Satisfaction with *Planning and Role Setting for Public Libraries* and Recommendations for Its Use and Improvement — 113

Satisfaction and Problems Reported in the Literature	114
Satisfaction, Problems, Hindsight, and Suggestions Reported to Author	115
Toward Improved Use of the Planning Process	125
Librarians' Opinions of the Planning Manual and Their Suggestions for Its Improvement	128
Toward a Revised Planning Manual: The Author's Recommendations	138
Summary	148
Conclusion	151

References	153
Appendix A: All Public Libraries with Roles Included in the Public Library Data Service *Statistical Report,* 1988–1994	159
Appendix B: *Planning and Role Setting for Public Libraries:* Its Use and Impact	177
Appendix C: Inclusion of Study Libraries in Public Library Data Service's *Statistical Report,* 1988–1991	183
Appendix D: Problems Encountered During Use of Planning and Role-Setting Manual	191
Appendix E: Librarians' Suggestions for Improved Use of the Planning Process	195
Appendix F: Suggestions for Improving *Planning and Role Setting for Public Libraries*	199
Author Index	203
Subject Index	205

LIST OF FIGURES

2.1	Staff Involvement Library System A Staff	*38*
2.2	Staff Involvement Library System B Staff	*40*
2.3	Satisfaction with Goals & Objectives Staffs' Responses Compared	*42*
2.4	Satisfaction with Planning Process Staffs' Responses Compared	*42*
2.5	Local Funding for Library System A	*44*
2.6	Local Funding for Library System B	*45*

LIST OF TABLES

3.1	Number of Libraries Per State Reported in 1991 by State Library Agencies as Using or Having Used Revised Manual	*70*
3.2	Number of Libraries Adding Roles to the Public Library Data Service Statistical Report 1988–1994	*70*
3.3	Aspects of Planning Process Used by Libraries	*80*
3.4	Respondents' Opinions of Levels of Effort Expended	*84*
4.1	Respondents' Opinions of Changes Due to Process	*91*
5.1	Satisfaction with Planning Process and Its Various Phases	*117*
5.2	Helpfulness of Manual's Information on Various Planning Aspects	*131*

Acknowledgments

Assessing the Public Library Planning Process represents the culmination of a decade and a half of study of the public library's planning process, an unprecedented and revolutionary innovation in public library administration. I would like to thank Columbia University Melville Dewey Professor R. Kathleen Molz for sparking my interest and guiding my initial research; Charles R. McClure, both for his much-appreciated assistance and for his own extensive work with the PLA planning process; and Ablex Editor Peter Hernon for shepherding this work through its final stages. My dean and colleagues at the University of Alabama School of Library and Information Studies and my family and friends have also been instrumental in sustaining my efforts, and their support is greatly appreciated.

The author also wishes to thank the following publishers for permission to reprint parts of their works in this book:

Adapted excerpt from "Three Libraries' Use of the Public Library Planning Process: An Analysis Accompanied by Recommendations for Future Users," in *Advances in Library Administration and Organization*, Vol. 9, pages 57–82, 1991, JAI Press Inc., Greenwich, CT. Reprinted by permission of the publisher.

Adapted excerpt and Figures 1, 2, 3, 4 from "Staff Involvement and the Public Library Planning Process," *Public Libraries* 28 (May/June 1989):175–181. Reprinted with permission of the Public Library Association, A Division of the American Library Association.

Adapted excerpt and Figures 1, 2 from "Citizen Participation in Public Library Planning," *Public Libraries* 30 (May/June 1991): 150–155. Reprinted with permission of the Public Library Association, A Division of the American Library Association.

Preface

In 1980, the American Library Association (ALA) published an exciting new tool to encourage and assist public librarians' involvement in community-based comprehensive planning. *A Planning Process for Public Libraries* (Palmour, Bellassai, & DeWath, 1980) outlined a process by which librarians could work with trustees and citizens to plan programs of service based on the library-related needs of local communities, a radically different approach to public library planning.

Publication of this eagerly awaited planning manual was heralded in the library press and at national, regional, and state library association meetings. Workshops instructing librarians and trustees on the use of the process were conducted throughout the country, and many articles were published praising and critiquing the process and its manual. Fewer libraries used the process than had been anticipated, and although published and verbal reports indicated that some of these libraries reaped great benefits, others encountered substantial difficulties during their use of the 1980 planning manual.

Planning and Role Setting for Public Libraries: A Manual of Options and Procedures (McClure, Owen, Zweizig, Lynch, & Van House, 1987), a revised and expanded version of the 1980 publication, was developed to alleviate some of the problems librarians experienced with the earlier manual. This work incorporated much greater flexibility, emphasized the importance of role setting, and downplayed the attention paid to data collection by the previous edition. These improvements were greatly publicized, and the 1987 manual received far greater use than the previous version of the process.

Reports and conversations with librarians and researchers indicated that, as before, its users varied greatly in their success with and opinions of the second planning manual. Many librarians reported that they experienced few problems and received great benefits. Others appear to have encountered varying degrees of difficulty and to be aware of few benefits. Obviously these librarians' opinions of the value of the process and its manual are quite different; the process may be praised or condemned depending on whose opinion is solicited. Whether librarians decide to use the public library planning process may then be influenced by other librarians' use or misuse of the process or by unsubstantiated rumors.

This author has devoted a decade and a half to studying the public library planning process. She conducted an in-depth study of the use of the first planning manual by three Southern libraries and obtained the opinions of 255 librarians about their use of the second manual. She read over 50 articles and studies of the manuals' use. This book documents the development and use of the public library planning process and assesses its value. It also contains numerous recommendations for improving the use of the process and for revising its planning manual.

Chapter 1 presents the rationale and status of comprehensive library planning and the planning processes developed for different types of libraries. It provides background and a full description of the process developed for public library planning and explores the extent to which it was used and the benefits and difficulties experienced by a small number of the 1980 manual's users as reported in the professional literature or observed during the author's study of three Southern libraries.

Chapter 2 discusses the valuable lessons learned from libraries' use of the first planning manual. It includes a detailed analysis of the conclusions derived from the author's study, presents recommendations of other researchers and librarians whose findings and experiences were reported in Chapter 1, and summarizes analyses and recommendations of library leaders and educators who studied the 1980 manual and its use. The chapter concludes with a summary of the many important lessons learned from libraries' experiences and a brief discussion of the recommendations for revising the 1980 planning manual.

Chapter 3 traces the development and provides a description of the second manual, *Planning and Role Setting for Public Libraries* (McClure et al., 1987), analyzes the important ways in which it differs from the earlier planning manual and estimates the extent to which it has been adopted. It also summarizes several reports, studies, and critiques of the manual published from 1987–1993 and presents a detailed account of its use by the 255 libraries surveyed during the author's 1991 study.

Chapter 4 demonstrates the impact of the current process by relating the many perceived benefits and resulting changes reported by libraries in the professional literature and in response to the author's survey. The few negative effects of their use reported by librarians are included as well.

Chapter 5 reports these librarians' satisfaction with their use of the planning process and manual, the problems they experienced, and their ideas of what they wish they had done differently. It also includes the librarians' and the author's suggestions for improved use of the process and their recommendations for revising the current planning manual.

This book's value is that in exploring use of the two versions of the public library planning process, it examines the planning experiences of over 300 librarians who shared their successes and difficulties with the process, either through articles in the professional literature or by participating in the author's two studies. The many benefits realized by these libraries are described, along with the problems the planners experienced. Many suggestions for making better use of the process are included, and specific recommendations are made for revising the 1987 manual. It is the author's hope that this detailed assessment of the public library planning process will prove helpful to librarians and trustees who are either considering or presently using the process, to other researchers who are studying its use, and to those responsible for future revision of one of public librarianship's most exciting and important advancements in many decades.

Annabel K. Stephens

Chapter 1

Comprehensive Planning and the Public Library Planning Process*

The planning efforts of American business and industry have increased substantially since the early 1950s. During the 1960s and 1970s, the majority of large companies developed their own specialized planning staffs and elaborate long-range plans. According to noted planning authority, Peter F. Drucker (1974), these efforts were intended to prevent managers from

> uncritically extending present trends into the future, from assuming that today's products, services, markets and technologies will be the products, services, markets and technologies of tomorrow, and above all, from dedicating their resources and energies to the defense of yesterday. (p. 122)

Theorists and administrators alike realized that the type of planning necessary to accomplish the above-mentioned purposes was a form of planning known as comprehensive or strategic planning. As defined by Drucker, strategic planning is

> the continuous process of making present entrepreneurial (*risktaking*) decisions systematically and with the greatest knowledge of their futurity; organizing systematically the *efforts* needed to carry out these decisions; and measuring the results of these decisions against the expectations through organized, systematic feedback. (p. 125, italics in original)

---

* Portions of this chapter were published previously in "Three Libraries' Use of the Public Library Planning Process: An Analysis Accompanied by Recommendations for Future Users," in *Advances in Library Administration and Organization*, Vol. 9, pages 57–82, 1991, JAI Press Inc., Greenwich, Connecticut. Reprinted by permission of the publisher.

Strategic planning is concerned not only with defining an organization's goals and objectives, but also with designing policies, plans, and organizational structure and systems to achieve those objectives. Based on a concept of planning developed for use by the military during World War II, Formal Strategic Planning systems were introduced in the mid 1960s in the form of Corporate Planning, as advocated by Igor Ansoff and Stanford Research Institute and in the shape of Program Budgeting and Planning systems, as espoused by Robert McNamara and then President Lyndon Johnson.

Such planning has become increasingly necessary in the modern business world because of the growing difficulty of achieving corporate goals in a rapidly changing economic, social, political, ecological, and technological environment (Whittaker, 1978, pp. 3–4). In fact, as early as 1977, a survey found that when asked their most important responsibility, chief executive officers of America's 500 largest for-profit firms ranked "planning/strategy" first above "management selection/ development," "capital allocation/profits," "policy decisions," and "maintaining morale" (Heidrick and Struggles, Inc., 1977, p. 4). According to one study, 90% of these companies had some form of documented long range plan (Ang & Chua, 1975, pp. 99–102).

Today planning in the business arena is less likely to be strictly the province of large centralized corporate staff planning offices. It has become a more decentralized process in which those charged with implementing the plans (the line managers) are increasingly being given responsibility for their development. Although planners can no longer "start out with today and project it into the future," Drucker (1980, p. 61) points out that "one can have *strategies* for tomorrow that anticipate the areas in which the greatest changes are likely to occur, strategies that enable a business or public service institution to take advantage of the unforeseen and unforeseeable" (italics in original).

COMPREHENSIVE PLANNING FOR LIBRARIES

Public service agencies such as hospitals, schools and universities, and libraries are affected by many of the same rapidly changing environmental factors that challenge business and industry. As a result, some form of comprehensive planning has also become a more necessary facet of library administration. The need for such planning has been heightened by the present inflation coupled with shrinking library budgets, rising expectations of library users, advances in computer and communications technology, and the necessity of providing more essential services to meet the unique needs of changing and diverse clienteles.

Advocates of comprehensive planning for libraries assert that planning combats uncertainty and accommodates environmental change and is therefore required to maintain a stable organization (Evans, 1976, pp. 101–102). Such planning gives direction to growth and minimizes complexity in today's environment of uncertainty, thus preventing ad hoc decisions or decisions that unnecessarily narrow tomorrow's choices (Kemper, 1970, pp. 212–213). Its advocates also warn that the absence of planning will result in a state of "crisis management" in which constant attempts to solve "yesterday's problems" (McClure, 1978, p. 456) will make planning for the future even more difficult.

Specialized planning processes have been developed for large, medium-sized, and small academic libraries, for school media centers, and for public libraries. Thus far, no formalized planning process has been developed for special libraries, and there have been reports of the planning efforts of only a few special libraries, perhaps because special library planning is usually conducted as a component of whatever planning is done by the organization or institution of which the library is a part. Following a brief discussion and analysis of statewide planning and of the planning processes developed for academic and school libraries, the remainder of this chapter will review the events leading to the development of the public library planning process, describe the planning manual published in 1980, discuss the extent to which this manual was used, and report on the planning experiences of a small number of the libraries that used the 1980 manual.

Statewide Planning

In his review of the status of library planning in the mid 1980s, Charles R. McClure (1986) suggested three perspectives from which planning for statewide library services could be considered. One was that the state library agencies (SLAs) are responsible for coordinating planning; a second was that planning should be done by groups of libraries of the same type with a "key stakeholder" shouldering the responsibility; the third was that statewide planning should be multitype (rather than single-type) library planning and that all libraries should participate (p. 12).

Where statewide planning for library services occurs, it is usually coordinated for a single type of library (public, school, or academic) by a particular state agency. The SLAs would be the appropriate agencies to encourage and assist public library planning; the state departments of education would bear this responsibility for school libraries; and the state Regents or Chancellor's office would be the body that would oversee academic library planning.

McClure concluded that in 1986, statewide formalized planning for library services was minimal and that most such planning was directed by the SLAs for public libraries because of their need to develop standards on which to base state funding. He found that where multitype library planning existed at the state level, it was apt to be linked to a specific activity such as automation or resource sharing.

By the early 1990s, many of the SLAs had begun to take a stronger role in encouraging and assisting the planning efforts of their public libraries. Since 1987 when *Planning and Role Setting for Public Libraries* (McClure, Owen, Zweizig, Lynch, & Van House, 1987) and the second edition of *Output Measures for Public Libraries* (Van House, Lynch, McClure, Zweizig, & Rodger, 1987) were published, over 30 of the states had revised their standards statements. Most statements now emphasize the importance of planning and evaluation and self-assessment by local libraries, and many include planning components. Several states (for example, Ohio, Iowa, Wisconsin, Tennessee, Oklahoma, and Utah) stipulate that local libraries must select roles and define a mission. Eleven states—Delaware, Illinois, Nevada, New Hampshire, New Mexico, Ohio, Oklahoma, Utah, Virginia, and Wisconsin—require libraries to have a long range plan to meet state standards, receive state aid or federal or state grants, or qualify for system membershp. The long range plans must be based on the 1987 planning manual or an adaptation (Smith, 1994, p. 212).

SLAs in at least two states, Utah and Oklahoma, have developed formalized procedures for instituting statewide planning processes for their public libraries. Both Oklahoma's *Performance Measures for Oklahoma Public Libraries* (Oklahoma State Department of Libraries, 1982) and Utah's *The Upgrade Process: Planning, Evaluating and Measuring for Excellence in Public Library Service* (1985) have integrated a planning process with the use of standardized performance measures.

Kentucky, Tennessee, and North Dakota are among the states that have approached planning in a phased manner. In 1991, Kentucky's SLA worked with 20 counties with a modified version of the planning and role setting manual titled *A Long-Range Planning Workbook for Kentucky's Public Libraries* (Wiggins & Cone, 1989); plans were to "have all counties involved in [Long Range Planning] within five years" (E. Hilliard, personal communication, October 3, 1991). Tennessee's SLA conducted extensive training sessions in using the planning manual with local boards and librarians with the intention that all counties would develop long-range plans. North Dakota held statewide workshops on the Preschooler's Door to Learning, on role-setting, and on citizen participation in planning. These are examples of only a few of the state library agencies' attempts to encourage comprehensive planning by local public libraries. Further discussion will be included in later chapters.

Academic Libraries

In 1973, the Management Review Analysis Program (Webster, 1973), an assisted self-study approach for large academic libraries referred to by the acronym MRAP, was made available by the Office of Management Studies of the Association of Research Libraries (ARL). A systematic investigation of the top management functions of a research library, MRAP required its users to address fundamental aspects of long-range planning such as mission, goals and objectives, and internal structures for perceiving and negotiating internal and external environments. In libraries using MRAP, teams made up of staff and task forces studied the libraries' planning and control, organizational development, and personnel structures over a nine-month period. A study of MRAP's impact on participating libraries (Johnson & Mann, 1977) revealed that although there was general satisfaction with MRAP's goals, its value was perceived differently by different strata of library management, and there was concern over its cost in staff time and energy.

In 1979, MRAP was redesigned to allow libraries to undertake smaller-scale studies by choosing from eight program modules in management functions. A second process, the Academic Library Development Program (Morein, Boykin, Wells, & Givens, 1976), was developed for libraries with staffs of more than 20 and fewer than 50; together these processes make up ARL's Academic Library Program.

In 1980, ARL produced a third program, the Planning Program for Small Academic Libraries (Morein, Sitts, & Webster, 1980), for use by academic libraries with fewer than 20 staff members. ARL has also developed functional modules to assist academic libraries in planning for preservation, collection analysis, and public services.

Some individual academic libraries have taken part in formalized planning processes, often as part of their university's planning efforts, but academic library planning has not been widespread. For the most part, it has not been emphasized by smaller non-ARL university libraries, college libraries, or community and junior college libraries. Results of a survey of college library planning practices were included, along with formal planning documents from six libraries in *Formal Planning in College Libraries*, published recently as Association of College and Research Libraries CLIP Note 19 (1994).

McClure (1986, p. 13) criticized academic library planning for often emphasizing self-review techniques for allocating library resources rather than planning for patron services, focusing on specific functions such as automation rather than on overall planning, and giving inadequate attention to evaluation and to integrating measurement. Several sources have been published which may encourage and assist academic libraries in integrating measurement and planning. These include Cronin's *Performance Measurement for Public Services in Academic and Research Libraries* (1985) and Van House, Weil, and McClure's *Measuring Academic Library Performance: A Practical Approach* (1990).

School Library Media Centers

James Liesener's *Systematic Process for Planning Media Programs* (1976) was developed for use by school library media centers. Planning participants (media specialists, teachers, and administrators) are guided in defining program output alternatives, surveying perceptions of current services, determining service preferences and priorities as they relate to local needs, assessing resource and operational requirements of services, determining costs of preferred and/or current services, calculating program capability, communicating which preferred services are currently feasible, reallocating resources and implementing changes to provide the range and level of services selected, and providing evaluation of services offered and documentation of changing needs. Model instruments and techniques for implementing these steps are provided by this manual.

McClure (1986, p. 13) attributed the lack of planning by school media centers he observed in 1986 to most school librarians' lack of success in becoming part of their school's management and decision-making process, to their preoccupation with helping students perform well on standardized tests, to the few rewards for librarians who do plan, and to the poor national database of information describing school libraries. Although too soon to tell, it is hoped that the emphasis placed on the importance of planning by the 1988 school library media guidelines will lead to increased planning for school libraries.

Information Power: Guidelines for School Library Media Programs (American Association of School Librarians, 1988) informs media specialists that "planning is central to every facet of program development and implementation and development" (p. 44). Five pages devoted to planning describe the functions of a "sound" planning process; provide questions to use for organizing planning activities (preplanning); discuss defining the program mission, goals, and objectives; suggest types and sources of data needed; and offer points to consider in implementing the planners' recommendations. The importance of systematic evaluation to review goals and objectives as they relate to user needs is stressed (pp. 44–48). Liesener's work, referred to previously, provides a more detailed explanation of the process outlined in the guidelines; it also contains surveys and other tools for use by planners.

Another fairly recent work, *The School Administrator's Guide to*

Evaluating Library Media Programs (Yesner, & Jay, 1987), provides guidance for evaluating 60 components important to school media centers. Designed to help principals and school media specialists identify potentials and problems, set goals and objectives, structure evaluation plans, and initiate improvements, the work focuses on the evaluation process: recognizing positive and negative elements, identifying what is missing, and suggesting possible solutions. Examples of the evaluation forms used by the Montgomery County Public Schools are provided, as are sample student evaluation questionnaires.

Public Libraries

Prior to the 1980s, much of the planning activity for local public libraries was directed toward individual operational aspects such as the development of new services or products, the opening of new facilities, and the acquisition of new technologies. This led to little comprehensive or strategic planning, terms that are often used synonymously in the library literature (Palmour, 1977, p. 33).

Until the 1980s, what comprehensive planning was attempted for individual public libraries was mostly undertaken in the form of surveys conducted by consultants and professional research firms. Many of the surveys merely analyzed current library resources and services and paid little attention to the communities and individuals being served (Martin, A.B. 1976, p. 437).

An analysis of surveys conducted from the 1930s to the 1960s (Wight, 1968) revealed that the chief method used during that period was to compare a library's activities and resources with the standards for public libraries formulated by ALA, issued first in 1933 and subsequently in 1943, 1956, and 1966 (Standards for Public Libraries; ALA Committee on Postwar Planning; ALA Coordinating Committee on Revision of Public Library Standards; Public Library Association). Although examination of the standards documents may reveal "a progressive effort to add components of ongoing planning" (Martin, 1981, p. 253), it has been suggested (Palmour, Bellassai, & DeWath, 1980, p. 2) that the heavy emphasis on the use of national quantitative standards in planning actually exacerbated the lack of comprehensive planning in many local public libraries.

The recognition of diversity and the increasing necessity for the services of public libraries to be tailored to the needs of various clienteles, living in rural, urban, or suburban communities, resulted in increasing dissatisfaction with the type of institutional standards devised by the ALA. The standards were criticized for being oriented for institutions rather than for users, relying on the untested judgment of librarians rather than on research and input from citizens and political leaders, lacking relevance for current problems, and lacking a foundation of objectives indicating what standard services were meant to accomplish. They were also criticized for promoting sameness by applying the identical criteria to very different communities and resulting in mediocrity by stressing minimum standards (Bloss, 1976; Hiatt, 1967; Martin, L., 1972; Martin, 1981; PLA Goals, Guidelines, and Standards Committee, 1979).

Consequently, despite increased planning efforts of American businesses and industries, by the early 1970s only a few public librarians had reported formulating specific goals and objectives for their institutions. These libraries' early (pre-PLA planning process) experiences with goals and objectives setting were described by Larry Earl Bone (1975).

Although the necessity of reevaluating a library's programs and services and basing them on carefully devised unique goals and objectives had long been advocated, most public libraries had not participated in any type of goals and objectives formulation, and their statements of purpose had indeed been based instead on the ALA standards. This situation was verified by several studies conducted during the 1970s: George Morey's (1970) survey of public libraries in Michigan, Indiana, Illinois, and Wisconsin found that only 27.3% of the libraries aspired to goals other than those specified in the library literature; Allie Beth Martin's (1972) nationwide study found that the failure to formulate objectives was regarded as the sixth major problem facing the profession; and Norman Crum's (1973) literature review found little evidence of reported attempts at goals and objectives formulation.

The movement toward more comprehensive planning for local public libraries began in 1970, when the Public Library Association charged its Standards Committee with revising the 1966 standards. The committee, acutely aware of the profession's dissatisfaction, decided that a similar "traditional relatively minor, update" of the 1966 standards would not be appropriate and that library standards should start with the needs of community residents rather than with institutional needs, a radically different approach to standards development (PLA Goals, Guidelines, and Standards Committee, 1979, pp. iv–v).

The committee was aware of a number of significant research projects relating to its work. These included the 1972 A.B. Martin study referred to earlier, *A Strategy for Public Library Change: Proposed Library Goals Feasibility Study*; a second study titled *Measurement of Effectiveness of Public Library Service* (Beasley, 1970), a precursor of the output measures manual that developed procedures and measures to evaluate library services; and the work of the joint American Library Association/National Education Association Committee (Garrison, 1973), which recommended coordination of all library services and resources at the community level. The Committee was also aware of the growing nationwide interest in and emphasis on coordinated library access and new service patterns to meet expanding and emerging user needs.

Influenced by the recommendations of many of these research efforts, the committee decided to focus on service needs at the community level and asked that working papers be developed to provide its members with "a conceptual framework within which to consider the philosophic implications of total community library service on any subsequent and sequential development of public library goals, guidelines and standards" (Community Library Service, 1973, p. 21). The working papers were prepared by three task forces, each made up of 15 librarians working specifically with adults, young adults, or children, who were asked to describe the particular needs of each age group for library service. Their reports were published in *School Library Journal* in September 1973, with an introduction stating that the papers were not intended to be library standards and suggesting that "given the wide variations in our nation's public libraries, the profession may well want to develop diversity by design, so that communities may have the choice of alternative patterns of library service" (Community Library Service, 1973, p. 23).

Ruth Warncke, then the immediate past Deputy Executive Director of ALA, and Ralph Blasingame and Mary Jo Lynch, faculty members of the Graduate School of Library Science at Rutgers University, were asked to react to the task forces' papers and suggest further action for the Standards Committee. Blasingame and Lynch (1974) advised the committee to abandon the compilation of standards and to articulate the need for tools to help librarians analyze situations, set objectives, make decisions, and evaluate results.

Consolidated by members of the Standards Committee, the task force papers were published in the PLA Newsletter in June 1975 as "Goals and Guidelines for Community Library Services." This document described the conceptual framework for a plan for library service for "the total community" and proposed that communities examine needs and resources and develop a "coordinated approach to total library and information service for every individual in the community" (p. 10).

After much consideration the PLA Standards Committee, whose name was changed in 1974 to the PLA Goals, Guidelines and Standards Committee, concluded that it would be inappropriate for a committee of public library leaders to set a single set of standards for all public libraries. The committee proposed, instead, that a process by which individual public libraries could develop their own standards and plan and evaluate service programs appropriate for each community be designed (PLA Goals, Guidelines and Standards Committee, 1979, p. v).

The committee requested research proposals for designing just such a comprehensive planning process and interviewed prospective researchers for the project. A contract was awarded in 1977 to King Research, Inc., to conduct "The Process of Standards Development for Community Library Service," with Vernon Palmour as principal investigator.

A manual describing the recommended process of planning was developed and field-tested by three American and two British library systems. Revisions were made to reflect the experiences of the field-test libraries, and suggestions were offered by a group of library leaders asked to critique the manual in draft form, and the revised manual, entitled *A Planning Process for Public Libraries* (Palmour et al., 1980), was published by ALA in the Spring of 1980.

DESCRIPTION OF *A PLANNING PROCESS FOR PUBLIC LIBRARIES*

A Planning Process for Public Libraries (Palmour et al., 1980) was designed to enable a public library to "plan effectively without spending large amounts of time deciding how to proceed" (Lynch, 1980, p. 1133), thus allowing the planners to focus on analyzing information and developing recommendations for change. The planning manual instructed public library administrators in the formation of a planning committee of citizens and library board and staff members, in the compilation of information about the community and the library, and in the use of the resulting information to set goals, objectives, and priorities. Sample data-gathering instruments, tables for displaying data, and techniques to aid in group decisionmaking were included.

The manual emphasized the necessity of a period of careful preplanning before the actual planning process is begun. It stressed that the climate within the library must be hospitable to the changes and risks inherent in a process that requires reexamination and questioning of present assumptions about the library's community and its service priorities. Because the process also encouraged library staff to plan in conjunction with community members, the manual advised that the lay citizens on the committee would have to be carefully chosen. They would also need to be educated about current philosophies concerning public library service and provided background on the role of their library in its particular community.

Explicit instructions for a seven-step process were outlined in the manual. These steps included:

1. Assessing community library needs.
2. Evaluating current library services and resources.
3. Determining the role of the public library in its community.
4. Setting goals, objectives, and priorities.
5. Developing and evaluating strategies for change.

6. Implementing the strategies.
7. Monitoring and evaluating progress towards goals and objectives.

Step 1, the assessment of community library needs, included the construction of a profile of the community derived from census data, community planning documents, and a survey of the community's citizens. Questions by which the planning committee could assess their community's needs for general information, specific information, and coping information were suggested.

Step 2, the evaluation of current library services and resources, involved analyzing library statistics, performance measures, and the results of the citizen survey provided for the first step plus the results of two additional surveys, one for library users and another for library staff members. The purpose of this analysis was to ascertain the extent to which the library seemed capable of satisfying the information needs determined in step one.

Step 3, the definition of the role of the public library in the community, was the selection of the actual role that the library would take in its community during the planning period. Because step 3 forms the basis for the remaining steps of the process, it is crucial. The manual provided a sample form on which the planners could rank possible activity areas, types of services, and user groups. The chosen role might be a verbalization of the library's present service philosophy or a new, more relevant role.

In step 4, the development of goals, objectives, and priorities, the planners were to use the role statement developed in step 3 as a basis to define broad service goals specifying who should be served and how services are to be delivered, with specific objectives by which the service goals are to be realized. In addition, the planners were expected to develop resource management and administrative goals and objectives to support the service goals. The planners were then advised to establish priorities among objectives according to different funding contingencies and to take into consideration conflicting priorities of various interest groups.

Step 5, the development and evaluation of strategies for change, involved examining the library's traditional services and operations and devising new methods to achieve the goals and objectives chosen by the planners. Step 6, implementation of strategies, included devising specific plans for implementing the chosen strategies detailing who is to do what, and when and how they should do it. Step 6 also involved developing a system of management data and defining measurements necessary to establish baselines and measure progress toward achieving goals and objectives.

Step 7, monitor and evaluate strategies for change, was both the final step of a library's initial or primary planning cycle and the first step of its second cycle. The development of a system for monitoring, evaluating, and measuring begins the second planning cycle. Monitoring and evaluating progress was to be a continuing function of the planning committee; the manual stated that once the committee had determined the information needed to measure progress, it should periodically review specific objectives and revise the library's plan to reflect the changing conditions affecting the library.

The key characteristics attributed to the process by its supporters were that it was based on careful analysis of local conditions and needs, it was participative as librarians and community leaders were supposed to plan together, it was based on acquiring and examining "solid information" about the library and its community, it was cyclical, and it was flexible. Designed to be a framework to be adapted to local needs by a local planning committee rather than a "blue-print to be followed slavishly" (Lynch, 1980, p. 1133), the process combined tools and techniques previously used to some extent by library planners with a new emphasis on output-related performance measures and concepts of management derived from MBO (management by objectives) and participatory management.

LIBRARIES' EXPERIENCES WITH *A PLANNING PROCESS FOR PUBLIC LIBRARIES*

A Planning Process for Public Libraries (Palmour et al., 1980) became available for use by libraries in 1980. Its publication was announced with great fanfare in the library press and at national, regional, and state library association meetings, and workshops were conducted at regional, state, and local levels.

The next few years were somewhat disappointing ones for this new and eagerly awaited publication: Fewer libraries used it than had been anticipated, and although several reported very positive results, a number of librarians experienced substantial difficulty using the planning manual. Beginning with a discussion of the number of libraries that used the manual, this section explores several libraries' experiences by reporting the results of two surveys and summarizing articles by librarians describing their libraries' use of the manual. The last part of the section contains a detailed report of the planning experiences of three Southern libraries studied by the author.

How Many Libraries Used the 1980 Planning Process Manual?

Although no official figures exist, libraries that used *A Planning Process for Public Libraries* (Palmour et al., 1980) probably numbered somewhere in the hundreds. An unpublished survey of state, territorial, and provincial library agencies conducted by the PLA Goals, Guidelines and Standards

Committee in 1985 reported substantial use of the process by libraries in 19, and some use in 17, of the 39 states responding. According to this survey, a rough estimate of the number of libraries that had used, or were using the process, at that time exceeded 150.

The Adult Services in the Eighties project (Heim & Wallace, 1990), a 1986 survey of 1,758 library systems and more than 8,000 independent libraries, central libraries, and branches serving populations of over 25,000, found that less than one fifth (18.7% or 741) of the 3,969 libraries responding to a question about their use of the process indicated that it had been used. A 1989 survey of small- and medium-sized libraries serving populations under 50,000 (V.L. Pungitore, personal communication, August 1, 1971) found that the 1980 manual had been adopted by only 14.5% or 41 of these smaller libraries.

Summary of Surveys and Articles on Use of *A Planning Process For Public Libraries*

Librarians reported mixed reactions to their use of the new process. Several realized great benefits and felt that the time and effort involved was exceedingly well spent, even though they may have encountered difficulties along the way. Others experienced frustrations, disappointments, and fewer benefits.

The results of two surveys on the use of the 1980 process and several articles by librarians describing their libraries' experiences are summarized in the following pages. Most of the articles described the substantial benefits resulting from the libraries' use of the process; a few also discussed problems experienced by the libraries.

Directors of two of the libraries used as test sites for the process reported on their libraries' experiences. The director of the Prince William Public Library (Detweiler, 1981) wrote that their process was definitely worthwhile. It was a morale booster and an educational process for staff, helped with "big decisions" such as budget and capital improvement requests, prepared them for threatened budget cuts, provided a long-range emphasis, included valuable input from citizens, collected important data, and resulted in a referendum for construction of branches and the addition of a deputy director. The major problems experienced were the large amount of time required for data collection, an "overload of irrelevant information," and failure to collect some critical data (pp. 28–34). The director of the Baltimore County Library ("An Odd Euphoria," 1980) cited the effect on political bodies and processes as the most positive result of his library's planning process.

The director of the Oakland Public Library (White, 1981) reported that their process improved their reputation as managers and provided direction for their staff. It also resulted in three million dollars in community development funds for buildings and inclusion in the city's master plans for automation.

A 1981 survey of 26 librarians who had used the process found that 23 (90%) rated it as satisfactory or better (Harris, 1983). The majority of them reported that although the planning manual was satisfactory, it could be improved by less attention to data collection and more to other instruction in using the process; staff members' perceived rate of acceptance was good but never full, and seemed to be directly influenced by their sense of ownership of the process; the rate of acceptance by communities was perceived as high where evident; and any effect on relationships with community organizations was considered to be positive. Time involvement was listed as the biggest problem by 48% of the respondents.

The director of the Loudoun County (Virginia) Public Library (Hunt, 1982) described successful methods her library used for involving citizens. They formed a Citizens' Advisory Committee to react to suggestions from the board and staff planning committee; appointed special advisers with knowledge of the handicapped, community development, and fundraising; solicited volunteers to help with data collection; interviewed selected business leaders and local government officials; and met with local groups such as civic organizations and business associations. She explained that because funding the plans' major recommendations was the responsibility of the local governing body that appointed the citizen advisers, their participation in the planning process "may prove beneficial in the acceptance as well as in the development of the plan and in its successful implementation in the years to come" (p. 152).

Directors of two small, rural Colorado libraries wrote about their very positive experiences. At the Fort Morgan Public Library (Sertic, 1982), the library board, city council, and county commission members were sent planning information including annual reports, staff/management goals and objectives, and annual library action plans. The local political decisionmakers' perceptions of the library's organizational efficiency resulted in increased support of library programs and services. The director of the library in Steamboat Springs (Duquette, 1982) wrote that their staff survey was a "useful tool" that helped her learn more about the staff's perceptions of their library and their activity priorities, library service, and service group priorities and helped the staff learn more about themselves as a group (p. 20).

Spokane Public Library's data coordinator (Adams, 1982) provided a detailed description of the seven steps involved in developing their survey of library users. The survey was developed during a two-month period by the data coordinator with help from a consultant and the library's management-level staff.

The importance of preplanning was emphasized by the director of the Oil City (Pennsylvania) Library (Speer, 1983) who wrote that "the planning manual worked for the Oil City Library.... The manual can work for any size library, but a strong commitment to planning must exist" (p. 27). The assistant director of the Downers Grove (Illinois) Library (Welles, 1983) reported on the methods his library used to enhance the library's public image. He pointed out the process's potential for improving library service and predicted that properly promoted it could lead to recognition of the public library as a "cultural, recreational, and educational institution with a relevant mission and a clear sense of purpose" (p. 196).

The associate director of the Montgomery County (Maryland) Department of Public Libraries (Friedman, 1983) described how her library developed strategies to which they could be committed, writing that although costly in terms of staff time, the sessions produced high-level strategies that were included in the library's plan of work. Later, during the 1984 meeting of PLA's Planning Process Discussion Group (Betz-Zall, 1985), she reported that major problems remained to be solved despite the political success gained through their planning process.

The data coordinator of the Central Arkansas Library System (Davoren, 1983) described their "satisfying" and "productive" use of the process as an "unqualified success" (pp. 19, 24). Within a year after the completion of the process, the board had addressed nearly half of their plan's 42 objectives and had begun implementing those that could be accomplished by policy changes and physical reorganization.

A survey of 55 libraries identified in 1983 as using the process (Schremser, 1984) found that a few of the small number of libraries responding had had positive experiences. These libraries had used the process as a guide rather than a "bible," adapting it to local situations.

The survey also revealed some of the problems that librarians were encountering. With comments such as "seems such a major task, haven't mustered time and energy yet"; "too much emphasis on surveys"; and "somewhat confusing; too many surveys; too detailed," three librarians reported they had "hardly used" the process. The parts of the manual listed as least helpful by the respondents were those on data analysis and collection, theory and philosophy of the planning process, and the performance measures. Specific criticisms concerning data collection and analysis included the following:

- "Much emphasis was placed on the data collection but little guidance given to its interpretation. The sample surveys were too long and the responses in many cases were too general to be of actual use."
- "It is easy for people to get caught up in the process of collecting data rather than correlating and interpreting it."
- "Data collection emphasis is excessive. Creates false notion that knowing the numbers will obviate decision making."

- "There are alternatives to the use of surveys... including a wide range of unobtrusive methods for observing and recording behavior. I am far more comfortable making decisions on what people actually read and do than on what they say they read and do."

Ironically, other librarians cited the sample surveys, the information on survey development, and the general planning principles as being the most helpful. Respondents complained that the "sheer bulk" of the manual was intimidating, the process was not suitable for small libraries, and the "specific planning steps tied the group down when individual imagination might have been superior."

Librarians at the Grande Prairie Public Library, among the first small Canadian libraries to use the planning process (Chislett & Soltys, 1984), reported completing the process in only seven months while following the manual closely in the data-gathering stage and accomplishing substantial movement toward achievement of almost all goals within the first year. Writing that the process was a great success, the authors explained that the results were immediately applied to their plans for a new library, a new potential core of friends was developed, the data continued to be useful for planning, and the application of performance measures was meaningful.

Based on a three-week study tour of U.S. libraries, an English researcher (White, 1985) reported that the directors she interviewed considered the intellectual effort of redefining roles, setting goals, and developing objectives worthwhile; that the process had stimulated interest in the need to plan and had created a focus for discussion; and that the importance of matching library services to community needs was the predominant theme that emerged to outsiders.

Asserting that "it is the process' political merit that is paramount. Its value as a planning tool is, at best secondary," the director of Washington's Whatcom County Library (Halliday, 1985, p. 177) explained that much can be gained politically from surveying citizens and that although they would have been developed without the process, his library's goals and objectives stood a better chance of being funded because of it. He concluded that "anyone can develop a plan, but only through a process like PLA's can a plan acquire political acceptance in the 1980s" (p. 177).

Three of the directors attending PLA's Planning Process Discussion Group's 1984 meeting replied "maybe" (Betz-Zall, 1985, p. 18) when asked if the process had produced results worth the effort required. One of the directors reported that she did not find the surveys to be worthwhile.

Writing that "despite problems, every department at Daniel Boone [Missouri] Regional Library has benefitted from the long-range plan" (Carr & Wiese, 1987, p. 11), the system's regional services and public relations coordinators explained that although their planning process did not always function as a "well-oiled machine," its implementation was "valuable enough for the library to want to revise and improve upon the original document and continue to progress under such a plan" (p. 9). Their plan imposed a focus for all library decisions, helped them make educated budget decisions, and provided a sense of direction and purpose.

Three Southern Libraries' Experiences with *A Planning Process for Public Libraries*

The previous pages summarized the results of surveys on the use of the planning manual and articles by librarians who wrote about the benefits and problems experienced by their libraries. The remainder of the chapter contains a description of the planning experiences of three libraries whose use of the process was studied by the author.

From Fall 1981 to Spring 1984 the author conducted research on the use of the 1980 manual by three medium-sized consolidated library systems in three Southern states. The research included attending 27 planning committee, 4 staff, and 5 board meetings; examining all reports, memos, minutes, and documents generated; and conducting 36 interviews: 6 with library directors, 4 with Board chairmen, 3 with data coordinators, and 14 with citizen planning committee members. A questionnaire was used with staff members at two of the libraries. The following pages contain a detailed report of the planning experiences of these libraries, which will be referred to as Library A, Library B, and Library C.

Description of Libraries A, B, and C.

Headquartered in a large city, the largest of the three systems, Library B, is a multi-county regional library system serving approximately 296,000 people in two counties through a central library and six branches. Library C is a city–county library with headquarters in a slightly smaller but fast-growing city; its central library and seven branches serve a population of approximately 238,900. Library A has only one service outlet and serves approximately 78,000 people living in a much smaller medium-sized city and the county around it. According to the *American Library Directory 1994–95* (1994), current statistics reveal that the number of staff members and volumes owned by these three systems ranges from 116 to 16 and from 578,684 to 121,444. Incomes range from $3,494,864 to $627,826, and annual circulations range from 1,791,466 to 240,829.

Descriptions of Planning Experiences of Libraries A, B, and C

There was considerable variety in the number of planning committee meetings held and in the length of the three libraries' planning periods. Library A's full planning committee met 19 times during a period of almost two years. Library B's met only five times within a period of one year and three months; much of the Committee's work was conducted during meetings of subcommittees to which each planning committee member was assigned. Library C's planning process was prematurely ended after only three planning committee meetings had been held, the first and second within two weeks of each other and the third (and last) meeting a year and five months later.

The three libraries also differed greatly in several of the most important aspects of their use of the planning process. These included preparation for the process, collection and use of planning data, choice of a mission and goals and objectives, development of strategies and plans for implementation and evaluation, involvement of staff and community members in planning activities, and leadership provided to the planners.

Library A. Little time or effort was spent on preparing to use the process at Library A. Few decisions were made and there was little attempt to inform and involve the staff, Friends of the Library, city and county officials, and other citizens before the first planning committee meeting.

The planning committee was not provided with an adequate profile of the community. The committee was deluged with data on the library's current status, but the members were not encouraged to evaluate services and programs or to consider innovative services offered by other libraries.

Because of inadequate design and flaws in the ways in which their five surveys were conducted, the surveys were unable to supply reliable, in-depth information on the citizens' information needs or their opinions of the library's current services. Instead of thoroughly discussing and attempting to analyze the results of the individual surveys, all the results were added together, and the little time devoted to analysis was based on these totals.

No attention was paid to new services suggested by survey respondents. In fact, little attempt was made to use either the meager community profile or the survey results to analyze the citizens' information needs or the extent to which these were being met. Instead, the information about the community and the survey results were used merely to support the library's needs for more funding, staff, and facilities; these needs were repeated by the director and board chair throughout the process.

No attempt was made to choose a role or roles for the library. The committee selected goals and objectives that reflected the specific library needs reported by the director and board chair. Some of these goals were supported by the surveys. Others were not so clearly substantiated or had no relation to the survey results. The planning committee did develop strategies, but the director reported having no plans for implementing or monitoring the goals, objectives, or strategies developed by the committee.

Insufficient attention was devoted to involvement of staff members or the majority of community residents. Staff members were not kept informed about the process, and citizens were not even told their library was using the process until after the planning committee's third meeting. There was little staff participation in planning process activities, and citizens other than those chosen to attend planning committee meetings or assist with conducing surveys were given little opportunity to participate.

Library B. Library B's board and director devoted a year and a half to carefully and deliberately preparing themselves, the staff, and the community for the library's use of the process. Funding for the process was secured, and a preliminary planning committee made many important decisions. Numerous attempts were made to inform and involve the staff, Friends, city and county officials, and other citizens during this period.

Library B's planning committee received a full, very detailed community profile and an abundance of statistical data about the library. The committee members were given little assistance in interpreting or assimilating the community information, however. Although no explanation of the library-related data was made to the committee as a whole, staff members provided additional information during meetings of the three subcommittees.

The surveys and performance measures were conducted according to the planning manual's instructions, but the results were not explained as thoroughly as they could have been. The Planning Committee was concerned with improvement of current services and the addition of new services such as computer instruction, information and referral, online databases, and video collections, and they did give consideration to the few new services suggested by the survey respondents.

For the most part, the committee based its assessment of needs on responses to the surveys, comments and recommendations of the library's director and staff resource persons, and the personal opinions and experiences of the planning committee members. Little attention was paid to the community profile or the needs assessment questions in the manual. Evaluation of current services and resources also was based largely on the opinions of the administration, staff resource persons, and individual committee members, but the results of the surveys and performance measures were heeded.

A mission statement was adopted by Library B's planning committee, and goals and objectives were developed independently by three subcommittees. Several of the goals and objectives specified a new focus or called for new services to be offered. The subcommittee on programs and services developed goals and objectives that were indicative of its members' professional positions, but that were also well supported by survey results. The subcommittee on facilities relied more on site visits, a local planning agency's report, and the opinions of committee members and staff resource persons, but the survey results were consulted and did influence at least one of the group's choices. The subcommittee on collections relied heavily on the recommendations of its staff resource persons, but also referred to the survey results, which provided support for several of its goals and objectives.

Although the committee did not go through a formal strategy development process, many of their goals and objectives included or suggested strategies. A checklist, which assigned categories of objectives to Library B's board members and department heads for their consideration and implementation, was designed to serve as a monitoring device.

Library B's staff and community were kept informed and encouraged to participate. In accord with the director's belief that education and public relations are the main strengths of the planning process, staff and community involvement were essential elements of the system's planning experience.

Library C. Library C's director spent almost two years in preparation, securing a small grant and making tentative decisions concerning the process. The board and the staff were not involved in the preplanning decisions, although they were informed of the director's plans. Most of the Friends of the Library, city and county officials, and other citizens were not informed that Library C would be using the process.

At the request of enthusiastic planning committee members, the committee's first and second meetings were held less than a month apart. The planning committee received extensive information about its community and the system's services and programs, but there was little discussion or analysis of the information. The committee was not convened for a third meeting until a year and five months after the second meeting, a period during which the library's director and board made numerous far-reaching decisions regarding new services and a major building expansion.

After the third meeting, the City Council approved a bond issue for a new building, the library received a grant to automate its circulation system, and several opportunities for adding new services and programs presented themselves. Perhaps as a result of the considerable time and effort required for planning and implementing these projects, the planning process was discontinued. In May 1985 Library C's director wrote that the surveys discussed at the last meeting had not been completed: "There simply hasn't been time with the planning for the building and working for funding...." She explained that "right now I couldn't even tell you if we will ever get back to the [planning process] at all. The planning process seems so far behind us, almost unnecessary now."

Two surveys were conducted after the planning committee's final meeting. Few staff or community members were kept informed of the system's progress with the process or encouraged to participate in its brief planning efforts.

Results of Libraries' Planning Experiences.

With such differences in their use of the process, the three library systems could not be expected to have gained equal benefit. Library A failed to take advantage of the full potential of the process in any of its aspects. Library B received considerable value from its use of the process as a device for planning, staff development, and improved community relations. Library C terminated its planning efforts too early to have profited much.

Library A. Other than the potential for increased support by those few planning committee members who remained active, the most obvious result of Library A's two-year planning efforts was a set of five goals calling for incremental inputs (more funding, staff, facilities) to be awarded by the library's funding body. The absence of in-depth analysis of the library-related data as they applied to the community's information needs, combined with inattention to innovative services other than those desired by the director and board, severely limited the committee's planning efforts and caused undue focus on the needs of the library as perceived by its director and board. Library A also failed to realize the process's full potential as a mechanism for staff development and improved public relations.

Acknowledging that the main thing he had hoped to achieve was "broader support for the goals I had in mind," Library A's director felt that the process had accomplished "pretty much what I wanted it to." He did, however, express some doubt that they had used the process as it was meant to be used: "The process is supposed to have been a self-evaluation if you go by that book. We don't know if we actually did that."

One of its citizen members objected that the committee's planning had merely resulted in a set of goals requiring increased funding instead of a realistic plan for improving services in a no-increase economy. Protesting that "these [are the] results I could have predicted," this member exclaimed, "I think we should start over. We need to do [the planning process] again."

The chairman of the board conceded that rather than evaluating "where we are and what we should be doing, what a good library should be doing," the process had merely backed up what the administration and board had already discussed by giving them facts and figures that seemingly validated their previous thinking. Saying he had thought the process "would examine what you're doing, what is your purpose, what do you need to be doing—all of that," the chairman explained that he was considering hiring a consultant to conduct an evaluation of the library and its services.

Library B. Of considerable value to Library B, its planning process resulted in a community-based, staff-approved plan calling for a revised mission and both new and improved services. Their process provided excellent opportunities for staff and board development, higher visibility in the community, and increased rapport with local governing officials, as well as the possibility of increased support from citizen planning committee members. It also provided a vast collection of primary and secondary data that have been used for making collection development decisions, preparing grant proposals, and determining service reductions. Library B might have benefited even further, however, from a more thorough examination and explanation of the community profile and the data obtained from the surveys and performance measures.

Interviews with the director, board chairman, department heads, and several planning committee members revealed that they considered Library B's planning process to have been an "unqualified success." Two of the citizen committee members and one of the system's department heads suggested that their system's use of the process could serve as a model for other libraries.

Department heads described their process as a "good public relations tool" that provided "a lot of good information" and "a lot of contacts with the community, with community leaders"; helped "clarify our goals and objectives internally and administratively"; and "got us more in touch with the city officials." One department head said that the committee's report was

> something extremely valuable to take to the Quorum court and the City Judge and anybody who can fund us for anything because we're not going saying 'Well, we think this.' We've got the numbers; we've got the statistics; we've got something to back up any argument or request that we could make.

Another department head agreed, saying, "We're not a ship in the middle of the ocean adrift now; we have a destination that we are headed toward."

The director said that she thought the process "will be proven to have made a lasting contribution to the library system" and that it was "worth far more than all the money, time, and effort." Saying, "through this process we have developed strong library advocates," she credited their use of the process as going "a long way toward turning this institution around from being a passive 'done to' institution to [being] an active institution in the community."

Library C. Results of Library C's short-lived planning process include

COMPREHENSIVE PLANNING 23

data acquired by the two surveys; the compilation of information on the system's service area, its services, and programs, which was assembled for the committee; and the committee members' thereby increased knowledge of the community and library. An unknown factor is the effect their brief involvement with the process has had on the interest and support of the citizen planning committee members, three of whom were representatives of local governing bodies.

The director had indicated that one of her reasons for using the process was to "marshal our community should we have a tax millage proposal, should we need a bond issue passed for a building addition." Although this objective was accomplished without completing the process, she had also indicated that she intended it to enable her to "develop the kind of program that the community wants"; "make better use of our facilities, our monies, our staff"; "become better acquainted with community influentials"; and serve as a "tool for staff development and public relations."

SUMMARY

Comprehensive planning has become a necessary and essential facet of library administration in the 1990's, and specialized planning processes have been developed for three of the four major types of libraries. After a brief discussion of the rationale and status of library planning and the processes developed for use by academic and school libraries, the majority of the chapter reported on use of the process developed for public library planning outlined in the 1980 manual, *A Planning Process for Public Libraries* (Palmour et al., 1980).

The extent to which the 1980 manual was used by libraries was explored, and the benefits and difficulties experienced by a small number of libraries whose use of the process was either reported by librarians or studied by researchers were presented. The last part of the chapter contains a detailed description of the use (and misuse) of the process by three Southern libraries studied by the author.

The next chapter discusses the valuable lessons learned from these libraries' successful, and not so successful, use of the 1980 planning manual. It also includes the recommendations for improved use of the planning process and for revision of the manual offered by its users, researchers, library educators, and other leaders of the profession. Later chapters will reveal that many of these recommendations are still valid and quite worthy of consideration by users of the current version of the public library planning process.

Chapter 2

Lessons Learned From Libraries' Experiences With *A Planning Process for Public Libraries**

The previous chapter discussed the rationale and the current status of library planning and described the planning processes developed for different types of libraries, with emphasis on the process developed for use by public libraries and its 1980 planning manual. The planning experiences of a small number (less than 50) of libraries whose use of this process was either published in the professional literature or studied by the author were then reported. Although most of the published accounts discussed the benefits received by these libraries, a smaller number discussed the problems they encountered.

This chapter focuses on the important lessons learned from these libraries' use of the first public library planning process manual. It also includes recommendations for improving the use of the process and for revising the first planning manual.

The chapter begins with a detailed analysis of the conclusions reached by the author after observing the benefits received and pitfalls encountered by

---

* Portions of this chapter were published previously in "Three Libraries' Use of the Public Library Planning Process: An Analysis Accompanied by Recommendations for Future Users," in *Advances in Library Administration and Organization,* Vol. 9, pp. 57–82 (1991), reprinted by permission of JAI Press, Greenwich, CT; "Staff Involvement and the Public Library Planning Process," in *Public Libraries,* May/June 1989, and "Citizen Participation in Public Library Planning," in *Public Libraries,* May/June 1991, both reprinted with permission of the Public Library Association, a division of the American Library Association (50 E. Huron Street, Chicago, IL 60611).

the three Southern libraries whose planning experiences were discussed in the last chapter. The next section includes the recommendations of the other researchers and librarians discussed previously and a summary of the analyses and recommendations of several library educators and other leaders in the profession who have studied the process and its implementation but have not used it firsthand. The chapter concludes with a summary of the many important lessons learned from libraries' experiences with *A Planning Process for Public Libraries* (Palmour et al., 1980) and a brief discussion of recommendations for revising the 1980 planning manual based on the lessons learned.

AUTHOR'S CONCLUSIONS BASED ON THREE SOUTHERN LIBRARIES' EXPERIENCES

From the previous chapter's description of the three Southern libraries' planning experiences, it is apparent that the three libraries differed greatly both in many aspects of their use of *A Planning Process for Public Libraries* (Palmour et al., 1980) and in the benefits they received from its use. This section explores the important lessons learned from these libraries' use of the following important aspects of the planning process:

- Pre-planning or preparing to use the planning process.
- Use of citizens as planning committee members.
- Orientation of citizen members.
- Choice of leadership for the planning committee.
- Collection, analysis, and use of data.
- Choice of a data coordinator.
- Selection of appropriate roles and mission.
- Involving staff members in planning.
- Public relations for the planning process.

In discussing each of these aspects, the conclusion drawn (or lessons learned) from the libraries' experiences will be stated first. A detailed discussion of the pitfalls encountered and benefits received by the libraries will then be provided as explanation of each of the conclusions.

Preplanning or Preparing to Plan

Decisions made and actions taken during the preplanning phase can have considerable effect on the subsequent efforts of the planning committee. Careful preplanning can also help ensure a climate more hospitable to change.

Little prior consideration was given to the choice of a data coordinator or planning committee chairman, to funding or conducting the data collection, or to the number, timing, or scope of Library A's planning committee meetings. As a result, the work of the committee required 19 meetings spread over almost two full years. With no additional funding or consulting assistance, the data collection became the responsibility of the system's director and the planning committee members, who spent over a year discussing methods of data collection and conducting surveys.

The staff was not asked to suggest prospective planning committee members. In fact, little attempt was made to prepare either the staff or the public for the planning process.

The year and a half spent in preparation for Library B's use of the process facilitated their planning efforts in several ways. The committee charged with the preliminary planning was able to make carefully considered decisions about the choice, timing, and conduct of data collection and the number, timing, and scope of planning committee meetings. It was also able to secure adequate funding to pay a data coordinator and to contract to have a Citizen Survey conducted and to select a data coordinator, planning committee chairman, and committee members recommended by board and staff members. Because decisions concerning data collection methods and arrangements for their conduct were made ahead of time, the data collection phase was completed in less than two months. As the board chair explained, "We didn't waste the time of the citizens on the committee. We had done all the leg work to get it started... and we cut it down to just a few meetings."

The director asserted that the system gained "as much out of [the process] as we did because we spent the time we did spend on the front end." She explained that dedicating sufficient time to preplanning enabled her to set the proper climate for the process by educating the board of trustees and staff about the process, encouraging the department heads and other interested staff members to read the planning manual, and informing and involving the Friends of the Library, city and county officials, and other citizens.

Preplanning activities at Library B included:

- Appointing a preliminary planning committee.
- Securing additional funding for the process.
- Selecting data coordinator, planning committee chair, and committee members recommended by board and staff.
- Making decisions about choice, timing, and methods of data collection and scope of planning meetings.
- Educating board, staff, Friends about the process.
- Informing the community and local government officials about plans for using the process.

Library C's director devoted almost two years to preparing for her system's use of the planning process. She secured a grant and made several tentative decisions. The process was discussed briefly at department head meetings, and six department heads were invited to serve on the planning committee. Attempts to involve staff below the level of department head were limited to brief notices in the staff newsletter and a short introduction to the process presented at a meeting of the overall staff a couple of months before the first planning committee meeting.

No invitation was issued for the community's residents to attend the planning committee meetings, and the majority of the Friends of the Library and the community's officials and residents were never informed that the system would be using the process.

Preplanning activities at Library C included:

- Securing additional funding.
- Making tentative decisions about data collection and planning meetings.
- Educating department heads and informing general staff about plans for using the process.

Citizens as Planning Committee Members

The inclusion of lay people on a library's planning committee produces citizens who are more knowledgeable about the local library and its problems. These citizens may also become more willing and able to support the library as a result of their experience.

During Library A's planning experience, lay citizens served on subcommittees that designed and conducted the five surveys used by the system and developed strategies to accompany its goals and objectives. Several of the lay citizens also attended the many meetings held to discuss the surveys and their results and to review the goals and objectives and strategies recommended by the committee members. The lay citizens received extensive information, both oral and written, about the library system and its problems.

At Library B, lay citizens were assigned to one of three subcommittees that focused on either the system's programs and services, its facilities, or its collections. To assist them in evaluating their areas and developing appropriate goals and objectives, subcommittee members were supplied with relevant information attained during the library data collection phase. Staff resource persons attending the subcommittee meetings provided additional information and explanations, as did the system's director and board chairman, who attended the five planning committee meetings.

Regardless of the differences in the manner in which they were involved in the planning activities, without exception those lay citizens who remained active throughout their libraries' planning periods indicated that serving as planning committee members had increased both their knowledge of their local libraries and their knowledge of the importance, and the problems, of public libraries in general. Perhaps even more importantly, the lay members of both committees indicated that serving as planning committee members had increased both their desire and their ability to support their libraries.

One of Library A's committee members reported that serving on the committee had increased her awareness "of what [the library] offers and what kind of job [the director and staff] do. It increased my knowledge of what was up there and appreciation for what we have." Another member said that she really did not know that the staff was "as overloaded as they are with work." She added, "I know they need more help." A third who said she now "saw the library a little bit more from the inside out" asserted, "Of course it increased my awareness of the need for people to support the library. I suppose I couldn't help but be a little more aware of the needs of the public library."

A citizen member of Library B's planning committee said that serving on the committee had made her "more aware of just how complex public libraries are" and had helped her to "appreciate them better." A second replied that she had become "more aware of the service that the library system offers" and that she felt that the library "has a greater impact or influence on our daily lives than I was aware of." She added that she had also learned "how important it is to our culture to preserve and maintain and enhance this facility—how much it means to the development of human beings and to our culture, society, and mankind in general." A third committee member explained, "I've learned a great deal. I've learned things I had no idea of about the inner workings of a library and the price tag of having a good library, [and] I've gotten an awareness of the necessity of having a library."

Illustrating the citizens' increased desire and ability to support their libraries, a lay member of Library A's committee reported that "being a little more familiar with [the library's] problems, and also being more aware of the people's needs in the community, makes me realize that [the library] is something that I will enjoy supporting and feel that I need to support." She added, "I feel like they need me maybe more than I had realized they did."

A second said that she might "take the initiative a little bit more in creating support and in supporting the library myself." A third pointed out that because serving on the committee had provided him with more information about the library, he "certainly would be in a better position to put in a good word for the library" if he were talking with a member of the County Commission. Yet another member said that he "would be willing to speak to those who have the responsibility of voting funds. I'd go to my magistrate and say, 'Look, I know [what the library is] doing. We made the survey, and this is needed. It's not just something off the top of their heads'."

A lay member of Library B's committee replied that he would have "probably made a token contribution in the form of money had I been asked, but now I would be willing to devote time in [the library's] behalf as well as money." A second member agreed that serving on the committee had given her "more ammunition, more reasons to support the library."

A third member explained that she could tell the public, "We worked on this concept, it's necessary because we investigated it and heard from people in the community, and that's something people are concerned about." Other members agreed, saying, "I can be a better advocate as a result of being on the long-range planning committee" and "Maybe we'll [the lay committee members] become advocates." One of the lay members explained her reason for being more willing to support the library after serving on the planning committee by saying,

> I did have the perception that librarians just kind of rocked along and did things the way they had already been done, and tax monies came in and they kind of bought a few books to replace the ones that were stolen, and that's just about all they did. And I do, from the planning process, see that they are trying to look ahead to the future and spend the tax money as wisely as possible.

Library A's director cited the planning committee members' increased knowledge of the library and how it operated as one of the chief benefits of his system's use of the process. The director of Library B reported that all of the citizen members she had talked with since their use of the process "are dedicated, committed library supporters and will remain so." She said she was sure "there is enormous word-of-mouth good will. I have felt that from talking to them." And although she acknowledged that they were probably already supportive of the library, the director speculated that the former planning committee members "are more active library supporters than they were before."

An additional benefit of having a group of citizens whose experience as planning committee members has stimulated their increased willingness to support the library is the establishment of a pool of potential library board members who are already very knowledgeable about the library and its programs and problems. Library A chose one of their planning committee members as a new board member, and Library B's planning committee, described by the system's director as "the absolute best training ground for Board of Trustee members," provided three new board members.

Orientation of Citizen Members

If lay citizens are included, an orientation session should be provided to explain the planning process and their roles and responsibilities to the citizen planning committee members. The citizen members should also be educated about public library organization, services, and issues.

Although the planning process was described during both Library A and B's initial planning committee meetings, citizen members from both committees expressed the need for a fuller orientation. A member of Library A's committee suggested that "definite guidelines for the committee should be spelled out more specifically for expediency and for the comfort of committee members."

One of Library B's citizen members objected that he "was really blank, had no idea where we were going, what our conclusions would be, what even our purpose was basically." Saying that she felt the committee was "floundering for a long time in not knowing how far to reach," another member explained that she did not understand "what the purpose of the whole thing was for a long time" and was frustrated that the committee had no "guidelines from the staff about what type objectives they wanted and what type of implementation."

A citizen member of Library A's committee suggested that staff members explain their particular jobs to a planning committee. One of Library B's citizen members suggested an "incubation period" during which the staff would educate the lay people about library issues and about "how libraries need to be run."

Committee Leadership

It is crucial that the person who will serve as chair of the planning committee be someone skilled in planning and in group leadership. The possibility of having this position filled by someone other than the library's director or board chairman should be considered.

Although it may not always be possible to have a professional planner as the committee chairman, even smaller communities have persons with experience in leading church and civic groups. Nearby colleges might be called on to provide training in group leadership, or a citizen could be sent to workshops or conferences to attain such skills. The important point is that the person chosen should be someone who can motivate the planners, elicit discussion during committee meetings from both library representatives and citizen members, and lead the committee in an objective examination of the library's current resources and services and in realistic planning for its future.

In addition to failing to motivate the subcommittees conducting data collection to proceed more rapidly, Library A's director/planning committee chair devoted an inordinate amount of the committee's time (most of twelve meetings) to discussion of the methods, rather than the results, of their data collection. Those few members still active then had to attend seven more monthly meetings to plan goals and objectives and strategies. He was also unable to elicit much input into discussions from the citizen members.

Both the director's misuse of time and the lack of response from the citizen members were criticized by the board chairman and several of the committee members. Saying, "he didn't do his homework like he should to keep it moving," the chairman objected that the director let the process "drag too much." One member objected that there "wasn't any input" from citizen members; another acknowledged there "could have been a little more response from the [citizens]"; and the board chairman voiced his disappointment that "some [of the members] didn't express more opinions or enter more of the discussions." A committee member pointed out that a committee's leader "needs to be real highly trained" in conducting meetings to "keep a meeting moving and directed [and] bring out the questions that need to be brought out."

More relevant to this library system's lack of success with the process, however, was the director/committee chair's inability to lead the committee members in an unbiased examination of his library's services and programs. One of the committee members made the somewhat obvious point that a planning process should be led by someone who would not be so "affected by the results." She explained that a planning committee chairman needed to be someone who could say, "Look, we need to look at our services and what we're offering. Are we meeting the demands of the public?"

A planner by profession, Library B's planning committee chairman was praised by the system's board chairman, staff, and several committee members for making the best possible use of the members' time. A committee member said, "Time was used wisely. The meetings were conducted with the minimum of time wasted." The chairman of the board also praised the committee chair's group leadership skills. She attributed the "good mixture" during committee discussions "to the expertise" of the committee chair and said that "it could have easily bogged down if [he] hadn't been such a skillful leader." The director insisted that "having a professional planner chair that committee contributed to its overall success." Both the director and board chair, who served as ex-officio members, and the staff who attended committee meetings as committee members or staff resource persons expressed satisfaction with the extent of their involvement in committee discussions.

Library C could have benefited greatly from having someone other than the system's director chair its planning committee meetings. Perhaps having a citizen chair would have motivated the director to continue the process, even though many of the results she had hoped to accomplish through the process were obtained otherwise. At least having someone to share the work of conducting the process could have allowed the director more time to devote to the planning and implementation of her other projects while continuing with the planning process.

Data Collection, Analysis, and Use

Careful consideration should be given to the amount and type of primary and secondary data that are collected. Once gathered, the meaning of those data and their implications should be explained adequately. Planning committees should limit their data collection to that information which can be collected, analyzed, interpreted, and understood by those involved. The data collected should also be limited to that which is necessary for planning and decision making. A small body of relevant data adequately explained would obviously facilitate planning much more than a larger amount that is not used.

Because little or no consideration had been given to how any of the data were to be used, Library A's planning committee was not supplied with an adequate community profile but was inundated with data concerning the system's current status and with results from five different surveys. The large number of surveys took such a long time to design and conduct that several committee members lost interest and stopped attending meetings; they also produced more data than the director was able to analyze or interpret.

There was little discussion or explanation of the meager community information or of the results of the individual surveys. Committee members agreed that "there was not much discussion or analysis of individual surveys" and said that the survey results should have been presented to the committee as "This is what was discovered. What should our mission be? What should our goals be?"

Instead, little attempt was made to use either the primary or secondary data to identify or analyze the information needs of the citizens or the extent to which they were met by the library. In fact, the data appear to have been used mainly to support the library system's needs for additional funds, staff, and facilities.

Reflecting those needs pointed out by the system's director and board chairman throughout the process, a few of the goals and objectives chosen were well supported by the planning data. Others either were not so clearly confirmed or had no relationship to the results.

Because it was feared that they might be easily overwhelmed by the amount of data collected, the citizens on Library B's planning committee were assigned to focus on either the system's services and programs, its facilities, or its collections. The members were supplied with a full and very detailed community profile, an abundance of data on the system's current status, and the results of five surveys, but were given little assistance in interpreting or assimilating the information. The only library-related data referred to by committee members as having been used were the availability analysis; the statistics tracing the library's funding over several years; the comparison of its funding, holdings, and expenditures with those of other libraries; and the information on the age, size, and physical condition of its facilities.

Several staff and committee members objected that the results of the surveys and patron observations were not explained adequately. One committee member complained, "Data were not presented [as] they should have been; everything was dumped on them with no explanation." Another said, "I would have preferred to have had someone sit down and have a detailed explanation... because some of [the data] were a little confusing." When asked if she thought members had read the surveys, a third answered that "some had and some hadn't; some people can't understand a bunch of figures until someone explains them." A staff resource person said there was a "lot of information on the surveys, [an] overload. A presentation with graphs and charts would have been helpful."

Saying, "We only pulled them out [if] they had something to do with what we were talking about; we referred to them; we didn't sit down on a one-to-one basis and analyze them," and "The objectives came from our own personal experience... from our background training," the committee members indicated that the survey results were used primarily as support for their personal and professional opinions. Although the majority of the goals and objectives chosen were well supported by the planning data, a more thorough presentation of the data might have resulted in a fuller attempt to identify potential community library needs and to evaluate current library resources with those needs in mind.

Data Coordinator

If surveys are to be conducted, it is crucial that the person who will serve as data coordinator be competent in survey design and random sampling techniques. Data coordinators not already possessing these competencies should be trained prior to beginning the process and should be assisted by a competent researcher throughout the process.

Although it may not be possible for smaller, less well-funded libraries to obtain the services of a professionally trained data coordinator, attempts should be made either to secure funding for consulting assistance or to train a staff member who can be released from other duties to devote adequate time and attention to data collection. It is totally impractical for a busy library director without adequate training or assistance to attempt such a time-consuming and crucial undertaking.

The lack of prior knowledge of survey design and sampling techniques combined with inattention to the data collection methods in the planning manual prevented Library A's director/data coordinator from providing adequate assistance to the subcommittees designing and conducting the surveys and patron observations. As a result, both of these activities were poorly designed, and the validity of their results was compromised by methodological flaws in the number and identification of survey respondents and patrons observed.

The utility of the results for the committee's planning efforts was questioned by the chairman of the board, who wondered whether they had "put into the survey more of what we want rather than questions that [would] enable us to find out what we really need to know." He admitted that throughout the process he had feared that "our preparation of the surveys, our make-up of the surveys, the questions we asked, were either too slanted or not comprehensive enough to let the real truth shine forth." One of the committee members objected that "the surveys were not conducted randomly or scientifically" and that "the questions on our surveys were skewed to get the results [some of the members and the director] wanted." Their usefulness for future planning will be minimal as well.

All surveys and performance measures used for Library B's planning efforts were designed and conducted in full accord with the planning manual's instructions by a data coordinator trained in statistical research or by a professional research team. The board chairman, library personnel, and planning committee members expressed confidence that their efforts resulted in reliable data for the planners. In fact, the chair attributed a great deal of their success to having "a data coordinator to handle every bit of [the data collection]," and a staff member wrote that he "would strongly urge that any library undertaking this process hire a data coordinator as we did" because "it would have been a much longer and more difficult process without her." The data have also been used in making collection development decisions, preparing grant proposals, and determining service reductions, and they will be instrumental in the library's planned employment of output measures.

Choice of Roles and Mission

The planning committee should at least make a tentative choice of roles and begin to develop a mission statement for the library prior to beginning goals and objectives formulation. In choosing roles, the committee first should examine the effectiveness of the library's current roles and services in meeting the information needs of the community's citizens. The point is not that a planning committee must choose new roles or services but that it at least should consider the appropriateness of the library's present roles (where such exist) and its current services. It must then plan appropriate roles and services for the library's future. Once a committee begins to formulate concrete goals and objectives without the philosophical context of a mission statement, it is very unlikely that it would go back to consider such an abstract assignment. If an attempt were made to select roles after formulating goals and objectives, it is highly likely that a committee would merely choose roles to fit the goals and objectives already selected.

After devoting twelve meetings to data collection, Library A's planning committee immediately began formulating goals and objectives with no consideration of an appropriate role or roles for the library even though the director had previously said the committee might choose to reconsider and revise the role statement issued by the board several years earlier. Committee members' comments of "I don't know that I saw us giving much attention in that direction" and "I made all those meetings, and we did not do that" indicated that the library's role in the community was never explored.

With no role or direction to guide their efforts, all the goals and objectives suggested by the committee members merely called for increases in either the library system's inputs or outputs. The system's director remarked that he didn't think that "the committee members discussed at any length the different services, whether they should be eliminated, changed, or improved to any great extent." One of the citizen planning committee members criticized the outcome and suggested that the committee repeat the process and look more "not at what we need to increase so much as to what we need to keep the same or change."

Library B's role statement was developed by the subcommittee on programs and services and later amended and approved by the entire planning committee. The statement both reflected the system's present philosophy and practice and indicated a new focus for its future. It specified that the system should "plan for the increased use of technology and educate the public in the uses of it in our changing world"; "provide services and programs that reflect the variety of cultural heritages of all groups in the community"; and "be an active agent in teaching the public how they can add to the cumulative body of human knowledge and experience." The role statement also stressed that "library programs, services and needs should be marketed aggressively to the public." The goals and objectives concerning Library B's services and programs were said by the subcommittee members to have come directly from the role statement.

Staff Involvement

Library staff members' satisfaction with the goals and objectives chosen by the planning committee and with their library's overall planning experience is related to their perceptions of involvement with the planning process. Extensive involvement of staff should make the changes necessary to accomplish the goals and objectives more likely to be accepted; it will also assist in staff development.

Staff Involvement at Library A

The director of Library A spent little time in preparing his staff for the planning process. According to the director, only two staff members had been informed of the process until it was "briefly discussed" at a staff meeting one month before the planning committee's first meeting. The system's one professional staff member (other than the director) was not involved in the decision to undertake the planning process or invited to serve on the planning committee.

Attempts to keep staff members informed about the system's use of the planning process were limited. Although the final goals and objectives were announced during a brief meeting after the process was completed, there was no evidence that staff members were kept informed about the process during the system's two-year planning period. Unfortunately, the director's failure to explain the purpose of one of the data collection methods, the observation of patrons' library use, created concern among the staff over how the results would be interpreted and used. The record of low library use caused once by a local fair and a second time by a local football game, alarmed members of the staff who feared the planning committee would think the library overstaffed.

Participation in planning process activities by Library A's staff members was also limited. None of the staff members was appointed to the planning committee, and staff members were not invited to committee meetings to discuss their areas of expertise. The staff's only input into planning deliberations was their response to the staff survey. Although staff had not been involved in formulating surveys or reviewing their results, three were asked to help with the mechanics of data collection.

Observation of low staff involvement was confirmed by a questionnaire distributed to Library A's staff members after the completion of the planning process. No staff respondent agreed that the staff had been kept informed. One staff member replied, "I know that I knew about the planning process but cannot say about the other staff members." Another insisted that, "the staff wasn't informed." Also none of the respondents agreed that staff members were encouraged to participate in planning process activities.

With no staff meetings devoted to staff discussion of planning activities and no representation on the planning committee, it was no surprise that only one eighth of those responding agreed that staff members were given sufficient opportunities to express their points of view. The respons-

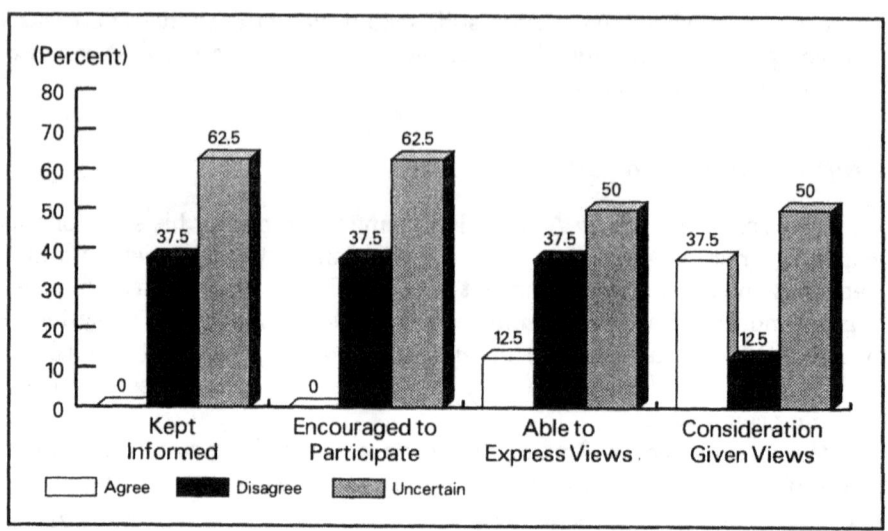

Figure 2.1. Staff involvement: Library System A staff

es of Library A's staff members to these four items are displayed in Figure 2.1.[1]

Staff Involvement at Library B

In accord with her expressed intention to use it as an educational process, the director of Library B devoted considerable effort to preparing her staff for the planning process. The system's assistant director was appointed to the preliminary planning committee; he also attended a regional library association workshop on the process. Department heads were informed of administrative and board plans for using the process at their monthly meetings and expected to convey what they learned to their respective staffs. The department heads, and the three assistant department heads, were also asked by the director to read the planning manual and journal articles about the process. Additional efforts to inform and involve staff during the preplanning period included three articles in the staff newsletter, a request to staff for recommendations of people to serve on the planning committee, and a system-wide staff meeting.

Library B's staff members were kept informed of planning process activi-

---

[1] Figures in this chapter reprinted with permission of the Public Library Association, a Division of the American Library Association, (50 E. Huron Street, Chicago, IL 60611) from "Staff Involvement and the Public Library Planning Process," *Public Libraries,* May/June 1989 (Figures 2.1–2.4) and "Citizen Participation in Public Library Planning," *Public Libraries,* May/June, 1991 (Figures 2.5 & 2.6).

ties throughout the planning period. Staff were informed of dates and times of planning committee meetings and supplied with reports of the meetings and results of the surveys and performance measures through eight articles in their staff newsletter. Information and decisions about the process reported at department head meetings were passed on to the rest of the staff. The department heads, told by the director that their major responsibility during the planning cycle would be to keep their respective staffs informed, posted their notes or talked with their staffs after each department head meeting.

Copies of the performance measures and each of the surveys, complete with tabulated results, were sent to each branch and department along with a profile of the community developed by the data coordinator. A detailed explanation of the planning committee's final report was presented at a meeting of the entire staff. Copies of the final report were also sent to each branch and department.

Library B's assistant director and department heads participated extensively in the system's planning activities. One of the department heads served as the staff representative on the planning committee, and the assistant director and four other department heads served as staff resource persons to the planning committee's three subcommittees, attending all planning committee meetings as well as their appropriate subcommittee meetings.

Although less extensive, attempts were also made to include participation by staff members below the level of department head. All staff members were invited to attend the planning committee meetings. Preliminary copies of the community and user surveys were sent to each department and branch for staff review. Staff were encouraged to make suggestions through department heads and their representative to the planning committee; staff input was also obtained by the staff survey. Methods of involving staff included:

- Assistant director included in preplanning decisions and sent to workshop on process.
- Department heads informed about plans for using process and told to inform their staff.
- Department heads asked to read planning manual and journal articles about process.
- Articles in staff newsletter prior to beginning process.
- Staff asked to suggest prospective planning committee members.
- Staff meeting held to introduce process and explain how it would be used.
- Staff member on planning committee and department heads served as liaisons to committee.
- Department heads posted notes and/or discussed planning activities with staff throughout process.
- Articles in staff newsletter throughout process.

- Drafts of surveys sent to each department.
- Survey results and other materials generated during planning and final report sent to each department.
- Staff meeting held to present final report.

The author's observations were supported by the responses of Library B's staff members to the questionnaire administered after the process was completed. Of those responding, 85% agreed that the staff had been kept informed; 65% agreed that the staff were encouraged to participate in planning process activities; and almost half agreed that staff members were given sufficient opportunities to express their points of view. The responses of Library B's staff members are displayed in Figure 2.2.

Library B's director credited their planning process with having great educational benefit for the staff, especially for the system's department heads. The director asserted that "all of [the department heads] without reservation are much stronger middle managers than they were three years ago." She explained that when assigned to implement some of the planning committee's recommendations, "because they had been involved in that process" the department heads had taken their assignments much more seriously than they would have previously, working in a very "thoughtful" manner "towards structuring how to fulfill particular objectives." The director also said that as a result of interacting with, and observing her interacting with, the planning committee members, the department heads had gained far more confidence, put aside a lot of self-protectiveness and defensiveness, and become more objective, more open, and more professional.

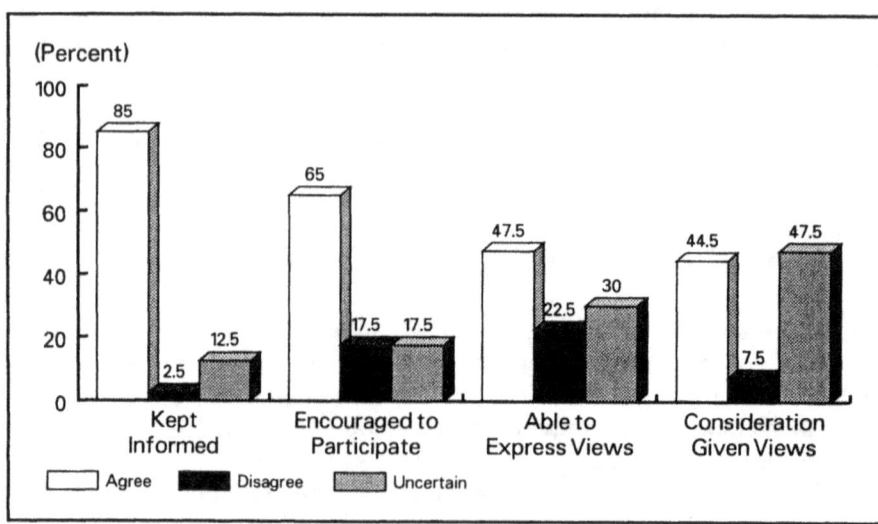

Figure 2.2. Staff involvement: Library System B staff

Although she was "less clear" about the educational value to staff members below department head level, the director said they were taking their role in the staff association much more seriously. Additional benefits mentioned were that the process had allowed staff at all levels greater interaction with the director and that the department heads were interacting with their staffs at a higher level, tending to delegate more, and exhibiting a "more open management style," an improvement that would eventually benefit staff at all levels.

Comparison of the Two Staffs' Attitudes Toward Goals and Planning Process

Both the interviews and the responses to the survey conducted after the library systems' planning periods indicated a considerable difference in the two staffs' attitudes toward the goals and objectives chosen by their planning committees. Similar variation was found in the staffs' attitudes toward their systems' overall use of the process.

Library A's staff members were less than enthusiastic about both the goals and objectives chosen for them by the planners and about their library's experience with the entire process with which they were so minimally involved. In fact, only 12.5% of the responding staff members agreed that they were completely satisfied with the goals and objectives. One staff member wrote, "The goals are a dream. If wider use by the public is wanted, we need guards at night, not goals on a paper. It's a joke."

As for their library system's overall experience with the planning process, only 14.2% agreed they would describe it as totally satisfactory. A staff member explained his dissatisfaction with Library A's planning experience by writing, "I feel the planners should have been more aware of low pay for employees; the library is in need of security. I feel these things must be [accomplished] before long range goals can be met."

Attention devoted to keeping staff informed and encouraging their participation in planning process activities proved to be an important aspect of Library B's planning efforts. A majority of the staff members indicated acceptance of the goals and objectives chosen by the planners and satisfaction with their library's overall planning experience.

Library B's department heads played an important role in their library's use of the process. All department heads responding to the author's questionnaire agreed they were completely satisfied with the goals and objectives selected by the planning committee. Those interviewed responded that they felt "very good about [the objectives] overall"; thought the committee "got at most of the things that were important"; and were "pretty much in agreement with the consensus that was reached." In fact, of all those staff members responding, over three fourths agreed that they were completely satisfied with the goals and objectives.

All department heads responding to the questionnaire also agreed they would describe the system's experience with the process as totally satisfactory, as did almost two thirds of all responding staff members. Some of the few staff members who disagreed offered reasons pertaining to their perceptions of insufficient involvement with the process. One wrote, "From what my supervisor told me it was a good thing. I was told that it was going on but did not feel directly involved." A second complained that "certain levels (or categories) of staff were given attention while others were not." Responses of Library A and Library B's staff members to the items discussed above are displayed in Figure 2.3 and Figure 2.4.

The relationship between the staffs' perceptions of involvement with their libraries' use of the planning process and their perceived satisfaction with both the goals and objectives chosen by the planners and their libraries' overall planning experience was examined by the use of a statis-

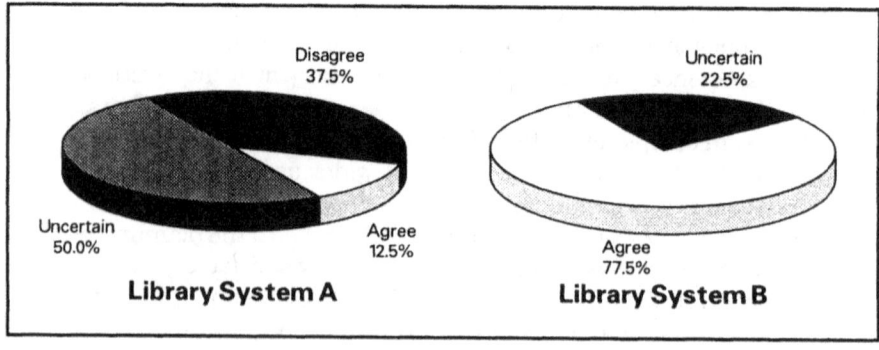

Figure 2.3. Satisfaction with goals and objectives: Staffs' responses compared

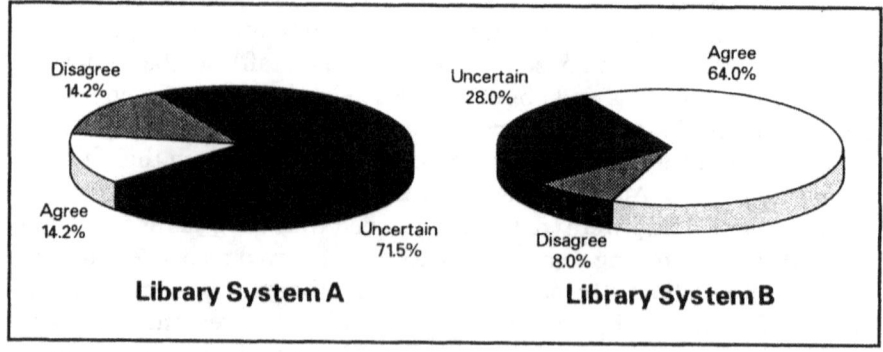

Figure 2.4. Satisfaction with planning process: Staffs' responses compared

tical test, the chi-square. Perceived satisfaction with the goals and objectives and with the libraries' overall experiences with the process was, indeed, found to be related to staff members' perception of being kept informed, being encouraged to participate in planning process activities, and being given sufficient opportunities to express their points of view. Perceived satisfaction with the libraries' overall experiences with the process was also found to be related to the perception that the staff members' points of view were taken into consideration.

Public Relations

Efforts devoted to publicizing a library system's use of the planning process result in increased visibility, which can in turn benefit the library system. Special attention directed to informing and involving local government officials can be of considerable benefit to a library system.

Public Relations at Library A

Two members of the Friends of the Library served on Library A's planning committee. The annual Friends' luncheon for elected officials, held soon after the board accepted the planning committee's final report, provided an excellent occasion for the director to present an overview of the planning committee's work and an explanation of its recommendations.

Local citizens were informed of the process through two articles and an editorial in the community's newspaper, and four lay people assisted the planning committee with its data collection efforts. A city commissioner served on Library A's planning committee, and selected city and county officials were interviewed during a survey of community leaders. Members of a local government-appointed study group attended three planning committee meetings and participated in conducting one of the surveys. The goals chosen by the planning committee were announced at the county's annual budget hearing and presented at the annual Friends' luncheon for elected officials.

Methods used by Library A included:

- Members of Friends as planning committee members.
- Local government officials as planning committee members.
- Articles in local newspapers.
- Citizens helped with data collection.
- Interviews with local government officials.
- Local government-appointed study group attended planning committee meetings.

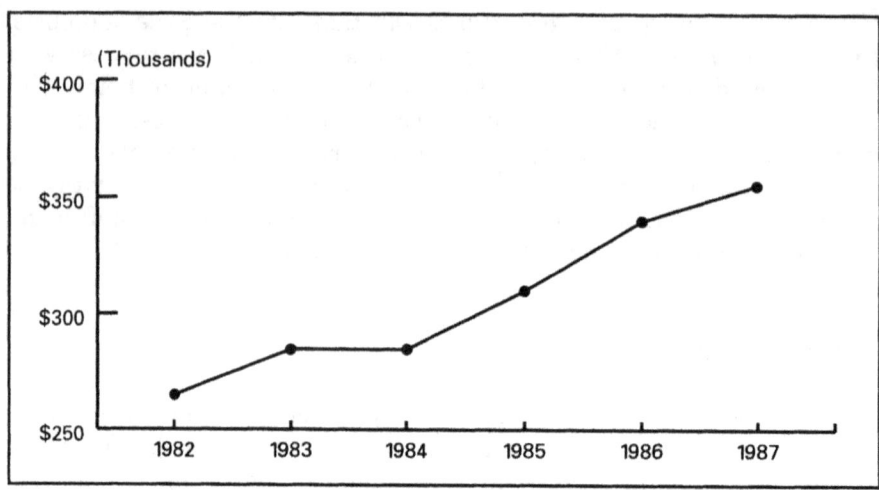

Figure 2.5. Local funding for Library System A

- Final report presented at Friends' luncheon and county commission annual budget hearing.

Although not positive it was a result of the planning process, Library A's director reported that since beginning the process the library had been asked to conduct two all-day radio broadcasts about the library and its programs and services. In the five years immediately following the beginning of their planning efforts in 1982, a time during which many libraries experienced cutbacks or level funding, the system's local appropriations were increased by 33%. The gain in Library A's local support, depicted in Figure 2.5, substantially exceeded the rate of inflation during this time period (the Consumer Price Index rose by approximately 17% from 1982 to 1987).

Public Relations at Library B

At Library B, the executive director and one member of the Friends of the Library were involved in preliminary planning, and three members were appointed to the planning committee. Six articles in the Friends' newsletter kept the members well informed both before and throughout the planning period.

Library B's planning committee meetings were open to the public. An article in one of the local newspapers prior to the first planning committee meeting explained the process and the rationale for its use, listed the planning committee members, and invited the public to attend the meeting. Five additional articles published during the planning period described the surveys and reported their results, announced the dates and summarized the events of subsequent committee meetings, and presented the committee's recommendations.

In addition to representation on the planning committee, several attempts were made to interest and involve service area governmental officials in Library B's planning process. Prior to its beginning, the officials were informed about the process and asked to support a grant application to fund the process. The Quorum Court judge and the chairman of the court's tax committee were sent the results of a sales tax question included on the surveys, and 26 selected officials were asked to complete the system's user survey. All service area city and county officials received personal invitations to the meeting at which the planning committee's report and recommendations were presented.

Methods used by Library B included:

- Members of Friends involved in pre-planning.
- Members of Friends as planning committee members.
- Local government officials asked for support.
- Local government officials as planning committee members.
- Articles in Friends' newsletter.
- Articles in local newspapers.
- Public invited to planning committee meetings.
- Local government officials surveyed.
- Survey results sent to local government officials.
- Local government officials invited to final planning committee meeting.

The director reported that the "higher visibility" resulting from the many efforts to publicize the planning process had been of considerable benefit.

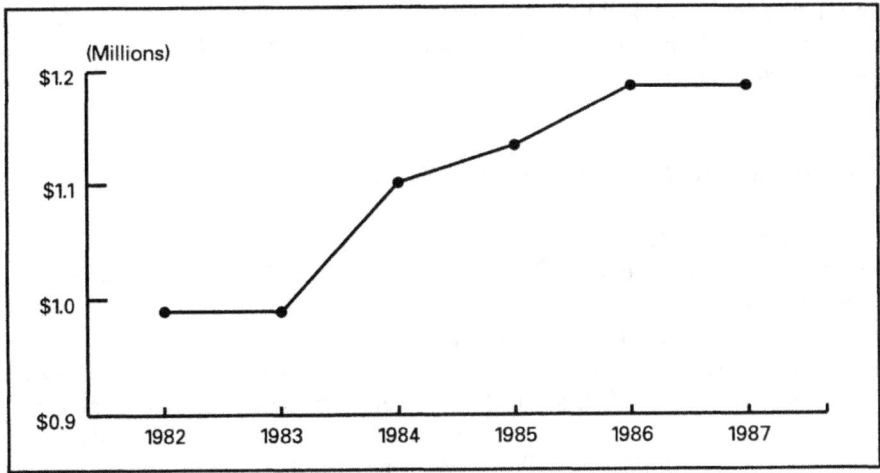

Figure 2.6. Local funding for Library System B

She said that the system was asked to prepare a public service announcement to be televised during the city's promotional campaign, a local state senator volunteered for the first time to sponsor library legislation, and the library was being taken "far more seriously than we were before."

According to the director, the efforts to inform and involve local government officials benefited her library almost immediately. She reported that a previously cut appropriation had been restored, the officials had become "much easier to work with," the system didn't have to "fight as hard for funding" as they had in the past, and the library was "being perceived as a serious part of the total city services in a way perhaps that we were not before." The director also reported that the mayor of the area's largest city had told her that the planning process had "increased [the library system's] credibility." Library B's local funding increased by approximately 20% in the five years following their adoption of the planning process. The increase in local funding, which slightly exceeded the 17% increase in the Consumer Price Index, is shown in Figure 2.6.

RECOMMENDATIONS OF LIBRARIANS AND OTHERS WHO USED AND STUDIED *A PLANNING PROCESS FOR PUBLIC LIBRARIES*

The suggestions discussed above are based on the observations of one researcher who made an extensive study of three libraries' use of the 1980 planning manual. Users of the current planning process manual can still benefit from paying close attention to both the wise choices and mistakes made by these libraries and to the following recommendations offered by the other researchers and librarians whose findings and planning experiences were discussed previously and by leaders within the profession and other library educators who studied the process and its implementation.

Recommendations of the Manual's Users

The director of the Baltimore County Library ("An Odd Euphoria," 1980) recommended the use of staff and trustees, rather than lay people, as planning committee members. He also criticized the lack of adequate measurement techniques in the 1980 manual.

To avoid problems such as the large amount of time required, the failure to collect some critical data, and an "overload of irrelevant information" (Detweiler, 1981, p. 34) experienced during their data collection attempts, the director of the Prince William (Virginia) Public Library recommended that libraries hire a professional agency to conduct and tabulate surveys, rearrange and interpret readily available data, and consider what information is needed and where else it is available before conducting surveys. She also recommended a high level of staff involvement, broad community representation on planning committees, wide distribution of survey results, holding public hearings, and interviewing local officials during planning.

The director of the Oakland Public Library (White, 1981) also recommended broad staff and community input. She too stressed the importance of involving local officials and library board members.

The respondents to the 1981 survey on the use of the manual (Harris, 1983) suggested the need for the following: less emphasis on data collection, improved guidelines for collecting and using data and for using planning committees, advice on simplifying the process, discussion of the implications of various choices, structured methods for examining various aspects of service, a less wordy style, and measurable and output oriented goals and objectives. Additional findings were that staff members' acceptance seemed to be directly influenced by their sense of ownership of the process, that the rate of acceptance by communities was perceived as high where evident, and that any effect on relationships with community organizations was reported to be positive.

The director of the Loudoun County (Virginia) Public Library (Hunt, 1982) offered the following suggestions for using citizen groups effectively: define roles and point out limits to authority, exchange minutes and reports between the various groups involved, appoint representatives to attend other groups' meetings, and have some joint planning meetings. She also suggested that librarians consider community receptivity toward citizen participation, availability of administrative time for coordination, and attitudes of staff and trustees in determining whether Loudoun's structure for involving citizens could work in their situations.

The director of the Fort Morgan (Colorado) Library (Sertic, 1982) found that sending the local decision makers planning information such as annual reports, staff/management goals and objectives, and library action plans improved their perception of the library's management and resulted in increased support of library programs and services. Spokane Public Library's data coordinator (Adams, 1982) recommended that libraries make one person responsible for overall development of survey instruments, hire a data coordinator from outside the system and a consultant expert in tasks that complement the librarian's areas of expertise, seek suggestions from all sources, and evaluate the suggestions objectively. She suggested that consultants should be accessible, interested, competent, easy for a librarian to work with, and hired for a specific sum.

Guidelines for preplanning offered by the director of the Oil City (Pennsylvania) Library (Speer, 1983) included understanding the process, communicating both the process and the library's current planning needs to staff and board, assessing available resources for planning, assembling a preplanning committee to develop plans for using the process, scrutinizing all proposed planning activities so that only essential steps are taken, and deciding the planning committee's role in data collection.

Pointing out that the planning process "has opportunities for raising the profile of the public library at every turn" (Welles, 1983, p. 194), the assistant director of the Downers Grove (Illinois) Library recommended selecting a broad-based planning committee, contacting local planners and community agencies, carrying out "well-executed" (p. 195) surveys with the help of community groups when feasible, holding a public meeting to publicize the completion of the initial planning phase and to recognize those who contributed, and paying careful attention to distribution of the final report. He advised librarians to keep their communities apprised about their planning efforts and pointed out that surveys can focus library services and bolster civic support for change.

Central Arkansas Library System's data coordinator (Davoren, 1983) listed eight elements that she felt were invaluable in their successful use of the process. These included the following: board support; preplanning to guarantee groundwork; a budget to cover extra expenses; a representative planning committee; a data coordinator able to devote an intense amount of time to data-gathering; easy-to-use data that were scientifically collected, well documented, and graphically illustrated; professional assistance in conducting surveys and prioritizing objectives; and a supportive and informed staff that was consulted and kept well informed (p. 24).

Respondents to a survey of libraries identified as using the process in 1983 (Schremser, 1984) suggested revising the data collection section to provide much clearer explanation of the reason for and use of the surveys, how to create a survey to fit local situations, how to interpret and use the data collected, and information on SPSS and computer coding. Other recommended changes included the following: offering alternatives to the recommended process; showing other formats, such as a matrix, to use for the plan itself; discussing the use of the process in small libraries and the role of consultants; focusing data collection on areas of interest by having the planning committee "brainstorm" prior to collecting data; omitting jargon; using the output measures; paying more attention to techniques of community analysis; and emphasizing "goals setting, dreaming, and connecting actions to goals and objectives."

The director of the Whatcom (Washington) Library (Halliday, 1985) recommended that libraries continue to use citizen committees and to survey citizens. He explained that "city and county councils and other funding authorities that are used to ignoring librarians find it hard to ignore the recommendations of citizen committees that are based on citizen surveys" (p. 177).

One of the directors attending the 1984 meeting of PLA's Planning Process Discussion Group (Betz-Zall, 1985) made several recommendations based on his experience. He advised keeping the planning group small, using information already available, relying on staff's experience and knowledge, using outside group facilitators, generating results quickly, knowing the current situation before beginning planning, and using a three-year planning cycle.

Admitting that "writing and conducting surveys without fully knowing how the resulting information would be analyzed turned into something of a private nightmare," librarians from the Daniel Boone (Missouri) Regional Library (Carr & Wiese, 1987) warned that "you can bog yourself down in a hurry with extraneous information" (p. 11). They recommended careful preplanning prior to beginning data collection; educating the staff about what the process can accomplish; helping staff understand the difference between goals, objectives, and strategies; and reviewing and revising the plan on an annual basis.

The above recommendations were made by librarians who had used the 1980 planning manual. The articles reviewed included helpful suggestions on:

- Preplanning.
- Make-up and use of planning committees.
- Data collection and use.
- Use of consultants.
- Involvement of library staff members.
- Involvement of community and local officials.
- Publicizing the planning process.
- Format and timing of the resulting plan.
- Revising the planning manual.

Analysis and Recommendations of Library Educators and Other Leaders of the Profession

This section contains a chronologically arranged summary of the analyses of *A Planning Process for Public Libraries* (Palmour et al., 1980) and its use offered by library educators and other leaders within the profession. Their recommendations for both improving the use of the process and revising the planning manual are included.

Mary Jo Lynch (1980), Director of the ALA Office for Research and coordinator of the "The Process of Standards Development for Community Library Service," (the proposal for developing the 1980 planning manual), recommended that librarians engage in careful preplanning, including defining the role of the planning committee, educating lay people about libraries and about the process, and thinking through the entire process before starting to estimate the minimum amount of data needed. She advised planners to feel free not to do all four surveys and to modify the sample surveys and stressed that determining the role of the library was important and would pay off in later planning.

David McKay (1980), then North Carolina's State Librarian, warned that the manual's surveys were expensive, time-consuming, and required expertise. He suggested that a revised manual include an explanation that the appropriate purpose of planning is to determine whether strategies and policies are appropriate to reach desired future objectives, not to forecast; a discussion of project management techniques and contingency planning; and an emphasis on the responsibilities of the library leadership as well as those of the planning committee.

Nancy Ruccio (1980), Director of the Westmoreland County (Pennsylvania) Library Board, noted the concerns of directors of small and medium-sized libraries, discussed the importance of planning to satisfy citizen needs, and encouraged librarians to have the self-confidence to study the manual and choose methods that best suit their situations. She provided a detailed explanation of each of the planning steps and listed the manual's recommendations for accomplishing each.

Robert Rohlf (1981), then president of the Public Library Association, spoke on the process at over 20 state and regional library association meetings. He characterized the manual's surveys as weak and warned that planning would probably be stressful but pointed out the value of getting the public involved. He advised using community planners and making sure the climate was hospitable to planning.

In her *Library Quarterly* review, Dorothy Sinclair (1981), then of Case Western Reserve University, warned that the manual provided insufficient attention to data analysis and that staff would not like having their productivity studied, and she criticized the manual's examples as appearing to favor demand, being mostly quantitative, capable of formulation without using the process, and misleadingly evaluating programming as a means of attracting users. Sinclair also pointed out that the "main theme" was that libraries should use the manual selectively and develop objectives based on their own communities and values and concluded that the process was a "valuable tool" if used as intended (pp. 212–213).

John Hawgood (1981), Director of Computing at the University of Durham, England, suggested dividing the manual's primary cycle into subcycles for training, thinking, and measuring; postponing data collection until the third planning cycle; and considering problems in their full complexity with existing data rather than diverting attention to data gathering early on. He explained the ABACON chart he developed and suggested that it be used earlier than indicated by the manual to record importance-ranking of goals, the measuring scales, the existing measuring values, and the target values for each goal, in addition to its use as a visual aid for evaluating strategies.

Betty Turock (1981), of Rutgers University's Graduate School of Library and Information Studies, reviewed what she considered to be the strengths of the process: its stress on participative planning and flexible implementation, explanation of the purposes of the methods and instruments suggested, provision of scientific data-gathering methods, suggestion of modification according to size, inclusion of warnings and pitfalls, and stress on planning's cyclical and ongoing nature. She expressed concern that the manual advocated use of a telephone survey for citizen input and gave only slight attention to the political nature of the process, group processes and values, and education for planning. Turock suggested that librarians develop a plan for using the process that would consider a library's planning history and its purpose, goals, and objectives for planning; operational level action steps; and continuing education and public relations activities.

Characterizing the process as comprehensive, flexible, adaptable, educational, stressing realism, participative, ongoing, and exciting, Marcia Bellassai (1982), consultant with King Research and a coauthor of the planning manual, enumerated the benefits and problems experienced by libraries and suggested helpful solutions. Bellassai pointed out that the process can result in local standards relevant to library needs and community resources; empirical data to aid in making and justifying decisions; a framework for future decision making; priorities for different funding contingencies; and broad staff and community participation, which help create an environment and support for any necessary change, provide a forum for airing differences in service philosophy, aid communication, and can play an important educational role.

Bellassai (1982) listed the following problems experienced by libraries: confusion over the planning committee's role; citizens' lack of understanding of library resources and services; staff's lack of exposure to management problems and their lack of concept of the library as a whole; committee members being reactive rather than active; data collection slowing momentum; planners becoming swamped in detail, having difficulty determining the importance of the findings, and being unaware of or forgetting relevant data; and hurt feelings resulting from staff surveys. To alleviate these common problems, she suggested being realistic in knowing what planners can do and then carefully explaining the role of the committee; summarizing planning objectives, community characteristics, services currently provided, and service potential; emphasizing service alternatives and tradeoffs; and having a subcommittee prepare positions for the full committee's consideration. Other suggestions included completing data collection before planning begins; presenting only data that have been analyzed, interpreted, and summarized in terms of implementation for relevant planning steps; having one person responsible for collecting, processing, and interpreting data during initial and secondary cycles; and encouraging planners to view data in perspective.

Citing the process as an important tool for change, Barbara Conroy (1982), a Colorado consultant, advised that libraries capitalize on possibilities for developing staff members' knowledge, skills, and attitudes through broad staff involvement. She recommended, conversely, that libraries with a need for comprehensive staff development consider the process as a vehicle.

Mary Jo Detweiler (1983), the director of the Prince William (Virginia) Public Library, one of the field-test libraries for the process, analyzed the planning manual and the planning documents submitted to ALA by 27 libraries. Her analysis mixed criticism of the manual based on space devoted to different aspects of planning with statistics on how many libraries completed various aspects of the process. She found that the manual devoted only five pages to the mission statement and only five pages to strategies; that over two-thirds of the manual was devoted to surveying; and that only 12 out of the 27 libraries had mission statements, only two had sections on strategies, and nearly half had submitted only survey summaries without roles, goals and objectives, and strategies. She criticized the manual for paying insufficient attention to developing mission statements and strategies and to the political environment, for overemphasizing data collection, wrongly advocating the process as a budget defense tool, not differentiating between planning needs of small and large libraries, and assuming wrongly that librarians could design and conduct surveys.

Mary Jo Lynch (1983) criticized Detweiler's methodology and refuted her conclusions. She asserted that the manual did not neglect to inform its users that choosing a mission was more important than data collection or that data should be collected only when needed. She also pointed out that libraries had sent planning documents at different times and at different stages in their planning cycles so that those examined may not have described the entire file of documents or the libraries' actual experiences.

Patrick Williams (1983), then of the University of Chicago Graduate Library School, criticized the manual as being illogical and incoherent and warned that planners attempting to use it for comprehensive planning would be defeated by the document and would produce incoherent plans. Insisting that the manual prescribed two separate processes that were incomplete and inconsistent with each other, he wrote that the first process, outlined in Chapters 5 and 6 of the planning manual, was incomplete because it ignored public demand and neglected to offer prescriptions for determining priorities or forming goals and objectives related to needs, and that the second process, beginning with Chapter 7, elicited a statement of purpose that used undefined and overlapping categories and recommended a simplistic method for establishing priorities.

Robin Gault (1986), then a member of the PLA Committee on Service to Children, recommended methods by which the specific needs of children's services can be taken into account in the planning process. She offered specific suggestions regarding the makeup and orientation of the planning committee and the relevant types and sources of information needed, and she provided questions to use in data analysis.

Donald Sager (1986), then director of the Milwaukee Public Library, discussed what he saw as the unique aspects and commonalties of planning for libraries serving populations over 500,000 and under 10,000: the need for participation, clarity, momentum, and macro- and micro-planning. Offering both general suggestions and suggestions and observations specific to large and small libraries, he recommended that board, staff, and community be involved; that planning committees be told their responsibility, the final product required, the level of support, and their deadline; that the committee's progress be monitored; and that the process be completed within six months to a year.

For larger libraries, Sager recommended greater selectivity and balance in choosing committee members, greater input into the process, delegating elements of planning to task forces and/or using specialized consultants, defining the respective roles of the planning committee and the task forces (the committee identifies general goals and objectives, whereas task forces develop specific strategies and refined objectives), and encouraging committee representatives to make a greater commitment to the plan's success. He pointed out that smaller libraries have a greater possibility of achieving fuller participation; their plans include greater specificity and may risk overspecificity; their planners may have a greater knowledge of community resources, which could cause overly conservative plans; there is greater opportunity for relating planning to planning activities of other institutions; and they may rely on their cooperative systems to develop plans and then fit their plans into the system's plan.

LESSONS LEARNED AND RECOMMENDATIONS FOR REVISING THE 1980 PLANNING MANUAL

What can be learned from the experiences and comments of librarians and others who used and studied *A Planning Process for Public Libraries* (Palmour et al., 1980)? An obvious lesson is that libraries and their communities definitely benefited from its use. An equally obvious lesson is that more than a few librarians experienced major difficulties, some because of their lack of understanding or misuse of the process, some the fault of the planning manual. The reports and analyses summarized in this and the previous chapter offer valuable suggestions for improved planning. Several also contain very specific recommendations for revising the planning manual. The benefits accrued and difficulties encountered by libraries are reported in the following section, and the lessons learned from these difficulties are discussed. A summary of recommendations made for revising the 1980 planning manual follows the discussion of lessons learned.

Benefits of Using the Planning Process

The chief benefits reported were political in nature. Local governing officials' improved perception of efficiency led to increased support; libraries' public images were enhanced; involving citizens and especially local officials helped in a plan's acceptance and implementation. The public became more aware of services offered by local libraries, as well as the expense and necessity of having good library services. Citizens became more willing to work on the behalf of libraries, new Friends groups were formed, and knowledgeable prospective board members were discovered.

Staff members learned to accept more responsibility and to be better managers; they too gained a greater understanding and appreciation of the overall context and the problems faced by their directors. Directors learned more about their staffs' perceptions; communication and morale were often improved. The process also collected data useful for both current and future planning, served as a focus for decision making, led to new and improved services, helped in making budget cuts, and most important, provided a sense of purpose and direction. Hopefully it has also resulted in better use of management data and in planning becoming an established function of library management.

Difficulties

The difficulties experienced by libraries indicated that some librarians lacked skills needed to use the methods outlined in the manual; others may not have studied the manual carefully or may have misunderstood its instructions. In some cases the manual's inadequacies were at fault. The following pages discuss the important lessons learned from the difficulties encountered, many of which are still highly relevant to today's planners.

Preplanning

It is crucial that libraries develop a plan for using the process. Staff and financial resources must be assessed, and a realistic estimate made of the costs of the process. Extra money may need to be obtained for hiring a data coordinator, group facilitator, or consultant or for contracting for data collection or other services. Staff and board must be educated about the process and possibly about the library's services and needs; their involvement and support is crucial. Decisions must be made about the role and makeup of the planning committee, the extent of data collection, and the means of informing and involving staff and community residents.

Involvement of Lay Citizens, Including Local Officials

Differing opinions exist about including lay citizens as planning committee members. Their inclusion produces citizens who are knowledgeable and concerned about the library and its problems; these citizens may also become more willing and able to support the library. However, if lay citizens are involved, their role and responsibilities must be carefully defined, and they must be given a thorough orientation to the library and to the planning process.

Numerous other opportunities exist for involving citizens. They can be appointed to focus groups, invited to attend town meetings or hearings, interviewed, or surveyed. Obtaining input about citizens' interests and information needs helps develop more relevant plans; it also gives citizens a sense of ownership of the plan.

Data Collection and Analysis

Data collection and analysis caused the greatest difficulty for most users of the 1980 manual. Some libraries collected enormous amounts of data without thinking about what data were needed or how they would be used; they became overloaded with irrelevant data and failed to collect some of the data needed. Some libraries did not follow the manual's instructions for conducting the surveys properly; many used the manual's samples without adapting them.

Librarians should place less emphasis on the data collection aspect of the process. Before any surveying is done, they should think carefully to decide what data are essential for planning; they should then check to see if the data are already available. If surveys are used, the data coordinator must be (or must become) competent in survey design and random sampling techniques, or the library must contract for professional services. Once collected, the data must be carefully analyzed and interpreted for the committee.

Responsibility of Director and Board

Directors and board members must be very involved in the use of the process, attending committee meetings and taking part in all decisions. In some cases it is a good idea for a director, board chair, or member to chair the process; in other libraries someone other than the director or board chair might be a better choice. The chair must be skilled in group process; it is equally important that the chair be someone who can be objective and open to considering new ideas.

Selection of Mission and Strategies

Many libraries failed to devote adequate time or thought to developing a mission statement, a crucial step that should precede and guide the development of goals and objectives. Other libraries neglected to develop strategies for accomplishing their goals and objectives. The mission is the unique reason for a library's particular goals and objectives; the strategies are the means of accomplishing them. The mission is the "why"; the strategies are the "how." Without these there seems little reason for having goals and objectives.

Staff Involvement and Public Relations

Many opportunities exist for involving and informing the staff and public. Staff can tell planning committees about the aspects of the library and its services that they know best; they can answer committee members' questions and serve on subcommittees. The more involved and better informed staff are, the better they will accept the decisions made by the planners. The planning process can also be an excellent means of staff development.

The public relations opportunities of the planning process are also numerous. In addition to their providing valuable input, it has been established that the more that citizens and local officials are involved and kept informed, the more they will grow to care about the library and its needs. Their increased knowledge and caring and their improved perception of the library's management often leads to increased support of the library.

Flexibility and Time Involvement

Several libraries that had successful planning experiences noted that they used the manual as a guide from which to choose rather than a bible that had to be followed rigidly. Others attributed their success to taking as little of the citizens' time as possible. At these libraries, much of the behind-the-scenes work was done before the committees were appointed or between committee meetings. The planning committee was used to brainstorm or build on work done by staff.

Suggestions for Revising the 1980 Manual

The manual was criticized chiefly for an overemphasis on data collection and a lack of attention to data analysis and interpretation, development of a mission statement and strategies, group process, and the needs of small libraries. Goals and objectives given as examples were said to favor demand and to be mostly quantitative and capable of formulation without the process. In addition to omitting jargon and using a less wordy style, suggestions included the need for less emphasis on data collection, improved guidelines for collecting and interpreting data and for using planning committees, advice on simplifying the process and adapting it for use by small libraries, discussion of the implications of various choices, structured methods for examining various aspects of service, and measurable and output-oriented goals and objectives. It was recommended that options be provided for using the process, and that librarians should be encouraged to choose methods that fit their planning needs. The section on data collection should discuss the reasons for conducting surveys and advise librarians on how to create surveys to fit their situations, and it should include information on computer coding and statistical packages. More emphasis should be given to developing mission statements and strategies, to the responsibilities of the director and board, and to group process, the political environment, and to providing education for planning.

SUMMARY

The three libraries studied by the author differed greatly in their use of *A Planning Process for Public Libraries* (Palmour et al., 1980) and in the benefits received from its use. This chapter included a detailed analysis of the conclusions drawn from the author's study. It also contained the recommendations of librarians who had used the 1980 manual and a summary of the analyses and recommendations of other researchers, library educators, and other professional leaders who studied the process and its implementation.

After summarizing the many important lessons learned about preplanning, involvement of lay citizens and local officials, data collection and analysis, responsibility of director and board, selection of mission and strategies, staff involvement and public relations, and flexibility and time involvement, the chapter concluded with a brief discussion of the recommendations made for revising the 1980 planning manual.

The next chapter introduces and describes the PLA's second planning manual, *Planning and Role Setting for Public Libraries* (McClure et al, 1987). After a discussion of its development and the changes incorporated into the new manual, many of which were recommended in the reports and articles discussed in Chapters 1 and 2, the author will begin to report on the use of the revised planning manual.

Chapter 3

The Revised Planning Manual: *Planning and Role Setting for Public Libraries: A Manual of Options and Procedures*

Designed to incorporate the many valuable lessons learned through libraries' use of *A Planning Process for Public Libraries* (Palmour et al., 1980), the second version of the planning process, *Planning and Role Setting for Public Libraries: A Manual of Options and Procedures* (McClure et al., 1987), was published as a component of the PLA Public Library Development Program (PLDP). Other components of the PLDP included a revised version of *Output Measures for Public Libraries* (Van House et al., 1987) and a customized national data service for use by librarians seeking comparative data from libraries that have completed a preselected group of input and output measures.

This chapter traces the development and provides a description of the new manual, analyzes the important ways in which it differs from *A Planning Process for Public Libraries* (Palmour et al., 1980), and estimates the extent to which the revised process has been adopted by libraries. Next, several reports, studies, and critiques of the manual's use published from 1987 through 1993 are summarized. The chapter concludes with a detailed account of the use of the 1987 planning manual by 255 libraries surveyed during a 1991 study conducted by the author.

INTRODUCING *PLANNING AND ROLE-SETTING FOR PUBLIC LIBRARIES*

In the June 15, 1986 issue of *Library Journal,* Kathleen M. Balcom, then Vice President/President-Elect of the Public Library Association, announced:

> Next Summer the Public Library Association (PLA) will unveil its major new management planning tool at the ALA Annual Conference in San Francisco. The work, called the Public Library Development Project (PLDP), is guided by PLA's New Standards Task Force. The completion of the project and its introduction to the profession will certainly be a major objective of my presidency. (p. 36)

One component of this new management tool was to be "a revised, shortened, but enhanced version of the *Planning Process for Public Libraries*" (p. 38).

After listing the problems encountered by users of *A Planning Process* (obsession with data collection, failing to use readily available data or to identify research questions prior to data collection or to develop goals and objectives that related to data collected, losing impetus before developing strategies), Ms. Balcom discussed the improvements to the new planning manual. She explained that the new manual would suggest different levels of planning effort, provide more options and flexibility at the data-gathering stage, discuss the relationship of planning to the budget cycle, incorporate practical suggestions offered by librarians, and include a role-setting component that would help planners differentiate among various roles and identify essential resources and performance measures for each role.

Ms. Balcom (1986) also pointed out that the manual would help planners relate role-setting to community analysis; integrate the role-setting process with planning, measurement, and evaluation; and understand the political implications and the value each role brings to the community. It would offer libraries a choice of planning components and allow them to match their efforts to their resources. This flexibility was designed especially to meet the needs of smaller libraries by the manual's developers who continually asked, "Is a one-librarian library reasonably able to complete this step?" (p. 39).

How Did This New Manual Come Into Being?

In July 1981, only a year after publication, PLA's Executive Board asked the PLA Research Committee to consider revising *A Planning Process*; development and publication of a revision was approved by the board at the 1982 ALA conference. Charged with its production, the Goals, Guidelines, and Standards Committee established a subcommittee to revise the manual by 1985.

In 1983 Nancy Bolt, then president of PLA, appointed the New

Standards Task Force. Its members included state library personnel, library directors, and people who had worked with smaller and medium-sized libraries as they used *A Planning Process*; in fact, most had been actively involved in developing and/or using the first manual. Originally appointed for one year, this task force was charged with making recommendations "on the feasibility and desirability of new standards for public libraries." The task force's recommendation was "to continue on the path started by the Planning Process for Public Libraries and not to return to the more directive standards of the past" (Pungitore, 1989, p.55).

Influenced by a 1982 consulting report in which Lowell Martin outlined suggested alternative roles for the Free Library of Philadelphia, the task force began to explore the possibility of incorporating the concept of role statements into the planning process. Martin's belief that libraries should select a limited number of roles to attempt to fulfill was incorporated into the new manual's role-setting concept.

At the end of its initial year, the task force recommended that, rather than merely revising the earlier manuals, new planning tools should be produced for public libraries. It recommended a "new approach" to planning that would shift emphasis from data collection to role setting and tie planning more closely with evaluation. Its recommendation was approved, and the task force was retained to organize and oversee the development of the new planning tools. The PLA Research Committee recommended that the new manual be made easier for inexperienced planning libraries and that it include better survey tools and a section on working with data analysis and consultants (Pungitore, 1989, pp. 56-57).

In May of 1984, PLA had submitted a draft proposal to the Department of Education to fund the revision of *A Planning Process*. When this proposal was rejected, a fund-raising effort, spearheaded by Charles Robinson, director of the Baltimore County Public Library System, was begun to request funds from state library agencies and individual public libraries. The Chief Officers of State Library Agencies (COSLA) and the Urban Libraries Council (ULC) initially donated $80,000 (Pungitore, 1989, p. 58). By April 1987, nearly $200,000 had been contributed. In addition to COSLA and the ULC, money was received from 33 state library agencies, 10 library associations, and 177 public libraries and public library systems (McClure et al., 1987, pp. xiv–xvii).

In 1985 a team of consultants was hired to produce the new planning tools; their work was guided by the New Standards Task Force, which met with them periodically to discuss, critique, and offer direction, test the concepts, and approve or veto the team's work. By January 1987, the consultants had completed the new planning manual; they had also revised the output measures manual and completed the design and specifications for the public library data service (Pungitore, 1989, p. 58).

The publication of the new "fresh approach to the planning process" (Anthony, 1987, p. 55) was heralded in the summer issue of *Public Libraries* by New Standards Task Force member Carolyn Anthony, who discussed the addition of the role-setting concept and the level of effort option. Pointing out that "the inclusion of such levels is but one of the ways in which PLDP has responded to experiences with the earlier manuals and other comments from the field" (p. 56), Anthony concluded that

> *Planning and Role Setting for Public Libraries* is truly a one-size-fits-all manual. Smaller libraries that regarded *A Planning Process* as too cumbersome to attempt and larger libraries that got bogged down in the planning process will welcome the clear presentation of choices in effort levels. (p. 56)

The initial efforts to disseminate the new manual and the other components of the Public Library Development Program were organized by PLA, which set up state library agency workshops to train consultants to work with the planning process and responded to requests from library organizations for speakers. After the manuals were published, supervision of their dissemination became the responsibility of the Goals, Guidelines, and Standards committee (Pungitore, 1989, p. 59).

DESCRIPTION OF *PLANNING AND ROLE SETTING FOR PUBLIC LIBRARIES*

The new planning process manual outlines options and procedures to help public librarians "plan more successfully" (McClure et al, 1987, p. 2). Its numerous options and very specific procedures assist planners in preparing for planning, gathering information about their libraries and communities, selecting roles and defining a mission, establishing goals and objectives, selecting activities and tasks, reporting results, evaluating planning accomplishments, and recommending future actions.

Divided into eight chapters, the manual (McClure et al., 1987) begins by introducing the purpose and benefits of planning, the planning cycle, levels of efforts, and the seven planning phases. Each of the remaining chapters outlines a series of specific steps for conducting one of the seven planning phases listed below (pp. 1–6).

Chapter 2, "Planning to Plan," offers options for tailoring a library's planning process to its planning needs, purposes, and resources by helping planners clarify planning purposes, balance the library's level of planning effort, define planning responsibilities, allocate resources, establish a planning schedule, establish the planning committee, and educate planning participants (pp. 7–14).

Chapter 3, "Looking Around," explains the process of collecting information about a library and its community. Planners are instructed to determine level of effort, prepare for collecting information, decide what information is needed, gather information, study the information, and report results (pp. 15–24).

Chapter 4, "Developing Roles and Mission," introduces eight service roles from which libraries may choose and explains the link between these roles and the library's mission statement. Planners are to determine level of effort, study library roles (each describes service aspects, benefits, critical resources needed, and output measures to explore), select and prioritize roles, and write the mission statement (pp. 27–44).

Chapter 5, "Writing Goals and Objectives," assists the planning committee in writing goals and objectives that support the roles and mission statement, respond to community characteristics and information gathered previously, and take the library's resources into consideration. The following steps are discussed: determining levels of effort, reviewing existing information, generating and screening goals, generating and screening objectives, making objectives measurable, writing a draft set of goals and objectives, ranking objectives, and reviewing the final goals and objectives statement (pp. 45–56).

Chapter 6, "Taking Action," helps the committee and staff translate the objectives chosen previously into activities and tasks. Steps include determining level of effort, identifying possible activities for each objective, selecting activities, changing the planning perspective (staff implements plans, committee reviews process and writes planning document), managing implementation, monitoring the implementation process, and reviewing objectives and activities (pp. 57–66).

Chapter 7, "Writing the Planning Document," offers guidelines for developing a written planning document, outlining three possible versions based on three different levels of effort. Steps include preparing to write the document, determining level of effort, writing the document, reviewing the document, obtaining formal approval, and presenting and promoting the document (pp. 67–74).

Chapter 8, "Reviewing Results," completes the process by suggesting a way to identify areas where planning can be improved for the next cycle. Its steps include determining level of effort, reviewing the plan, reviewing the planning process, and recycling the information (pp. 75–83).

Procedures and Workforms

A large portion of the manual consists of procedures to help planners accomplish the various steps and tasks necessary to the process. Detailed instructions are provided for each step of each of the planning phases.

64 STEPHENS

Specific suggestions are made for what to include in the letter inviting people to serve on the library's planning committee; how to prepare a planning budget; how to educate people about the process and the library; what to do and not to do during data collection; types of information to consider about the community and the library and methods of data collection; organizing, interpreting, and reporting the information collected; studying, selecting, and prioritizing roles; writing the mission statement; developing, writing, and ranking objectives; identifying and selecting activities; managing and monitoring implementation; writing the planning document; and reviewing the plan and the planning process.

Eighteen sample workforms are provided. These are included in an appendix with the instruction that many can be duplicated directly but others have to be revised or reformatted; reduced forms are found at the appropriate points within the text.

Forms are provided for planners to use in preparing simple planning budgets and planning charts; listing planning information; translating the findings of looking around; selecting library roles; drafting mission statements; assessing the measurability of objectives; ranking objectives; writing a summary of roles, goals, and objectives; listing activities; reporting the status of implementation activities; assessing activities and objectives; reviewing goals, roles, and mission statements, information gathered by looking around, and the overall planning process; and making recommendations for the next planning cycle. Other figures include an overview of the planning cycle, a sample planning road map, do's and don'ts for looking around, a sample information needs list, suggested outlines for reporting the results of the looking around process, the public library roles, recommendations for the number of roles, a sample role selection tabulation sheet, mission statement and goals and objectives for a fictional library, a chart of the objectives cycle, output measures for typical library service areas, a chart for comparing alternate activities, a sample planning chart, a list of factors affecting level of effort for writing the planning document, and planning document guidelines for each of the three levels of effort.

HOW DOES *PLANNING AND ROLE SETTING* DIFFER FROM *A PLANNING PROCESS*?

Its preface declares that "this planning manual is not a revision of *A Planning Process for Public Libraries*. Rather, the new manual is a new approach to public library planning. The manual offers a new and simplified process" (McClure et al., 1987, p. xix). This description is entirely accurate. The only clarification needed is to point out that the process itself (reviewing existing conditions and services, defining roles and mission, setting goals and objectives, choosing strategies, and evaluating results) is basically the same as that outlined by the previous manual. It is in its approach to carrying out these components of the process that the new manual differs substantially.

The major suggestions for change incorporated in the 1987 manual include the following: offer specific direction on how to prepare to use the planning process, limit the amount of needs assessment and data collection, describe a range of levels of effort, include a set of typical service roles from which libraries may select, specify possible outlines for a planning document, detail procedures for implementing the plan, and make the process "easy to use, flexible, and doable" (p. xix). Most of these recommendations were mentioned or alluded to in the articles and research summarized in the previous chapters; many of the other specific recommendations included in those pages were also included. The many suggestions for revision resulted in changes in the following aspects:

- Format and style.
- Planning components.
- Flexibility.
- Citizens as planning committee members.
- Planning to plan.
- Data collection.
- Developing roles and mission.
- Formulation of goals, objectives, and strategies.
- Output measures.

Format and Style

The 1987 manual looks much more like a true manual or workbook, with plenty of white space, lists, charts, pictures, and workforms. It is much shorter (only 83 pages of text) and more concise. The style is less formal and more direct, with clear wording and a minimum of jargon. It has a practical step-by-step approach that includes many helpful tips for conducting most of the procedures included.

Planning Components

Although renamed, many of the seven planning phases are very similar to those in the earlier manual. Phases on preparing to use the process (preplanning) and on writing the planning document were added. The previous manual's steps on assessing community library needs and evaluating current library services and resources were combined into one step, "Looking Around," and those on developing and evaluating strategies for change and implementing the strategies were combined as the "Taking Action" phase.

Flexibility

The newer manual's flexibility is one of its most obvious improvements. Although *A Planning Process* advised librarians to tailor the process to their needs, this aspect was not stressed and few options were outlined. Beginning with the inclusion of "options" in the subtitle, *Planning and Role Setting* emphasizes the concept of choice. Planners are told in the preface that the manual "offers a general approach" to planning and that they "should use those techniques most appropriate to their situation and adapt others" (McClure et al., 1987, p. xix).

A major device for encouraging and enabling librarians to tailor the process to their needs and resources is the concept of levels of efforts. Although the choice of a basic, moderate, or extensive level of effort for the overall process serves as a framework, planners can set different levels of effort for each of the major phases and for specific steps within the phases. In fact, choosing a level of effort is either the first or second step of each of the planning phases. Succinct instructions for each of the three levels are included in boxes within each chapter; guidelines for specific steps are also included in the narrative. An excellent example of the choices encouraged is the chart providing varying guidelines for writing each section of the planning document according to level of effort chosen.

Flexibility is allowed in the order in which the planning phases are attempted. A "likely route" is laid out for a library completing the planning cycle for the first time, but planners are told, "The route for subsequent objectives will vary from this pattern, as may the route you develop for your library" (p. 4). An example is the choice of the order of the "Looking Around" and the "Developing Roles and Mission" phases. Although it is assumed that the full process will eventually be completed, libraries may postpone some phases to later cycles.

Numerous options are suggested for many of the steps within major phases. For example, the chapter on writing goals and objectives discusses options for the following: organization for writing goals and objectives; for relating roles, goals, and objectives; for the number of goals and objectives; and for the sequence of writing goals and objectives. Other examples include options for educating planning participants, organizing planning information, selecting roles, and generating alternative activities.

Citizens as Planning Committee Members

One of the main differences found in *Planning and Role Setting* is the deemphasis on including lay citizens on the planning committee. Although broad-based citizen representation was a basic tenet of the first process, the revised manual states, "Some libraries seek citizen representation on the planning committee; others do not. Planning committees may include any combination of the following: the director, key staff, board members, and citizens" (McClure et al., 1987, p. 10). Options for citizen involvement such as serving as informal reactors or advisers and holding public hearings are suggested.

Planning to Plan

Although the earlier manual briefly discussed the need for preplanning, "Planning to Plan" has been made the official first step of the revised process, and a full chapter is devoted to preparing for the use of the process. Concepts presented include public relations, planning for libraries with multiple outlets, clarifying planning purpose, balancing levels of effort, responsibility of the different participants, funding the process, the planning schedule, establishing a planning committee, and educating planning participants.

Data Collection

The heavy emphasis on surveying was deleted. Unless planning at an extensive level of effort, planning committees are encouraged to select only a small set of data from that available from printed information sources, agencies and organizations, and existing library statistics. Those planning at the extensive level are referred to other sources (including *A Planning Process*) for data collection methods such as surveying and interviewing, which are "beyond the scope of this manual" (McClure et al., 1987, p. 23). Greater emphasis is placed on deciding what information is needed and on organizing, interpreting, and reporting the results of the information collected.

Developing Roles and Mission

A major addition to the process is the concept of role selection, a new and innovative concept in 1987. The service aspects, benefits, and critical resources needed are described for eight possible roles or profiles of service emphasis. Planners are encouraged to choose a small number to emphasize for the planning cycle; the roles chosen provide a framework for the remaining steps of the process. The role-setting process is linked to the data-collection phase and to the use of output measures, and attention is paid to the political implications of choosing a role and the value each role brings to the community.

Formulation of Goals, Objectives, and Strategies

Greater assistance is provided in the mechanics of developing goals and objectives. Much more attention is given to developing and prioritizing strategies and to managing their implementation.

Output Measures

The manual ties the use of output measures with planning. An appendix summarizes the output measures, defining and providing the means of calculating and data collection for each. Suggested output measures are included for each of the roles, and output measures are discussed in connection with data collection and objectives development.

EXTENT OF LIBRARIES' USE OF *PLANNING AND ROLE SETTING FOR PUBLIC LIBRARIES*

Since its publication, *Planning and Role Setting for Public Libraries* (McClure et al., 1987) has been widely heralded in the library press. It has also been heavily promoted and discussed at national, regional, and state library association conferences.

Many of the state library agencies have encouraged libraries in their states to use the revised process. In fact, a 1989 survey (Pungitore, 1989, pp. 82–83) found that nearly half or 48.6% of the state agencies had decided to take a significant role in its dissemination, as compared to the 26% that took a significant role in disseminating the earlier manual.

The state agencies reported in 1989 that they had used a variety of techniques to encourage and facilitate the manual's use, including consulting (90%), conferences (71%), articles in journals (65%), both introductory (52%) and "how-to" (42%) workshops, and mailings promoting the manual (36%). One fourth (26%) of the agencies reported bringing in outside presenters and one fourth (26%) reported actually working with libraries as they used the process. A small percentage (7%) of the agencies reported that they mandated its use (Pungitore, 1989, p. 88).

The most recent study of state library agency involvement (Smith, 1994) included responses from 35 agencies, 33 of which reported that they encourage planning and the use of the PLA planning manual. Methods range from formal presentations and instruction on using the manual to urging its use in particular libraries. Most states provide continuing education workshops and consult with individual libraries. Several recommend use of the process to trustees. One state conducts the "looking around" step for small libraries headed by nonprofessionals; others modified or adapted the manual for their libraries' use. Eleven states require that libraries use the manual (or an adaptation) to receive state aid or federal or state grants, join a system, or meet state standards. Smith concluded that the responses to her survey "testify to the adaptability of the document and its widespread acceptance as the profession's standard planning manual" (p. 211).

As was the case with the 1980 planning manual, although over 17,000 copies have been sold (McClure, 1993, p. 199), no official figures exist for the number of libraries that have actually used the planning and role-setting manual. It is estimated, however, that the number of libraries that had used it by 1994 was far greater than had used *A Planning Process for Public Libraries* (Palmour et al., 1980) in the seven years between its publication and that of the revised planning manual.

In the 1989 survey of state library agencies referred to previously, 20 of the agencies reported that a total of 441 libraries in their states had used the manual by 1989. At that time an additional nine agencies had also reported its use by from one to 100% (for an average of 36%) of their libraries (V.L. Pungitore, personal communication, August 1, 1991). It is also possible that additional libraries in these states (and in the other 21 states) may have used the process without their state agencies' knowledge.

In reply to a 1991 survey of state library agencies conducted by the author to discover which libraries had used or were using the revised planning manual, 29 of the agencies supplied names of a total of 1,354 libraries in their states. Five state agencies (Alabama, Delaware, Hawaii, North Dakota, and West Virginia) reported that no libraries in these states had used the revised manual; 16 agencies did not respond. The director of Field Services Division of the state library of Kentucky wrote that her agency was currently using a modified version of the manual with 25 counties and that she hoped to have all counties involved in long range planning by 1995 (E. Hilliard, personal communication, October 3, 1991). Table 3.1 lists the number of libraries reported by each of the state library agencies as using or having used the manual.

A total of 304 libraries' roles were reported to the Public Library Data Service for its *Statistical Report* from 1988 through 1991. Many of these were also among those libraries reported to the author by the state library agencies. Although the libraries' inclusion of their roles would seem to suggest at least some use of the planning manual, this is evi-

Table 3.1. Number of Libraries per State Reported in 1991 by State Library Agencies As Using or Having Used Revised Manual

State	Number	State	Number
Alabama	0	Massachusetts	19
Alaska	2	Mississippi	2
Arizona	2	Montana	2
Arkansas	9	New Mexico	4
California	19	New York	71
Colorado	20	North Dakota	0
Connecticut	52	Oklahoma	10
Delaware	0	Oregon	13
Georgia	14	South Carolina	9
Hawaii	0	South Dakota	19
Idaho	22	Tennessee	176
Illinois	618	Texas	7
Indiana	157	Virginia	5
Kansas	2	Vermont	44
Kentucky	20	West Virginia	0
Louisiana	3	Wisconsin	9
Maryland	3	Wyoming	1

dently not always the case since at least nine librarians whose libraries' roles were listed in the report wrote the author that they had not used the planning manual.

Another 313 libraries' roles have been added to the statistical report's listing since 1991, for a total of 617 libraries (see Appendix A for names of libraries) listed to date (Public Library Association, 1988–1994). Table 3.2 lists the number of libraries' roles added each year, beginning with 1988, the first year the report was published.

To repeat, no official figures exist for the number of libraries that have used, or are using, the planning and role-setting manual. The manual certainly is being used, however, although much more heavily by libraries in some states than in others, and its use appears to be growing steadily.

Table 3.2. Number of Libraries Adding Roles to the Public Library Data Service Statistical Report 1988–1994

Year	Number of Libraries
1988	70
1989	83
1990	103
1991	48
1992	82
1993	113
1994	118

PUBLISHED REPORTS, STUDIES AND CRITIQUES OF LIBRARIES' USE OF *PLANNING AND ROLE SETTING FOR PUBLIC LIBRARIES*

The first two reports of role setting by libraries appeared in the same 1987 issue of *Public Libraries* as Carolyn Anthony's article introducing the Public Library Development Program. The director of the Conant Public Library (Baker, 1987), a small Massachusetts library serving a community of 6,000, discussed her library's involvement with a study done for the Options for Small Libraries Committee. Trustees, librarians, and community leaders identified appropriate roles for their libraries from a list of 11 roles similar to those listed in *Planning and Role Setting for Public Libraries*. The committee recommended that, regardless of size, Massachusetts libraries should consider being an interlibrary access point, a recreational reading and viewing center for adults, and a recreational reading and viewing center for children as their basic roles.

Tucson Public Library's Main Library Regional Manager (Miller, 1987) reported on her library's planning efforts, which to some extent mirrored the progress of the Public Library Development Program. After a presentation on planning and role setting made by Charles McClure in 1985, a staff subcommittee proposed six roles for the library based on those in early drafts of the new planning manual. Small committees then studied each role, provided relevant supporting data, refined definitions, and developed objectives for each. Matrices reflecting the resources needed to provide basic levels of service for each role at various service units and projecting expanded levels of service were developed.

The system's coordinator and consultants (Metz, Van House, & Scarborough, 1989) reported on a joint project for simultaneous local planning engaged in by the Bay Area Library and Information System (BALIS) member libraries. The libraries developed individual approaches and progressed at different paces and levels of effort but benefitted from joint training and information sharing through attendance at workshops on each of the planning steps and meetings of the libraries' planning team chairs. The authors found that the system's simultaneous approach to planning proved valuable for each library and for the cooperative relationships within the system; also the information and experience gained will assist with system-level planning.

The former director of Pine Mountain Regional Library System (Hopper, 1991), the poorest of Georgia's regional systems, related the many dividends received from her system's successful use of the process. Ms. Hopper ended her description of the library's positive planning experience by insisting that "planning is success" and that "those who do not have time or other resources for planning should start immediately" (p. 22).

The director of the Free Library of Philadelphia presented a brief account

(Quinn & Rogers, 1991) of the Five-Year Plan resulting from his library's two-year planning process that included community and staff meetings, task forces, and professional user surveys. The largest metropolitan library to date to adopt the PLA planning process, the Free Library used the manual as a "guide" rather than as a "recipe" (p. 14). Adapted from those in the manual, the library's four major roles are to:

1. Be Every Learner's Library—an educational materials resource for all ages.
2. Be The Answer Place—a reference materials center.
3. Provide From Bestsellers to Business Week—a popular materials center.
4. Open A Big Door for Little Readers—preschool activities. (p. 14)

The director of the Crawford Memorial Library in Monticello, New York (Barrish & Carrigan, 1991), a small resort town, discussed his library's use of the process, which resulted in defined roles for its service patterns that gave meaningful direction to collection development within their budget constraints. He asserted that the planning process "set the Crawford Memorial library on a course to far better service within the constraints of its current budget" (p. 285).

St. Paul, Minnesota, Public Library's Public Service manager and planning process consultants (D'Elia, Rodger, & Williams, 1991) described the procedures used to gather input from that library's community. Nominal group techniques were used to interview five groups of stakeholders (adult patrons of the central and branch libraries, institutional representatives, students, educational providers, and community leaders) and library staff members to determine how patrons used the library, their opinions of its strengths and weaknesses, and possible new services the library might provide. Responses concerning materials and collections, reference and information services, access to and dissemination of information, networking with community agencies, adult and educational programming, outreach services, children and young adult services, community relations, staff and staffing, technology, and facilities and equipment were generated and then used to develop surveys of the library's users. Steps for using nominal group techniques and other helpful suggestions for conducting group interviews were included.

Brett Sutton (1991), a researcher at the Library Research Center of the University of Illinois' Graduate School of Library and Information Science, presented a preliminary summary of the results of his study of the long-range planning efforts of four medium-to-large urban public libraries. Some of the libraries followed the ALA handbooks more closely than others, although none used them as the only or principle sources of planning information. Aspects of planning discussed included the following: the libraries' motivation and impetus for planning, organization of the planning process, communication during planning, "sociology" of planning (organizational and personal factors influencing planning attitudes), data collecting, the planning document, planning cycles, planning and budgeting, keys to success, and benefits and hazards of planning.

Also in 1991, Verna Pungitore of the School of Library and Information Science at Indiana University reported the results of her research on the use of the planning process by six smaller (fewer than 25 members, 10,000–50,000 population served) libraries in four midwestern states. Based on interviews with directors, staff, trustees, and citizen planning committee members as well as statistical data, the study's findings revealed differences in the libraries' awareness of and adoption of the planning manuals, the makeup and use of their planning committees, implementation of various elements of the process, perceptions of participants, and planning outcomes. A 102-item bibliography on public library planning was included.

Elizabeth Richmond (1988), a Colorado consultant, criticized that the manual neither includes representatives from other local libraries and library systems in local planning nor provides tools to assess their impact on planning and role and strategy selection, thus diminishing its usefulness to regional systems, individual public libraries, and academic, special, and school libraries. Richmond advised "macro planning" (p. 30), systematically involving representatives of other local libraries, networks, or systems on planning committees or through open meetings, surveys, or hearings; using focused techniques to determine areas of similarity and difference and considering written information about other libraries; and using group techniques to investigate the feasibility and development of joint strategies. Such planning, she asserted, is more realistic for today's libraries, rationalizes the role-setting process, aids in other cooperative efforts, makes limiting services easier, is politically wise, improves funding strategies and communication to other libraries, and widens the context for strategy development.

Writing that "some of the most active and successful library planning today" is being done by public libraries, Brooke Sheldon (1989, p. 200), Dean of Texas Woman's University's School of Library and Information Studies, outlined the strengths of PLA's and other current planning processes: an awareness of the importance of careful needs assessment and evaluation of strengths and weaknesses; good participation by representatives of clientele groups; skill in developing mission, goal, and objective statements; resourcefulness in choosing strategies; strong participation by directors and leaders of local organizations; and a new understanding of quantitative and qualitative methods of evaluating effectiveness. She recommended focusing on one or two service areas that are problematic rather than surveying entire communities, identifying problems capable of being alleviated, making planning a cyclical process carried out by various departments and tied to performance objectives, interweaving environmental trends and forecasts into the planning process, developing plans that allow for longer or shorter diffusion rates, translating goals into a "tangible credo that all employees can both identify with and visualize" (p. 206), and welcoming and rewarding new ideas proposed by staff.

Several researchers have conducted studies to determine which of the manual's eight roles have been chosen as primary and secondary by libraries using the process. Some were quite critical of the libraries' choices; other researchers have criticized the roles themselves.

Carolyn Smith (1989), a master's student at the University of North Carolina, reported the results of her study of the status of role setting by 42 Florida, Georgia, North and South Carolina, and Virginia library systems with budgets of one million dollars or more. Thirty-nine (93%) of the systems had made role selections. Most had chosen only two dominant roles; none had picked more than six for primary emphasis, and only 10% had chosen more than four. Popular Materials Library was chosen most often as a primary role, followed by Reference Library and Preschoolers' Door to Learning. Although Community Activities Center (CAC), Community Information Center (CIC), Formal Education Support Center (FESC) and Research Center (RC) were usually not primary, six systems had chosen CAC, three had chosen CIC and three FESC, and two had chosen RC as such for one branch. Thirty systems (71%) had allocated resources according to the roles selected.

Joan Durrance and Catherine Allen (1991) analyzed data in the PLDS *Statistical Report '90* (Public Library Association) and compared roles selected by 199 libraries with activities undertaken by these libraries to promote literacy, economic development, and democracy, the themes of the 1991 White House Conference on Library and Information Services. Three roles predominated: Popular Materials Library had been chosen as a primary role by nearly 83% of the libraries and either as a primary or secondary role by 95%; Reference Library had been selected as a primary role by slightly over half (52.3%) and as either primary or secondary by 76.4%; a little over one in five had chosen the Preschooler's Door to Learning as a primary role and half chose it as secondary, with more than two-thirds of the libraries choosing it as either primary or secondary.

When the libraries' role choices were compared with their activities to promote literacy, democracy, and productivity, it was discovered that two roles, Reference Library and the Independent Learning Center, were more likely to foster literacy activities; none were directly related to either economic development or democracy; and the Popular Materials Library role was associated with low support of all three. The researchers concluded that role selection does impact public library activities and recommended that a revision of the planning manual should "address explicitly how to incorporate activities that foster democracy and economic development into the role-setting process" (Durrance & Allen, 1991, p. 43).

George D'Elia (1993) first surveyed 1,001 members of the general public and 300 opinion leaders (newspaper editors and editorial writers, TV and radio news directors; elected or appointed public officials; business and civic leaders; and educators). Respondents were asked to evaluate the importance to their communities of the planning manual's eight roles plus two additional roles, an "information center for community businesses" and a "comfortable, quiet place where residents could go to read, to think or to work" (p. v). Roles considered to be very important to their communities by a majority of the general public are listed below, followed by the percentage of respondents ranking them thusly: Formal Education Support Center (88%), Independent Learning Center (85%), Preschoolers' Door to Learning (83%), Research Library (68%), Community Information Center (66%), Information Center for Community Businesses (55%), a Comfortable Place for Residents... (52%), and Popular Materials Center (51%). Six of the roles were also considered very important to their communities by the opinion leaders. These roles (followed by the appropriate percentages) included: Formal Education Support Center (also 88%), Preschoolers' Door to Learning (81%), Independent Learning Center (78%), Community Information Center (65%), Research Library (56%), and Popular Materials Center (53%).

D'Elia subsequently conducted similar surveys with a national sample of African Americans and Hispanic Americans. When combined with those obtained by the general public poll, the results indicated that among all three groups (Caucasian, African, and Hispanic Americans) the highest percentages of "very important" responses occurred for the three educational roles of the public library (Formal Education Support Center, Independent Learning Center, and Preschooler's Door to Learning). D'Elia's report provides detailed comparisons of role evaluations by various demographic groups within each sample that could be used to generate a tentative set of roles for a library or for branches of library systems. These could then be tested by a small community survey, interviews with representatives of various groups within the community, or other appropriate means.

Kenneth Shearer (1993) compared roles reported by 311 libraries to the 1992 edition of the PLDS *Statistical Report* with those selected by random samples of opinion leaders and the general public conducted by George D'Elia. He found that Popular Materials Library was the only role chosen as primary by a majority (77%) of the libraries, although nearly half (49%) had chosen Reference Library as primary, with Preschoolers' Door to Learning a primary choice of over a fourth (28%) and a secondary choice of 50% of the responding libraries. When primary and secondary roles were combined, Popular Materials Library was given a priority by 94%, Preschoolers' Door to Learning by 78%, and Reference Library by 78% of the libraries, whereas Formal Education Support Center, Independent Learning Center, and Preschoolers'

Door to Learning were the top choices of both groups of citizens surveyed. Citing the opinion poll as an indication that citizens wanted libraries to support lifelong learning, Shearer criticized libraries for emphasizing the role of circulating popular materials and warned that "public libraries must stop confusing the most commonly occurring activity in the public library with the most important activity in the public library" (Shearer, 1993, p. 197).

In the last of these published critiques, written in 1993 by one of the planning manual's coauthors, Charles McClure (1993) warned that continued reliance on the manual in its present form "may be detrimental to public libraries." McClure described the manual as "innovative and feasible" (p. 198), praised it for introducing the concept of service roles, addressing the difficulty of trying to be all things to all people, and significantly increasing awareness of the importance of ongoing planning, but criticized its "too traditional, somewhat out of date" service roles, "lack of attention to technology and to adequate information infrastructure to support service provision" (p. 199), and assessment of needs via a preexisting menu for data collection.

Asserting that "PLA and the public library community need to develop an approach to update and expand the manual" (p. 199), McClure offered several suggestions for its revision. He recommended that a revised manual offer possible planning approaches from which individual librarians could develop appropriate planning processes drawing on unique and situational factors particular to their libraries, encourage librarians to design innovative and dynamic service roles especially appropriate for their libraries, better integrate the use of management information systems and evaluation with planning, and recognize the importance of integrating technology and developing a technological infrastructure to empower service provision.

RESULTS OF AUTHOR'S STUDY OF THE USE OF *PLANNING AND ROLE SETTING*

The remainder of the chapter introduces the results of a national study on the use of the planning and role-setting manual conducted by the author during 1991 and early 1992. The study explored how, and how successfully, libraries were using the revised manual and examined the impact that its use had made on the libraries that had adopted the manual.

Survey Population and Description of Libraries Returning Author's Survey

To include the experiences of as many as possible of the libraries that had used *Planning and Role Setting*, questionnaires (see Appendix B for copy of questionnaire) were sent to over a thousand libraries in 44 states and 8 provinces. All libraries with roles listed in the Public Library Data Service *Statistical Report* from 1988 through 1991 were included in the survey population, as were libraries nominated by their state or provincial library agencies as currently using or having used the planning process since 1987. Names of libraries were supplied by 29 state and 4 provincial library agencies. Five state and 4 provincial library agencies responded that none of their libraries had used the planning manual.

Replies were received from 303 libraries, less than a third of those sent questionnaires. Nine of the librarians who had sent their libraries' roles in to the Public Library Data Service *Statistical Report* sent letters explaining that they had not used the planning manual, as did 29 of the librarians whose libraries were nominated by the state and provincial library agencies. Other librarians wrote that the process had been used by previous directors who had left little documentation.

Usable responses were received from 255 libraries (see Appendix C for names of libraries) in 32 states and 2 provinces. The median population served by these libraries is 26,673, which means that half of the libraries serve smaller populations and half serve populations larger than that. Seventy-four of the libraries serve under 10,000, and 66 serve populations over 100,000. One hundred and fifteen serve between 10,000 and 100,000 people. The majority of libraries, 59%, are single libraries without branches. Thirty-six percent are consolidated library systems (systems with branches and one board), and only 3% are federated systems (systems with member libraries that have their own boards).

Planning Participants

First, the librarians were asked to indicate which members of their staffs and communities were involved with their libraries' planning efforts, and whether these individuals served as planning committee members. They were also asked which individuals chaired planning committees or directed the process in those libraries not forming committees.

Seventy-seven percent of the responding libraries indicated that they had formed planning committees; another 2% plan to do so. Library directors served on planning committees in 74%, associate or assistant directors in 31%, and branch or department heads in 38%, of the libraries. A fifth (20%) of the libraries included professionals other than the above, and 23% included paraprofessional and clerical staff on their planning committees. Seven percent indicated that heads of a system's member libraries served on their planning committees.

Over half (57%) of the libraries included board members, and over a third

(38%) included their board chairmen. A third of the responding libraries (33%) included citizens other than board members, Friends, and local officials on their planning committees; a fourth (25%) included Friends of the Library members. Local officials served on planning committees in only 14% of the libraries. Ten percent listed consultants as planning committee members.

Less than half of the libraries responded with the identity of the person who chaired their committee or otherwise directed their planning efforts. In over a fourth (27%) of the libraries this was the director; in 6% a library board member; in 3% either the chairman of the library board or an associate or assistant director; and in 2% either a citizen other than a board member, Friend, or local official or a branch or department head.

Of those libraries indicating categories of planning participants other than those who served as planning committee members, paraprofessional and clerical staff were included by almost one third (30%), library directors by 23%, branch and department heads by 22%, "other" professionals by 19%, and associate or assistant directors by 13%. A third (33%) included library board members, 26% included board chairs, 14% included Friends, 13% included local government officials, and 10% included other citizens.

Use of Various Aspects of the Planning Process

Because libraries vary greatly, the planning process was designed so that local planners could shape the process according to their own libraries' planning needs and resources. One result of this flexibility is that libraries may (and often do) use different aspects of the planning manual during different planning cycles. To determine the extent to which each was being used, the librarians were asked to indicate whether they had used, or anticipated using, each of 14 aspects of the planning process.

Although a majority of the libraries had used (or will use) each of the 14 aspects, some were, or eventually will be, used much more often than others. The parts of the process reported as being used (or scheduled to be used) the most were those that dealt with choosing roles, writing a mission statement, and developing goals, objectives, and strategies. Those dealing with choosing levels of effort, conducting interviews and/or surveys, calculating output measures, and reviewing the planning process were the aspects used (or intended to be used) less often.

As reported above, 77% of the responding libraries had formed planning committees. Use of the remaining aspects will be reported in the order in which the aspects are introduced by the planning manual.

Because libraries have different planning needs and varying amounts of resources to devote to planning, the manual recommends that before beginning the process planners determine a level of effort (extensive, moderate, or minimum) to devote to the overall planning process and to each of its aspects. Although this is a major feature of the flexibility built into the revised process, only 70% of the librarians either had chosen or planned to choose a level of effort for the process as a whole, and only 56% had chosen or planned to choose levels of efforts for the individual phases and steps. Ten percent of those responding to the overall survey did not respond to the former, and 16% did not respond to the latter, of the questions regarding levels of effort, perhaps indicating that they were unfamiliar with, did not understand, or were unsure whether they would use this option.

In gathering information about the library and its community, 86% had used, or planned to use, printed sources and library statistics; 63% had conducted, or planned to conduct, interviews and surveys; and 70% had calculated, or planned to calculate, output measures. No responses to these questions were received from 11%, 13%, and 17% of the libraries respectively. Again, the high degree of nonresponse (17%) raised concern over whether the librarians were familiar with the use of output measures in evaluating a library's services and resources.

Ninety-two percent had selected, or planned to select, roles from those listed in the planning manual. Fifty-two percent indicated they had adapted the manual's roles or chosen other roles, or planned to do so. Over a third (88 or 35%) of the librarians checked that they had both used the manual's roles *and* adapted its roles or chosen other roles; 2% plan to do both.

The librarians were asked to list all roles that were chosen for their libraries. The vast majority of those who did, 114 (57%), listed roles exactly as they are described in the manual, 56 (28%) had used the manual's roles but changed their wording or definition, and 16 (8%) had used or adapted some of the manual's roles but had also added some original ones. Twelve libraries (7%) had originated all of their roles rather than using or adapting any of those listed in the planning manual. Fifty-six (22%) of the libraries did not provide their roles.

Popular Materials Center was the role selected by the largest number of libraries, 180. Preschoolers' Door to Learning was next; it was chosen by 119 libraries. Another 34 libraries enlarged this role to Children's Door to Learning and 6 to Youth's Door to Learning. Reference Library was listed by 115, Formal Education Support Center by 80, and Independent Learning Center by 74 of the libraries. Community Information Center was selected by 40, and Community Activities Center by 32 of the libraries. Research Center was chosen by only 7 of the libraries.

Ninety-five percent had written, or planned to write, a mission statement; 97% had developed, or planned to develop, goals and objectives; and 92% had selected, or planned to select, activities and tasks to accomplish objectives. Along with role setting, these were the aspects of the process receiving the greatest use.

Table 3.3. Aspects of Planning Process Used By Libraries

	Yes	No	Plan To	No Response
Formed planning committee	77% [194]	21% [53]	2% [4]	2% [4]
Chose level of effort for process	66% [150]	31% [70]	4% [9]	10% [26]
Chose levels of efforts for phases and steps	51% [108]	45% [95]	5% [10]	16% [42]
Used printed sources and statistics	83% [189]	14% [31]	3% [7]	11% [28]
Conducted interviews/surveys	57% [126]	37% [83]	6% [13]	13% [33]
Calculated output measures	63% [133]	30% [64]	7% [15]	17% [43]
Selected roles from manual	88% [212]	9% [21]	4% [9]	5% [13]
Adapted roles or chose others	48% [102]	48% [103]	4% [8]	16% [42]
Wrote mission statement	90% [226]	5% [12]	5% [12]	2% [5]
Developed goals and objectives	88% [221]	4% [9]	9% [22]	1% [3]
Selected activities and tasks	75% [184]	8% [20]	17% [43]	3% [8]
Assigned implementation responsibility	62% [145]	17% [40]	21% [48]	9% [22]
Wrote document	72% [176]	11% [27]	17% [41]	4% [11]
Reviewed plan	57% [134]	14% [32]	29% [69]	8% [20]
Reviewed process	32% [73]	30% [70]	38% [88]	9% [24]

Although 92% had selected, or planned to select, activities and tasks to accomplish objectives, only 83% had assigned, or planned to assign, responsibility for their implementation. Eighty-nine percent had prepared, or planned to prepare, a planning document; 86% had reviewed, or planned to review, their plan. Only 70% of those responding had reviewed, or planned to review, their library's overall planning process, making this one of the less used aspects of the process, along with choosing levels of effort for the overall process and for individual phases and steps, conducting interviews and/or surveys, and calculating output measures. A sizeable number of those responding (30, 31, 45, 37, and 30%, respectively) indicated that they had neither used, nor anticipated using, these important aspects of the planning process.

From comparing the number who indicated they had actually accomplished particular steps with those who plan to do so, it appears that many of the librarians were between the "Writing Goals and Objectives" and "Taking Action" phases at the time they received the survey. Table 3.3 lists the percentages, followed by the numbers, of librarians who marked "yes," "no," or "not yet—plan to," when asked to describe their libraries' use of various aspects of the planning process. The percentages and numbers of libraries not responding to each of these items are also provided. The percentages for the "yes," "no," and "not yet—plan to" categories are based on the number of librarians who responded to each item; those for the "no response" category are based on the total number of surveys returned.

Levels of Effort Expended for the Process and Its Phases

As pointed out previously, a major feature of the revised process' flexibility is the concept of levels of effort, the acknowledgement that it is permissible (perhaps even desirable) for libraries to devote varying degrees of effort to various stages of the process. Librarians were asked to indicate the level of effort they had expended on the planning process as a whole and on each of 10 major aspects of planning. They were then asked whether the levels of effort expended were "far too much," "too much," "about right," "too little," or "far too little." Although only 66% had indicated in the previous question that they had selected levels of effort for the overall process and only 51% had done so for individual phases and steps, most of the librarians were able to report and evaluate the levels of effort actually expended. (The nonresponse rate for each of these items was less than a third and was often less than one fifth.)

Over half (60%) of those responding to this question reported spending a moderate level of effort on the process as a whole; a fifth (20%) had spent either an extensive or a minimum level of effort. Almost three fourths (73%) reported feeling that the level of effort expended on the overall process was about right; 10% considered that it was too great, and 17% felt it was too little.

The first phase of the process, the "planning to plan" step, gives planners the opportunity to lay the groundwork for the rest of the process. It is during this step that planners shape the process to fit their libraries' needs and resources, define the responsibilities of major planning participants, and select and train the planning committee.

Forty-five percent of the librarians reported spending a moderate, and 42%, only a minimum level of effort. Only 13% reported spending an extensive level of effort on this important step. Seventy percent felt that the level of effort they had expended was about right, and only 9% felt it was too great. Almost one fourth (22%) felt the effort expended for this step was too little, however.

The second phase of the process, "looking around," is the step during which the planners study their communities and review their libraries' resources in an attempt to assess residents' information needs and the libraries' abilities to meet these needs. Demographic figures and other published and unpublished information about the community and its library are studied; surveys and interviews with knowledgeable citizens may be conducted. Close to half (46%) of the librarians reported a moderate level of effort expended for this step; almost one fifth (19%) reported an extensive level, and over one third (35%) reported only a minimum level. Over half (67%) felt their level of effort expended was about right, and only 6% felt it was too great. Again, over one fourth (27%) felt the level of effort expended for this step was too little.

Responses to the next two phases, "developing roles/mission" and "writing goals and objectives" were almost identical. During the role-setting step, planners choose which of eight roles their library will emphasize over the next few years; the mission statement consequently developed articulates these choices. Goals and objectives that will guide the library in fulfilling its chosen roles are then written. The choice of roles and mission thus guides the goal-setting step.

Fifty-five percent of those responding indicated spending a moderate level of effort on each of these two steps. Twenty-seven percent had spent an extensive level for the role-setting step, while 26% had done so for writing goals and objectives. Nineteen percent had expended only a minimum level of effort for each of these steps. The vast majority of respondents (82%) felt the level of effort expended for the role-setting step was about right; three fourths (75%) responded thusly for the goal-setting step. Nine percent reported that their level of effort for role-setting was too great; another 9% felt it was too little. Nine percent also felt they had expended too great an effort on goals and objectives setting, while 16% felt they had expended too little effort.

Once goals and objectives are developed, planners devise specific strategies or activities by which they can be accomplished. This step is known as "taking action." Fifty-three percent of those responding reported a moderate, 19% an extensive, and over one fourth (28%) only a minimum level of effort expended for this phase, which is the step that determines the strategies the library will use to try to meet its goals. Sixty-nine percent felt their level of effort was about right, and only 4% felt it was too great. Over one fourth of the librarians (27%) felt the level of effort expended on developing strategies was too little, however.

The mission statement, goals and objectives, and strategies developed by the planners are to be detailed in an official planning document. Forty-eight percent of the librarians reported a moderate, 21% an extensive, and 31% only a minimum level of effort expended for this step. Almost three fourths of the librarians (72%) felt their level of effort expended was about right,

10% felt it was too great, and 18% felt it was too little.

"Reviewing results" is the last phase of the process. During this step planners review both the library's progress toward reaching its goals and objectives and the library's planning process itself. Forty-six percent of those responding reported spending a moderate level, 7% an extensive level, and 47% only a minimum level of effort for this step. Fifty-nine percent felt their level of effort expended was about right, and only 3% felt it was too great. Over a third of the librarians (39%) felt the level of effort expended for this step was too little.

As can be seen from the above account, around half (from 44 to 55%) of the librarians reporting level of effort expended indicated devoting a moderate level of effort to each of the seven phases of the planning process. The majority of the librarians, from 59 (for "reviewing results") to as high as 82% (for "developing roles and mission"), reported the levels of effort expended for each of the steps as being about right. However, almost a fourth (22%) reported they had devoted too little effort to the "planning to plan" phase, over a fourth (27%) reported too little effort put into the "looking around" and "taking action" phases, and over a third (39%) reported spending too little effort on the "reviewing results" phase.

It is also interesting to note the number of those responding to the overall questionnaire who did not report levels of effort expended. This number increased from a fifth for the earlier steps to closer to a third for the last three steps (taking action, writing the planning document, reviewing results) of the process. The number of those who did not give their opinion of the amount of effort expended was much lower (from 6 to 22%), although this number also increased as the steps progressed. The decline in those responding to questions concerning levels of effort expended for those phases usually attempted toward the end of the process was probably a reflection of where the librarians were in their use of the process. It should be remembered that a similar decrease was noted in the number of persons reporting they had used a particular step.

Level of Effort Expended on Staff Involvement and Attempts to Inform and Involve the Library's Public

Forty-four percent of those responding reported spending a moderate level of effort on involving library staff members in their planning efforts; 23% reported an extensive, and one third (33%) reported only a minimum level of effort devoted to staff involvement. Well over half (66%) felt their efforts at staff involvement were about right, and only 5% felt their efforts were too great. Almost a third (30%) felt they had devoted too little effort to staff involvement, however.

The majority of respondents, 58 and 60%, respectively, reported spending only a minimum level of effort on informing or involving their communities' residents. Only 4% reported an extensive level, while 38% reported spending a moderate level of effort on informing the public. Only 8% reported an extensive, while 33% reported a moderate level of effort spent on citizen involvement.

A majority of the respondents (57 and 51%, respectively) felt they had expended too little effort on each of these important aspects of the planning process. Less than one percent (.9% and .5%, respectively) felt they had expended too much effort on either aspect, while those reporting that efforts to inform and to involve the public were about right were 42% and 49% respectively.

Table 3.4 lists the percentages, followed by the numbers, of librarians who marked "far too much," "too much," "about right," "too little," and "far too little" when asked to indicate their opinion of the amount of effort expended by their libraries on the planning process as a whole and on each of its phases and aspects. The percentages and numbers of libraries not responding to each of these items are also provided. Again, the percentages for the categories labeled "far too much," "too much," "about right," "too

Table 3.4. Respondents' Opinions of Levels of Effort Expended

	FAR TOO MUCH	TOO MUCH	ABOUT RIGHT	TOO LITTLE	FAR TOO LITTLE	NO RESPONSE
Overall process	2% [4]	8% [20]	73% [176]	13% [31]	4% [9]	6% [15]
Planning to plan	3% [6]	6% [14]	70% [166]	16% [39]	6% [14]	6% [16]
Looking around	1% [3]	5% [12]	67% [158]	23% [54]	4% [9]	7% [19]
Dev. roles/ mission	.8% [2]	8% [18]	82% [194]	6% [14]	3% [8]	7% [19]
Writing goals & obj.	.4% [1]	9% [20]	75% [172]	11% [25]	5% [11]	10% [26]
Taking action	.9% [2]	3% [6]	69% [148]	21% [45]	6% [13]	16% [41]
Writing document	2% [4]	8% [17]	72% [155]	11% [23]	7% [16]	6% [40]
Reviewing results	0% [0]	3% [5]	59% [118]	29% [58]	10% [19]	22% [55]
Staff involvement	.4% [1]	4% [8]	66% [150]	22% [51]	8% [18]	11% [27]
Informing public	0% [0]	.9% [2]	42% [92]	43% [96]	14% [31]	13% [34]
Involving public	0% [0]	.5% [1]	49% [107]	36% [80]	15% [32]	14% [35]

little," and "far too little" are based on the number of librarians who responded to each item; those for the "no response" category are based on the total number of surveys returned.

SUMMARY

This chapter traced the development and provided a full description of *Planning and Role Setting for Public Libraries* (McClure et al., 1987). The new manual's format and style; planning components and flexibility; deemphasis of citizens as planning committee members; introduction of a planning to plan step; instruction on data collection and developing roles and mission, goals, objectives, and strategies; and its inclusion of output measures, all areas that differed greatly from those in the earlier manual, were analyzed.

The chapter also contained a description and critique of the use being made of the revised manual as reported both in the professional literature and in response to the author's 1991 survey. The next chapter will begin the author's assessment of the planning process by examining the tremendous impact that the use of the planning and role-setting manual had on a sample of the libraries that adopted it during the period 1987–1991.

Chapter 4

The Impact of *Planning and Role Setting For Public Libraries* on Its Users

What difference has their use of *Planning and Role Setting for Public Libraries: A Manual of Options and Procedures* (McClure et al., 1987) made to the many libraries that have adopted it? How have these libraries been affected and what changes have resulted from their use of the public library planning process and its manual?

In assessing the value of the process, it is crucial that its impact on its users be considered. Libraries that use the public library planning process devote extensive time and resources to this endeavor. If few benefits were derived and/or the status quo remained unchanged, the cost would certainly be questionable.

The previous chapter reported on libraries' use of this process and its planning manual, based on the professional literature and the results of a national survey of its users. This chapter attempts to demonstrate the important impact of the process on its users by relating the many perceived benefits and resulting changes and the few negative effects reported by librarians who have used the revised manual to guide their libraries' planning.

The impact of the process on a small number of libraries whose planning experiences were reported in the professional literature and discussed briefly in the previous chapter will be presented first. Following this discussion, its impact on those libraries whose directors' opinions were obtained by the author's 1991 survey will be examined.

87

IMPACTS REPORTED IN THE LITERATURE

Roles chosen by libraries in Conant, Massachusetts (Baker, 1987) and Philadelphia, Pennsylvania (Quinn & Rogers, 1991) were reported. Tucson Public Library's use of the process to set roles, develop objectives, and design matrices showing needed resources and projected expanded levels of service was described more fully (Miller, 1987). The libraries in California's Bay Area Library System were credited with deriving the following benefits from their simultaneous use of the process (Metz, Van House, & Scarborough, 1989): improved data collection, clearer direction, explicit decisions about priorities, improved staff morale and communication, action toward needed changes, validation of current practices, good interaction with boards and advisory groups and other departments, and increased funding for member libraries.

Georgia's Pine Mountain Regional Library reportedly benefited from increased communication between library and community and between administration and staff, improved staff morale, increased responsiveness to community needs, planning committee members communicating their support to funding bodies, and a mission leading to more effective decision making and more focused action. A 91% increase in local funding, replacement of a leaky roof, attention paid to collection development and evaluation, increase in support staff, faster decision making, more consistent policies and procedures, attention and resources given to system development, and an end to crisis management were also attributed to their use of the process (Hopper, 1991).

The Crawford Memorial Library (Monticello, New York) made several specific changes based on its choice of roles. Weeding, use of materials dumps and other merchandising techniques, shifting books from reference to circulation, renting popular titles, increasing paperbacks and multiple copies of best sellers, book lists, press releases, and adult book discussion programs were initiated in support of their popular materials role. Designating 50% of the materials budget for children, sponsoring workshops on parenting and babysitting, purchasing new furniture and remodeling the children's room, and displaying children's art work were strategies chosen for the role of Children's Door to Learning. Because Reference Library was not chosen as a primary role, the decision was made to refer some reference questions to larger libraries. Other benefits mentioned were a direction and purpose that had been lacking, more efficient and effective service, and an explanation for why patrons sometimes have to rely on interlibrary loan (Barrish & Carrigan, 1991).

As part of St. Paul Public Library's use of the process, interviews with five groups of stakeholders generated 777 responses. These were used to survey 1,036 patrons as to the importance and quality of the library's current services and the relative importance of several new services and service roles being considered (D'Elia, Rodger, & Williams, 1991).

Pungitore (1991) enumerated the many benefits achieved by the libraries whose planning experiences she studied. She wrote that the process demonstrated the importance of longer-range planning, provided direction, guided decisions concerning materials and services, helped staff members work together, and encouraged staff participation in decision making, which led to greater understanding of staff expectations and increased pride and initiative. It also generated information on perceptions and information needs of users and nonusers, increased respect of and improved working relationships with funding bodies, and provided justification for increased funding. Examples of specific results were decisions to weed parts of collections and deemphasize various roles not chosen as primary, the addition of staff members, quiet space for study, added space for computer terminals, increased numbers of talking books, a terminal for the handicapped, a theft-detection system, and distribution of long-range plans to funding agencies and potential donors.

PROCESS' IMPACT AS REPORTED TO AUTHOR

The librarians who responded to the author's 1991 survey had two opportunities to describe the impact of the planning process. They were first asked to indicate whether their libraries' use of the process had resulted in changes in the following 13 important areas: types of materials collected and services offered; numbers of materials circulated, reference questions asked, and borrowers registered; communication between administration and staff; community awareness of library services; morale of library staff members; library policies and procedures; numbers attending library programs; working relationships with local officials; reallocation of library budgets; and increases in library funding. The librarians were then asked to relate other ways, both positive and negative, that using the planning process had affected their libraries.

Percentages of Librarians Reporting Changes

A majority of the librarians who responded to these particular questions reported that, indeed, changes had occurred in 9 of 13 areas. Sixty-eight percent of these librarians indicated they had added, dropped, or changed emphasis on collecting in certain areas such as popular materials, reference materials, materials for children and students of all ages, and certain categories of audiovisual materials. Sixty-five percent of the librarians responding to this question reported that they had added, dropped, or changed emphasis on certain services (mostly in the areas of reference, services to children, and outreach services).

Sixty-five percent of the librarians reported increases in circulation, 61% reported increases in numbers of reference questions, and 57% reported increases in numbers of registered borrowers. Perhaps the changes in output measures for circulation, reference, and borrowers registered can be at least partially explained by the publicity resulting from the process, as 60% reported that their communities seemed more aware of the libraries' services. Improvement in communication between administration and staff was reported in 64% of the libraries, and 58% of the librarians indicated that staff morale had improved. Fifty-two percent reported that their libraries had changed policies and/or procedures as a result of the process. Others wrote that such changes were either expected or in process, and eight librarians indicated that they had developed written policies where none had existed previously. Changes were made in policies governing personnel, circulation and registration, selection and processing of materials, and hours of operation, with most changes resulting in increased access to library services and materials.

Although fewer than a majority, well over one third of the librarians reported changes in the four remaining areas listed. Forty-five percent indicated that program attendance had increased; 41% reported that local officials were easier to work with as a result of the process; another 41% reported that budgets had been reallocated; and 37% even indicated that their overall budgets had been increased.

The nonresponse rate for the 13 items discussed above ranged from 16 to 28%, which means that quite a few of the librarians did not reply one way or the other to particular items. Several wrote that they had only recently completed the process, and it was too early to tell what its impact would be. Others explained that they could not answer because they were still involved in the process. A few librarians (some who did and some who did not reply to questions about specific items) wrote that they could not be sure whether the changes that had taken place at their libraries were a result of their planning processes. It could be speculated that other librarians may also have been unsure whether the changes they reported were a result of the process but neglected to say so.

It is sometimes very difficult to know why change has occurred or to isolate a particular cause. What *can* be said with certainty about these libraries' experiences, however, is that the libraries *had* used the planning process, a majority of their librarians reported that changes had occurred in 9 of the 13 areas (with well over a third reporting changes in the four remaining), and only a few indicated that they were unsure whether these changes had resulted from their use of the process. Also, many of the librarians later related examples of very specific changes that they attributed to their libraries' use of the planning process.

IMPACT ON USERS 91

TABLE 4.1. Respondents' Opinions of Changes Due to Process

	Yes	No	No Response
Added/dropped/changed emphasis on certain types of materials	68% [136]	32% [64]	22% [55]
Added/dropped/changed emphasis on certain services	65% [130]	35% [70]	22% [55]
Increase in circulation	65% [133]	35% [72]	20% [50]
Increase in reference questions	61% [121]	39% [78]	22% [56]
Increase in registered borrowers	57% [114]	43% [85]	22% [56]
Improved communication between administration and staff	64% [129]	37% [74]	20% [52]
Community more aware of services	60% [126]	40% [84]	18% [45]
Improvement in staff morale	58% [111]	43% [82]	24% [62]
Changed policies and/or procedures	51% [95]	48% [88]	28% [72]
Increase in program attendance	45% [89]	55% [108]	23% [58]
Local officials easier to work with	41% [82]	59% [116]	22% [57]
Reallocation of budget	41% [81]	59% [118]	22% [56]
Increase in overall budget	37% [80]	63% [136]	15% [39]

Table 4.1 presents the percentages, followed by the numbers, of librarians marking "yes" and "no" to each of the items listed as potential changes that could have resulted from use of the planning process. The percentages and numbers of libraries not responding to each of these items are also provided. The percentages for the categories labeled "yes" and "no" are based on the number of librarians who responded to each of the items; those for the "no response" category are based on the total number of surveys returned.

Librarians' Positive Comments on the Process' Impact

Seventy percent of the librarians who returned surveys responded to the narrative question asking them to relate ways using the process had affected their libraries. The vast majority were very positive about the effect that using the process had had. A few stated explicitly:

- " I think it was a positive experience."
- " No negatives. This was one of the best things we have done."
- "I have no negative experiences to report."
- "The effort has only been positive."
- "All use of the planning process has been positive."
- "I think the planning process is the best thing the library has ever done."

Librarians described the planning manual as "a handy outline," "an invaluable resource," and "a great help," and commented that the process got their library "out of a rut" and gave them "the opportunity to be reflective."

One director remarked, "We feel that the process has been critical in providing us a foundation for achieving excellence, and for creating a vision of excellent service which can challenge and motivate the staff." Another wrote, "So far the major change is that we have been able to take advantage of opportunities that have presented themselves. Often, before we began the planning process, we didn't recognize opportunities when they came along." A third director explained,

> The planning process got us out of a "static" mode into a more "dynamic" mode, relative to our long-range objectives, particularly [our] branch development plan. Our thinking had been rather like this: Fill the existing library facilities with more books, and they will come. While this was true for our heavily used branch in the affluent part of town, it was not true for the unserved areas.

The vast majority of comments indicated that the planning process had affected libraries positively by helping the responding librarians manage their libraries both more effectively and more efficiently. Many pertained to aspects of management referred to previously such as collection development and service choice decisions, communication between administration and staff, community awareness of library services, staff morale, changes in policies and procedures, relationships with governmental officials, and funding and budgeting. Arranged according to topic, the directors' comments will be presented in the following pages in the order in which these topics were listed previously.

Following these comments are a large number of comments concerning additional aspects of library management about which respondents were not specifically questioned by the author. Beginning with the section titled "aid to new directors," these comments address aspects of management such as planning and evaluation, working with trustees and library staff members, and facilities and automation planning.

Changes in Materials

One-hundred thirty-six librarians (68%) responded that they had added, dropped, or changed emphasis on collecting certain types of materials. Most changes involved an increased emphasis on popular materials, reference materials, or materials for children and students of all ages, and addition, deletion, increase, or decrease of certain categories of audiovisual materials.

Thirty-nine librarians reported increasing emphasis on popular materials, with seven specifying increases in paperbacks and in multiple copies of current materials. Thirteen reported increased emphasis on reference materials, including periodicals; three reported decreasing their emphasis. Sixteen librarians indicated an increased emphasis on children's materials, while two had increased emphasis on materials for young adults. A few librarians reported an increased emphasis on student-related materials and literacy materials.

Other changes reported included addition or increased emphasis on large-print materials, self-teaching or self-improvement materials, career and educational guidance materials, black interest materials, and parenting materials. Four libraries have added computer databases, and two have begun collections of educational software.

Ten librarians wrote that they were now placing more emphasis on audiovisual materials, but did not specify particular formats. Others reported adding or increasing emphasis on specific formats such as videocassettes, audiocassettes, compact discs, and music cassettes. Two reported placing less emphasis on videocassettes. A few librarians reported discontinuing their collections of phonograph records, films, filmstrips, slides, and framed reproductions.

Librarians described the process' effect on their overall collection development efforts by writing:

- "We had no direction and now we know where we are going."
- "The planning process has increased awareness and initiated better decision making."
- "We've set some priorities. I hadn't really prioritized before."
- "We have extensively studied circulation to determine the most popular materials and reallocated our budget accordingly."

The process was also credited with influencing creation of collection development policies and plans. One librarian wrote that her library was "currently producing a collection development plan that will result in changed emphasis." Another explained, "One of our major objectives was development of a collection development statement and better allocation of the materials budget. We have done most of that."

Librarians commented that because of the process they had begun purchasing requested materials rather than relying on interlibrary loan; developed collection development agreements with university, community college, and special libraries; developed clearer selection criteria and easier budgeting formulas; and become more aware of patrons' requests. Others reported they had become more aware of the importance of weeding and better able to write collection management policies and access their collections.

Nineteen specifically indicated that role selection had greatly influenced their collection decisions. Examples of their comments included the following:

- "We changed statements in the selection policy to fit our roles."
- "Roles have had a definite impact on our collection development; this has been the most important area."
- "By defining each branch's roles, we have drafted a collection development plan for a collection to meet that role."
- "We are able to prioritize services and materials based on the roles identified in the plan."
- "[We] have focused collection development to roles [and] dropped minor activities that were draining away staff hours."

Two librarians echoed each other, writing, "Selecting roles allowed us to narrow our focus rather than 'being all things to all patrons.' We [now] select more heavily in popular fiction and children's materials and less in reference and business," and "As a result of choosing roles, it has been easier to make acquisitions and weeding decisions; we no longer need to try to be all things to all people." Another concluded that the role selection aspect would "ultimately have the most significance" because "it will directly impact the way in which materials budgets are allocated." He explained that their process made the staff consider "why we make the collection development decisions we make—what is our intent and what role does it support."

Several offered concrete examples linking particular roles with specific collection development decisions. Libraries choosing the role of Formal Education Support Center were expanding reference indexing to CD-ROM, placing more emphasis on obtaining materials corresponding with school assignments and curricula, and "trying to move toward purchase of more juvenile materials and realization of [our] role in supplementing K–12 school assignments—never articulated before." Conversely, a librarian who did not choose this role reported that "clarification of [our] role has underscored [the] need to strengthen local school libraries so public libraries can move beyond [a] default role and strengthen our own mission statement."

One librarian explained that her library had reallocated more funds to reference sources because Reference Library was chosen as its main role. Others reported adding more children's books to fit the role of Preschool

Door to Learning and emphasizing popular materials at branch libraries and increasing purchase of videos and compact discs in their Popular Materials Library role.

Changes in Services

Some 130 respondents (65%) indicated that their libraries had added new services or discontinued or changed emphasis on current services provided to their patrons. Librarians commented that their planning process "provided us with an excellent plan for expansion of services" and "allowed us to focus our services to highlight and exploit our strengths as a community institution." One wrote, "[The] planning process enabled us to focus on specific areas of service. It also provided us with the means to expand and improve upon those areas which we felt were important and where we believed we were succeeding." A second explained, "It's a great tool for reestablishing your roles in service or changing those that aren't working out. It keeps you tuned to your public. Defines your goals and keeps you on the road."

The majority of reported service changes were in reference, services to children, and outreach services. Eighteen librarians reported an increased emphasis on reference service, and one "created [a] reference service." Specific examples included: additional reference staff and materials; shorter waiting time at the information desk; increased use of interlibrary loan, database services, and telefacsimile; and increased emphasis on business reference and library user instruction.

Two librarians reported deemphasizing their reference service to adults. One emphasized young adult over adult reference; the other chose to refer patrons to other libraries for complete reference service and limit service to a few specific subject areas.

A few librarians reported an increased emphasis on general services and programming for adults, while a few others have dropped or deemphasized adult programming. Libraries have added readers' advisory services and services for adult independent learners. Some have concentrated more on adults and students of all ages, emphasizing formal education support for preschool, elementary, secondary, and literacy students, and designating a branch as a formal education center.

Thirty-four librarians reported an increased emphasis on services specifically for children, while six reported an increased emphasis on services to young adults. Specific examples included: beginning or increasing story hours and summer reading programs; offering after school activities, services for toddlers and for day care providers; and hiring of children's librarians. Five listed an increased emphasis on school visits.

Five librarians reported decreasing their libraries' services to children, however. Two have discontinued or cut back on class visits to the library, while one has discontinued service to schools.

In addition to those providing services to day care providers, 16 librarians reported adding or increasing emphasis on outreach services such as branches, bookmobiles, or talking book services and delivery of materials to the home-bound and to nursing homes. Others reported increasing services to older adults in the library as well as efforts to improve access for handicapped patrons. Librarians have also begun literacy services, services to Spanish language patrons, and classes in English as a second language.

Five libraries have added fax services, and two have added public-use computers. Pay phones, photocopy machines, typewriters for public use, and meeting rooms have also been made available as a result of the process.

Several librarians indicated that the role selection process had both guided their choice of services to emphasize and allowed them to place limits on services offered. Comments included:

- "This is a slow evolving process, but with roles in place for both our branch libraries and the main library we are realigning our expenditures."
- "We are keeping our roles in mind and are adapting our goals during any given year and from year to year."
- "We realized that we can't do everything we want to do so we have had to establish priorities among both existing and projected services."

Others explained that they "are better able to define what services we do not provide and why," have "focused on consistent services at main and branches and eliminated non-essential services," have "stopped trying to do all roles [and] concentrated on ones we chose," and have "given priority to four selected roles."

Several librarians offered examples of specific services added, dropped, or changed in emphasis because of particular roles chosen. Libraries have ceased providing typewriters and computers for public use, cut hours in their local history/genealogy section to emphasize Popular Materials Library as their number one role, increased activities to nursery schools and preschool children to support the role of Preschool Door to Learning, and built a database for a community information center to facilitate one of their selected roles. Other librarians reported adding readers' advisory services to support the Popular Materials Library role; giving greater priority to adult independent learner than to children's services; changing their secondary role to Formal Education Support Center for preschool, elementary, secondary, and literacy students; and strengthening the role of Children's Library by "liberating" their children's librarian from cataloging. Librarians not choosing Community Activities Center as an important role deemphasized this role by providing space but not staff time and using space previously dedicated to meetings and programs for direct service to users. Four other libraries had added meeting rooms in support of this role.

Improved Communication Between Staff and Administration

Of those responding when asked about the process' effect on staff members, 64% checked that communication between administrators and staff members had improved. Librarians reported that their process resulted in "better" and "greatly improved" communications between library administration and staff. One librarian explained, "We are currently in the process of developing and selecting roles with input from all of our staff. Communication has increased as a result." Others reported that "everyone has input into the direction of the library" and that their process "incorporated ideas from staff" and gave selected staff members opportunity "to participate in management and voice their opinions."

Respondents indicated that the planning process "got trustees together to talk about library service with staff" and resulted in improved communication among various departments within their libraries. Librarians reported that their process "enhanced a team philosophy," "helped very greatly in improving our internal coordination and communication," and "introduced a mechanism for staff input into library service. We now have regular staff meetings centered around planning." One librarian wrote, "We found the process highly effective in creating mutual understanding and cooperation among departments of the library. Communication improved. Staff attitudes became less compartmentalized." Others explained that involving staff at all levels "gave staff an opportunity to experience working in a group" and was "unifying" because "everyone has had multiple opportunities to participate and to contribute ideas."

Community Awareness

Sixty percent of those responding reported that their communities seemed more aware of their libraries' services. Librarians commented that the process served as an "educational experience" that "increased community involvement and awareness" and resulted in "greater enthusiasm for our services" and "higher visibility for the library in the community." One librarian wrote, "We felt we have been able to make the public more aware of the library services." Another explained, "The process increased the overall awareness of our system and the services offered. The tools (surveys/questionnaires) acted as educational tools as well as information-gathering sources."

Although increased community awareness of library services is certainly vital, numerous comments in the narrative section revealed that the process had played an even more crucial public relations role in many communities, that of increased community involvement. Some librarians listed "community involvement in [the] planning process" as one of the positive effects of their planning efforts. Others offered more specific examples such as "the idea of community, board members, and staff working together," "reactivated Friends of the Library," "closer work with schools, special work with businessmen of the town," and "cooperation with other businesses and agencies." One librarian wrote that her library's planning committee had "developed an extremely close relationship to the library. Members want to continue their involvement."

Enhanced communication between library and community was a positive result reported by many. Librarians responded that their planning process provided "more open communication with the community," "facilitated dialogue between community and library, stimulated discussion of library problems," "created stronger communication with community groups," and "helped with presentations to civic clubs and other groups."

Librarians have used the planning process and its attendant publicity to explain change; update community members' ideas of their libraries' mission statement, purpose, and image; clarify and justify roles; defend service choices; and respond to patron complaints. A librarian described how her library's roles improved communication by writing,

> In describing what we call a Tier I Branch (smallest, neighborhood-type facility) and its services, we can now say, 'This branch is primarily a popular reading library, and it also emphasizes services to preschoolers and their parents and to elementary school kids, it isn't big enough to help the high schoolers and it can't do anything more than minimal reference service.' Anybody can understand this because it is concrete.

Another replied that her library's roles "have helped us to defend what we are doing, and to define for others what we should be doing." Pointing out that "public libraries not only suffer from trying to be 'all things to all people,'" but they "also suffer from different people wanting them to be or do different things," she explained that "having extracted agreement on mission and roles from a relatively diverse planning group, it is now possible to deal sensibly with proposals for new programs, etc." A third librarian wrote that her library's mission had been used to respond to citizen complaints. She explained that when patrons complained that the library was too noisy, "the Board explained that our top two roles—Popular Material and Children's Door, are ones that do generate much activity and with it, noise."

Librarians reported that their use of the planning process had resulted in increased support from community members. One librarian wrote that "holding focus groups with various segments of the community was the best thing we did. This turned out to be a terrific way to win new supporters—people were pleased to be asked." A second librarian attributed the "encouragement, support, and good PR" received from a school media specialist to the increased emphasis placed on children's services in her area. A third felt that her library's process "increased [the] public's demand for quality service and consequently public support!"

Appreciation for their planning efforts, "increased respect," and "greater credibility with the community" were welcome results reported by several librarians. Two wrote, "It is apparent that the community is aware of our interest in discovering and using community needs as we plan," and "No matter what the results, I feel people are encouraged that we are interested in their opinion and concerned about the services we offer." Others explained that their process had "demonstrated to staff and the community that you could plan and make some judgment calls for the future" and had "given the library the boost it needed in the town's eyes. We are now seen as a progressive service."

In describing their formal planning documents, librarians wrote that their planning committees created "a good PR tool," that projected "a more professional image for the library," a "handy 'Business Plan' which can be articulated quickly and in concrete terms," and "a marketing plan—unique in this library—to unite the staff, Board, Friends, etc. in pursuit of the mission." One librarian explained, "What the planning process did for us was help us to put on paper a plan which several members & the community now know and which we have embraced."

Improvement in Staff Morale

Fifty-eight percent of the responding librarians marked that their staff members' morale had improved. Some merely listed "improved staff morale" as one of the ways using the process had affected their libraries, while others directly attributed the improvement to their staffs' involvement in planning. One librarian asserted, "Staff morale seems to have improved—they are more involved. Sometimes it seems we talk a topic to death, but they are interested—a definite plus." Three reported that at their libraries, "staff morale and sense of involvement is positive," "staff feel more involved because of committee assignments to achieve goals," and "staff morale has been positively affected with their ability to provide more input into the planning process." Two additional librarians explained that their staffs now have "the feeling of contributing to the future directions of the library system" and "a clearer sense of their relative importance."

Relationship with Government Officials

Although fewer than a majority, 41% of those who responded regarding their libraries' relationships with local government officials checked that officials were now easier to work with. Remarks in the narrative section indicate that the process has helped librarians communicate and clarify their libraries' mission and roles, allowed them to recommend actions and receive approval to remedy specific problems; and provided libraries with greater "visibility," "credibility," and "accountability."

A librarian replied that their Board of Supervisors now viewed them as "actively 'managing' the library program." Another wrote, "We were more prepared at budget hearings. Our rationales were better defined. It gave our village board a clearer idea of what we were trying to accomplish." Others explained that their use of the process brought "increased respect" and "greater credibility" from their City Councils "because we are organized and know what we are doing and where we are going" and because "they know we have looked ahead/planned ahead/made choices."

Additional benefits mentioned were that government officials who served as planning committee members have a "much better ongoing relationship with [the] library, and know more about our quotidian reality," and that librarians can "fall back on our planning document" when meeting with local officials. Other librarians reported that their planning process made sense to business people and elected officials and that it had helped them "in dealing with local government," "heightened the interest of the city administration in the library's future," focused the officials' attention "on the growth of library use and the transitions our libraries must make," and shown officials that libraries have "a socially redeeming legitimacy, a practical utility."

Budget Increases or Reallocations

Of those responding to questions concerning budget increases and reallocations, 80 librarians (37%) indicated that their libraries' overall budgets had been increased, and 81 (41%) that they had been reallocated. In the narrative section, a few librarians specifically mentioned increased funding as an example of how using the planning process had affected their libraries. Other librarians indicated that planning had also benefited the budgetary process by assisting with grantwriting, funding reductions and reallocations, and budget preparation and justification.

One librarian reported that her library's written plan was helpful in developing plans for a change in governance that increased library revenues by 26% or about $1.2 million. Another library's budget had increased from $1.8 to 2.8 million.

One librarian wrote, "We convinced the voters to double our operating tax by a 73% majority because we had such a detailed plan for improving services and resources during [the] next five years." A second remarked that passage of a successful tax referendum made her library better able to serve patrons. A third asserted that her library had received full funding increases as requested from three localities despite a climate of financial constraint because "money talks—evidently our localities were mostly convinced that we're on the right track, and have become proactive." A fourth librarian explained that because his planners produced a document "of substance with ambitious goals and measurable objectives,... our funding bodies are taking our requests much more seriously. Knowing what they are allocating money for makes it easier somehow for them to loosen purse strings."

In addition to receiving increased funding from local government and tax referenda, their use of the planning process benefited libraries in their attempts to secure grants. Libraries used information collected while "looking around" as evidence when submitting grants. One librarian explained, "Having the planning document has made it easier in applying for grants in that we can look to it for guidance in how to expend funds and showing that we have a reason and plan in requesting the grant."

Librarians reported that the planning process also provided the "unexpected 'benefit' of making cut-backs easier" by giving them a "clearer picture of where we should cut as funds diminish." One librarian explained, "In our years of rapid growth in the mid-1980s, we added services. When the cuts came, it was difficult to change our attitude to one of offering fewer services, but of equal quality." He continued, "We now face a period of relative stability with no real prospects for growth. The planning process allowed us to focus on what the priorities for our library are and to convince the staff to do the same." Another commented that the process "helped us deal with decreasing funding. We have priorities clearly established."

Librarians reported that their planning process and resulting document "helped in budget preparation" by providing "an administrative tool for budget decision making," which "clarified and simplified" budgetary decisions. The process provided "a focus for resource allocation and programming," "ensured better use of resources since we understand that we can't be all things to all people," and allowed libraries to "greatly improve our effectiveness by helping us target our limited resources."

One librarian wrote, "Having the planning document with selected roles makes the planning of expenditures easier. You don't spend for things that you are not doing and thus can concentrate on what you do best or need to do." A second explained, "We are allocating resources better. We are not embracing every new trend and then doing a lot of things poorly. Instead we adopt those that help us fulfill our stated goals and objectives."

The use of the process resulted in improved fiscal planning by helping librarians unify their planning and budgetary processes. Librarians wrote that their libraries' planning document kept the "direction of [the] library in line with [the] economy/budget," provided "an excellent 'handle' on needed funding and expenditures over the years of the plan," and started a "continuous cycle of plan–act–evaluate–plan coordinated with funding."

One explained, "We set our annual budget objectives using the plan we wrote. This year we celebrated our accomplishments by listing them in relation to our plan." A second pointed out that the process made "budgeting easier as our five year goals/objectives are the basis for our financial plans." A third librarian wrote that their process "was the impetus for our developing a five year fiscal plan. City Council asked for a fiscal plan after we presented our LRP to them. The fiscal plan has been a very helpful tool." Others wrote that their use of the process also made their trustees more aware of why their budget was constructed as it was and provided a document to present to their funding source justifying new budget items.

Aid to New Directors

A large number of comments revealed that using the process also enabled librarians to manage more effectively and efficiently by helping with other aspects of library administration than just those about which they were asked directly. The process appears to have been especially beneficial to directors who were relatively new to their positions. One wrote, "On a personal level, it was a great way for me (as a new director) to absorb a great deal of information about the community and the library," and a second described the process as "a great tool to help give shape to my need as the new library director to get a handle on our community's needs and desires." Another new director wrote that the process "forced [him] to see the library as a whole," and a fourth explained that it "aided me in getting a clearer perspective of the types of materials the public was interested in. This aided me in my buying decisions."

Planning and Evaluation

Librarians wrote that the process encouraged future thinking, provided a "structure" or "framework" for making long-range plans and managing change, resulted in improved information on patron needs, and provided them with a direction or focus for their activities. Many specified role selection and prioritization; development of goals, objectives, and strategies; and evaluation as management techniques provided by their use of the planning process.

Librarians commented that their use of the process got their "committee and entire Board thinking and planning in more long-range ways," steered them "towards the future of Library Services," encouraged "looking at the big picture, not many unconnected smaller parts," and provided "an enlarged vision with more sense of purpose." The planning process provided "a foundation from which to work and an overall picture of what library operations are all about," started librarians "thinking about our priorities and use of resources—and the structure of planning," and served as "the tool we used to gain direction at the management level—[it] provided a process."

One librarian wrote, "Our library is 126 years old and this was the first written long-range plan. It has helped focus staff and board on important work to develop and deliver quality library service for our community." A second replied that as a result of the process her "library board and staff have had consistent goals for three years, so the library has developed along planned routes, rather than by haphazard chance." A third librarian reported that her library's process had "set [the] course for [the] library for five years—something that was never done" and had "also given emphasis that planning is important."

The process provided "greater coordination," a "more systematic approach," and a "blueprint for change," enabling librarians to "become more action oriented" and to "concentrate on what needs to be changed." Librarians wrote that their process "replaced some of the complacence and 'stuck-ness' with an atmosphere of change" and helped them become "proactive and make change happen rather than being reactive to things imposed upon us."

The surveys and interviews conducted during the "looking around" step provided valuable information on desires, needs, and perceptions of library patrons and other community members. Librarians commented that the data collected helped them become "more aware of the patrons' needs" and "more aware of what is to be done to obtain the best library service for the community" because "we found out from our patrons what they requested most." One librarian stated, "The process has given us a better feeling of what our purpose in the community is. We are putting more emphasis on what seems to us to be what the community wants us to be." Another explained that because administrators were required to look carefully at service areas, existing services, and needs of the system, "emphasis has shifted from 'what do we want,' to 'how do we fit in to the various communities we serve' and 'what do our users want and need.'"

In addition to data about patron needs and desires, librarians reported that their surveys "showed us which areas needed work—but [that] also in many areas we were doing a good job" and "confirm[ed] a clearly and strongly positive perception of the library, and among long-time users, a sense that the library is better than it was." Mixed feelings were expressed by one librarian who wrote, "I can look at it two ways: (1.) I'm full of this information or have access to it and can't use it fast enough. Frustration! (2.) At least I have options and don't have to continue just 'as we've always done.' Hope!"

Twenty-three librarians commented that their planning process and plans provided a sense of direction and helped focus their resources. Fifteen of these actually used the words "directed," "direction," "focused," or "focus," explaining that the process "directed board and staff," "focused staff toward goals and objectives," "gave us a focus of areas and goals," and "provided direction for services and expenditures." Others conveyed the same concept in more general statements such as:

- "The process has been extremely useful in examining where we are going."
- "We now know where we have been, where we are now, and where we can be."
- "Trying to visualize where you want to go has helped us all to see where we are and where we are not but should be."
- "We are ready for the future by knowing where we are going in five years."
- "[The process] has made the trustees and administration more aware of what we are doing and where we want the library to go in the future."

One of its most beneficial aspects appears to have been the process' role selection and prioritization component, about which many librarians commented favorably. One wrote that the process heightened "awareness among members of the staff and the board of the philosophy of role selection for the library and the effect on collection development and services that selecting roles can have." A second explained that "the development or selection of roles and then writing of a mission statement has made decisions at all levels easier because of the ability to refer to chosen roles."

The process "defined and clarified roles for board and staff," helped "set priorities," and encouraged tackling "one problem at a time." Librarians explained,

- "Planning has been the map to follow in providing service; [it] helped us to make choices."
- "[The] process forces making choices—prioritizing is good for us."
- "We are always looking ahead and prioritizing our work. That's good!"

As discussed previously, use of the process seems to have "allowed" librarians to accept that their libraries cannot offer everything that communities might expect or want. One librarian wrote, "We have determined more clearly the roles we wish to play in our communities and have a better idea of how to achieve these roles, but we also see that in many instances our resources, both materials and personnel, are lacking." A second reported that his library's process "is causing us to cope more objectively and realistically with the fact that we cannot fulfill all roles without unlimited staff and funds. We are focusing on what we can contribute to best serve our community"; and a third responded that "by clearly identifying roles with staff and board we found we do not need to be all things to all people and because we put most of our effort into the three major roles we identified, we don't need to apologize for what we are not."

Development of goals, objectives, and strategies was also considered as particularly beneficial. The process was described as a "management tool" that resulted in "clear" "long range and short range" goals, created "a basis for annual setting of objectives/action plans to reach goals set in process," and operated as a "to do list." Librarians commented, "I feel by using the process we were better able to identify our goals within the community"; "We now know our realistic needs and can identify yearly goals"; "We are much clearer as a staff on our mission and 5-year goals"; and "We are in the middle of our 1989-1994 Plan of Action and are finding it very useful in keeping us on track with policy development review and revision."

The importance of the evaluation aspect was noted. The process and its resulting plans were praised as "a useful administrative tool—a way to judge progress" that provided a "basis for annual review." One librarian explained that as "action steps" are reviewed "we have an idea when to implement, and sometimes, when to drop an action step as a bad idea." Others commented that it was "great to be able to check off objectives as they are accomplished and know that our goals are being reached" and "helpful to have a document to refer to in accessing the year, setting priorities, and verifying why I am doing something or whether I should be doing something."

Working with Trustees

Directors commented on ways the planning process helped them work with their library boards. One used the process to "activate" a library advisory board, another as a "training method" for new board members. Others used it to "clarify roles," "focus the [board's] attention" on increased usage and needed "transitions," and "educate" board members "about what we do" and "about how libraries should be run and the nuts and bolts of actually doing it."

The process "encouraged trustees to look ahead more," "heightened [their awareness] of library roles and possibilities," and "increased expectations for what our library can be." It provided "an increased awareness of [the] need to be more directly involved as a library board with our staff education," informed board members "about services (ILL and reference) that do not show up on statistics," and helped them accept that "we cannot be all things to all people."

Directors wrote that their boards were "more willing to discuss policy than they were before" and that the process made it easier for the board "to make policy decisions, and to have a vision for the library's future." One explained that his library's process "forced the board to realize that big changes take more major planning and discussion of ramifications before jumping into," and another wrote that "it helps me as director to tell the library board we should be getting this done because it is in our five-year plan and let's keep up with the goals in the five-year plan." Others explained that as a result of their use of the process, their library boards have taken "ownership" of the library's plan and have become "more active advocates for library services" and "better able to articulate the library's mission and roles to other government officials."

Personnel Administration

The personnel administration function was positively affected in several ways. In addition to improving communication between administration and staff and overall staff morale, discussed previously, the process enabled libraries to "add staff to appropriate areas" and renew "attempts to increase salaries of staff." In several libraries it was also regarded as an "educational experience" for the staff and an "excellent staff development tool." A librarian who "worked with each department on how they contribute to the mission and to develop roles for everyone" wrote that her staff had "come to take planning and implementing the plan seriously."

At one library, planning has become "a way of doing business down into each of the units, who all have planning sessions for their own internal affairs." At another, using the process has meant that "every unit must consider the library's goals and their own objectives every month when compiling their monthly reports and will evaluate their progress at the end of each year."

The process was said to have "enhanced conceptual skills," "forced" staff members to "think in a systematic and logical manner," helped them "focus on work at hand," showed "staff involved some of our strengths & weaknesses," and "greatly assisted in self-evaluation and motivation of staff." Librarians reported that their process "created a 'system' focus among staff and committee members," that their staff "seems more aware of the library and where it is headed" and "more unified in its understanding of what we are doing and why," and that their "staff now has an idea about the 'Big Picture' rather than each person's individual contribution with no focus." Others wrote that their staff "is more aware of who we serve" and that their process "had a positive effect on customer service orientation and end-decision making among library managerial staff members and others" and provided a "framework to get staff to review practices re community [and] get away from librarian's library to community library, a real problem/concern for us."

In some libraries, involvement with the planning process had the added benefit of increasing staff support of plans developed for the library. Librarians commented that their process "empowered" and gave "ownership to the staff," that staff members were "interested in the plan because they were involved," and that staff "indicated support and as a result portions of the plan had a positive effect on the library." One librarian explained that at her library "many changes which had been considered but resisted by staff were able to be accomplished when reviewed in terms of importance as a role." Others commented that the process provided "direction to the staff who may not understand why they are being asked to perform certain tasks" and that "staff and other planning participants have become more active advocates for library services."

New or Renovated Buildings

Ten librarians reported that their processes had helped secure construction grants, start fundraising projects, or pass bond issues for new or renovated library buildings. The planning process also helped librarians and library boards evaluate and rearrange their libraries' current buildings, create building programs and preliminary designs for new and renovated buildings, and communicate these needs and plans to their funding bodies and other community members.

One library's process "creat[ed] the committee which was ultimately responsible for moving forward on an expansion/accessibility project." Others' emphasized their space problems and resulted in building programs to enlarge libraries. A library used information gathered during its process in writing an L.S.C.A. grant application for its new building. Another's community involvement in planning and documentation of its efforts and plans was "one of the critical steps... in achieving our goal," a construction grant of $4.7 million.

A library's long-range development planning document "laid the necessary groundwork for council acceptance" of a $6.1 million renovation to their central library. One that had assessed its buildings on the basis of objectives developed through the process and developed a capital improvement program to fulfill the objectives received "public support" for a $12 million bond issue for capital improvement by a 72% majority. Another library had identified space requirements and size for a new central library and site criteria for branches that were included in its strategy/needs statement for a successful $55 million bond election. Other librarians reported that their plans enabled them to expand their main library and build a new branch because these were "in the plan and we were ready when an opportunity arose" and "highlighted and underscored the need for new facilities at all branches [and] provided necessary documentation to pass the bond."

In addition to resulting immediately in new or renovated buildings, libraries' processes and planning documents proved helpful to their building program in other important ways. A library's board "became aware of the usefulness of the building and how it can be better used. Its hazards were pointed out. They are now working on what has to be done and how to get it done cost efficiently." Libraries' plans "assisted a great deal in rearranging the physical layout of the library and in helping us be clear about what we need in an expanded facility"; "proved very helpful when we next wrote a building program to know what we were trying to do"; and "became an important tool for the architect."

One hired a consultant to complete a facilities study and help the staff gather background and planning data, have long discussions of roles, and hold public hearings as part of the study. Another's staff was "able to speak to [the] community about why [their] building was designed with specific 'roles' in mind." Yet a third library decided to use their basement for a children's department rather than build an addition.

Automation

A few librarians reported that their libraries were automated as a result of their use of the planning process. When asked how the process had affected their libraries, one wrote, "It did give direction to add a computer system (circulation, acquisitions and database)," and another "recognized commitment to future automation." A third replied, "We have automated—as a direct result of the planning process." Other libraries have added online and CD-ROM resources and public-use microcomputers as a result of their planning processes.

NEGATIVE COMMENTS

As demonstrated above, the vast majority of comments about the process' impact were very positive. However, almost one fourth of those offering comments (23% or 41 respondents) either wrote negative comments about their libraries' experience or the process itself or indicated that the process had had little impact on their libraries.

Some of the negative comments expressed the librarians' disappointment that the process failed to provide budget and salary increases, money for new buildings, and increased awareness of local officials. Although many libraries did benefit in just those ways, the process manual certainly does not promise that such benefits will occur. Other comments indicated disappointment about things such as lack of interest, participation and acceptance of goals by staff and board members, failure to involve staff or citizens or to use their recommendations, inability to meet goals, plans that were overly simplistic, and use of plans for cutting budgets. It is the author's opinion that these disappointments resulted from the libraries' use of the process and were not the fault of the process but of the way it was conducted.

One director reported that "[neither] the board chair (nor I) were able to persuade participation" by board members who wanted "no outside interference" and were unwilling to "confront the kind of structure... which [the manual] advocated." A second who described the process as "100% pie in the sky and of very little value" wrote that his library's planning process "discredited the library in the eyes of both community and political leadership." A third reported that using the process had caused him "to realize that user surveys are political tools and do not contribute to planning." This librarian explained his belief that "a modern public library needs to define itself through the services it presents" and warned, "If you rely upon users to define what your library should be—you will find that they want you to either continue to be what you are or be the library they remember from their childhood."

Seven librarians expressed disappointment that use of the process had had "little" or "very little" effect on their libraries. One complained that the process "hasn't raised salaries; it hasn't helped heighten awareness with [the] county commission; it was a lot of work with minimal returns. We were spreading our money thin before, and we still are." Another wrote, "Unfortunately the implementation of a long-range plan has had little effect on our day-to-day operations. Activities are seen as extras and rarely get carried out the way they were intended to." He added that it "has been difficult to maintain enthusiasm for the process in the face of complete indifference from co-workers." A third who also felt his library's process had had little effect commented, "To be blunt, I think the process produces a document required for that year's per capita grant... and that's it. Maybe if the timing and situation had been different, I would have a more positive opinion of the process."

One librarian explained that his library's plan had not had much impact "mainly because it was such a simple, un-detailed plan that didn't really say much." Another commented that his process had resulted in few changes because "not one board member realized the importance of the planning process or implemented the document in our daily operations."

Along with their more positive comments about their process's impact, 30 respondents included negative comments regarding the time and effort required to complete the process and other negative effects on staff, lack of support by library boards, disappointment with results and use of data collection, frustration over inability to meet goals, and the process and planning manual themselves. Librarians described the process as "time and labor intensive" and "a lot of work" and noted that record keeping and revising the plan, increases in the volume of paperwork, writing the plan, and "trying to direct and prepare everything for the sessions along with managing the library" were particularly time-consuming. Others reported that "the length of the process has negatively affected staff morale," that there were "frustrations because of overload," and that staff members dreaded the words "output measures."

A librarian complained, "Too much is involved—the initial process as well as the ongoing evaluation and review process is almost an overwhelming task." Another commented that "the process takes so much time that staff, in particular, feel stressed out," but also wrote, "We are pretty sure it is worth the effort." One commented that "the books and the process as suggested simply took time which we did not have much of, so feelings of frustration came about in deciding the correct level of effort. Many compromises were made." Another reported feeling frustrated "because we couldn't make a greater effort."

One librarian responded that his library's process "caused distress among staff members (related to acceptance of change and also responsibility of participation)." Two reported that their library had "not yet achieved optimal acceptance of process and its value by middle managers and staff," and that "some people felt left out of the process (and they mainly were)—department heads and non-supervisory librarians had little input, paraprofessional staff the same." Others explained that there had been "some anxiety created among staff members [because] it is natural to perceive change as traumatic" and that "aging staff has not been happy with some 'changes' but are now coming around."

Lack of interest and support from board members was mentioned by several. In one library there was "negative reaction from two longtime trustees. No interest." In another, the trustees became so involved with a bond election and building project that "they didn't share the planning tasks as much as we had decided in the 'planning to plan' phase. The heaviest part of the responsibility fell on me, as director."

Two additional comments illustrated the necessity of ongoing board support for plans developed during the process. One director explained that "because the library board was not wholly supportive of the plan, its effectiveness was weakened." A second lamented that "once the document was done it was forgotten by the board. Work to review the document has been very minimal."

Lack of adequate citizen involvement and disappointment with planning data were mentioned. As one librarian described, his library's "only negative" was that "we still need to involve the public more." One complained that his library's survey "was so overwhelmingly complimentary that perhaps it made us a bit complacent. [We] went for a building plan which was turned down by the town." A second wrote, "Of course, everyone wants everything... [It's] hard for some patrons to be realistic and some board members not to want everything for patrons." This director warned that "with the wrong board, I think the surveys could work more against them for a limited staff library."

Another negative effect indicated was the inability of several libraries to meet goals developed through their processes. Librarians commented, "Need larger staff to meet all needs and goals"; "The negative side is slight dissatisfaction with goals that are too slow in becoming realized"; and "Without adequate funding and recession cuts, we haven't been able to meet every objective on schedule."

One director reported his library suffered "some loss of credibility (perhaps) with planning committee members, since we've had to abandon or delay some of our more ambitious planning activities." A second regretted that knowing that the "information from the public on their needs" had not been used as it should have been "has left the board with a feeling that we are still 'incomplete' even as we accomplish the goals and objectives that were set." Explaining, "The fact that no new resources have been dedicated to implement major portions of the plan has also had a negative impact," a third concluded, "It is obviously seen as a negative process if the plan has been used for budget cutting as it has in our case."

Librarians complained that "small libraries didn't really need a planning program made for all sizes of libraries in the state" and wrote that "[the] process is quite complicated for [a] small system.... Maybe we need an 'abridged' planning process." One director commented that restricting the number of roles a library can choose "is arbitrary and meaningless" and that the manual's vocabulary and definitions were "so cumbersome that [the] board quit (and lost interest) before [the] process was complete."

After writing that the process "helps us to visualize a dream and starts an 'unconscious process' in the community that will bring that about in a reasonably timely fashion," one librarian added that it was his observation that such efforts were helpful "only in focusing attention of important segments of the community on a vision for the future of the library, to interest the community in supporting funding needed to enlarge, mechanize, rebuild the facility when this becomes necessary." This director explained his belief by stating:

> These studies have never, in my experience, had much effect on day-to-day, gradual and organic growth that will happen better when left to a competent responsive management that is based on the realities present in any given moment. It is my opinion that they are largely a waste of time and effort.

SUMMARY

The professional literature contained librarians' and researchers' accounts of benefits and changes resulting from a small number of libraries' use of the revised process. Additional ideas about its impact were gleaned from the author's study of the use of the process by 255 libraries.

Asked whether their libraries' use of the process had brought about changes in 13 important areas, the majority indicated that changes had indeed occurred in 9 areas, and well over one third reported changes in the 4 remaining. Quite a few of the librarians did not reply one way or the other to particular items, but several explained that they had only recently completed the process or were still involved in it. Although a few librarians wrote that they were unsure whether the changes that had taken place were a result of their planning processes, almost three fourths of those returning surveys provided specific examples, the majority of which were very positive, when asked to relate additional ways using the process had affected their libraries.

Almost one fourth of those commenting either offered totally negative comments about their libraries' experiences, indicated that the process had had little impact on their libraries, or included negative comments along with their more positive ones. Some of the negative comments expressed librarians' disillusionment over the failure of the process to provide particular benefits, whereas others indicated disappointment that may well have been the result of how the process was conducted rather than the fault of the process.

By relating the many perceived benefits, specific changes, and the negative comments reported both in the literature and in response to a national survey of the manual's users, this chapter addressed the matter of whether, and in what specific ways, planning libraries were affected (impacted) by their use of the process. The next and final chapter will report planning librarians' satisfaction with their use of the planning process and its manual, the problems they experienced, their ideas of what they wished they had done differently, and their suggestions for improving the manual and its use. It will also include the author's recommendations both for improved use of the planning and role-setting manual and for its future revision.

Chapter 5

Satisfaction With *Planning And Role Setting for Public Libraries* and Recommendations for Its Use and Improvement

The previous chapter began to assess the value of the revised planning process by examining the process' impact on its users. This chapter continues the assessment by reporting planning librarians' satisfaction and problems experienced with their use of the process and its manual and their suggestions, along with the author's, for improving both.

The first section contains a brief presentation of the few problems and suggestions reported by planning librarians in the professional literature. The next section reports results of the author's questions regarding the survey respondents' satisfaction and problems experienced with their use of the planning process. It also includes these librarians' ideas about what they wish they had done differently. The librarians' suggestions are followed in the next section by the author's recommendations for improved use of the process. The last two sections contain the responding librarians' opinions of the helpfulness of the planning manual, their suggestions for its improvement, and the author's recommendations for those responsible for its future revision.

SATISFACTION AND PROBLEMS REPORTED IN THE LITERATURE

The previous chapter included a description of the many benefits derived by a number of libraries whose apparently highly satisfactory use of the revised manual has been reported in the professional literature. Only a small number of the authors revealed problems they experienced or observed, or made suggestions for future users of the process and its manual. The following discussion presents the few problems and suggestions gleaned from the literature.

Few problems were encountered by the member libraries of the Bay Area Library and Information System during their joint project for simultaneous local planning, which was considered to have been "valuable for each library and for the cooperative relationships within [the system]" (Metz, Van House, & Scarborough, 1989, p. 220). These libraries did find, however, that it was difficult to keep their processes at a basic level of effort, that high levels of staff involvement were time-consuming (but worthwhile), that the amount of data suggested for the comprehensive level was not needed, that roles often needed to be adapted to local priorities, and that they underestimated the time and effort required for setting goals and objectives. The authors suggested that libraries carefully consider the amount of time required, be realistic about whether the results of working at a basic level will be satisfactory, obtain funding for consultants' and specialists' services, devote adequate time and effort to discussing roles, and prepare brief, professionally prepared planning documents for communicating with the libraries' external environments.

Pungitore (1991) reported that the planning experiences of three libraries whose use of the revised manual she studied were also considered to have been highly satisfactory. Although one library's report was not adopted by its board, both director and board were pleased with their process. This library's director commented, however, that he played too passive a role by turning leadership over to the committee chair (plans were made without considering his recommendations), that it was a mistake to conduct surveys prior to forming a planning committee, that the data collection phase took too long, and that plans and completion dates were established with no regard to the budgeting cycle. His and the other directors' suggestions included the following:

- Use of a facilitator is very helpful.
- Directors should assume responsibility for the process.
- Plans should be tied to yearly budget cycles.
- Development of mission statements should be saved until late in the process.
- Staff and citizen input is crucial.

Although none of the libraries included in Bret Sutton's study of long-range planning (1991) used the planning and role setting manual as their only or principle source of planning information, its findings would still be helpful for the manual's users. Sutton's study found that successful long-range planning efforts exhibited good leadership (support by management and supervision by a planning coordinator), a process tailored to the local environment, a solid foundation and an orderly structure (events clearly scheduled, meetings at appropriate times, follow-through, staff receipt of planning information), appropriate involvement of staff at all levels, a means of overcoming resistance to long-range thinking (good organization, balanced attention to both immediate and long-term problems, and good communication), and specific, implementable goals.

SATISFACTION, PROBLEMS, HINDSIGHT, AND SUGGESTIONS REPORTED TO AUTHOR

Satisfaction with Use of the Planning Process and Its Phases

When the librarians surveyed by the author were asked about their satisfaction with their libraries' overall use of the planning process, over three fourths (81% of those who replied to the question) reported being from somewhat to highly satisfied (using the words "satisfaction" or "satisfied"). Although just under half (49%) checked that they were "somewhat satisfied," nearly one third (32%) were "highly satisfied" with their libraries' use of the overall process. Only 11% reported being from somewhat to highly dissatisfied ("dissatisfaction" or "dissatisfied"), with 3% marking "highly dissatisfied" and 8% marking "somewhat dissatisfied." Eight percent reported feeling neutral about their libraries' overall use of the planning process.

A clear majority (ranging from 57 to 85%) also reported being satisfied with their libraries' use of five out of seven individual phases or aspects of their process. Role setting and goals and objectives writing were the steps for which satisfaction was reported by the largest numbers, 84 and 85%, respectively. In fact, over one third of the librarians reported being highly satisfied with developing their libraries' roles and mission, and one third reported being highly satisfied with their writing of goals and objectives. Only 7% reported dissatisfaction with their libraries' experience with role setting, and only 8% reported dissatisfaction with their goals and objectives writing experience.

Almost three fourths (71%) of the librarians reported satisfaction with their libraries' planning of strategies (taking action); only 16% reported being dissatisfied. Sixty-nine percent indicated satisfaction with writing their libraries' planning documents, while only 11% indicated dissatisfaction. Sixty-nine percent were also satisfied with their looking-around activities. Only 13% were dissatisfied, but one fourth (25%) reported feeling neutral about their libraries' use of this important phase.

Although 62% of those responding to the question indicated that they were satisfied with involvement of staff members in their libraries' planning process, almost a fourth (21%) indicated dissatisfaction. Their response is not surprising as 30% had indicated earlier that they felt their libraries had devoted too little effort to staff involvement.

A smaller number of librarians, 57%, indicated that they were satisfied with their libraries' use of the planning to plan and reviewing results phases, the important first and last steps of the planning process. Fourteen percent reported being dissatisfied, while 29% reported feeling neutral about their preplanning efforts. Twenty-one percent indicated dissatisfaction, while another 21% felt neutral about the review of their planning results.

Less than half of the librarians indicated that they were satisfied with attempts made to involve or to inform their communities' taxpayers. Although 44% reported satisfaction with their efforts to involve the public, over one third (36%) reported dissatisfaction. In fact, 11% of the librarians indicated that their libraries did not do this at all. Forty-two percent indicated satisfaction with their libraries' attempts at informing the public, but over one third (36%) reported dissatisfaction, and 9% chose the "did not do" option.

A majority of librarians had indicated earlier that they felt too little effort had been expended on both these important public relations aspects. Fifty-one percent had reported too little effort put into involving the public, while 57% had indicated that too little effort was made to keep the public informed.

The category labeled "did not do" was offered as an attempt to keep librarians from reporting neutrality or dissatisfaction for those phases not yet used by their libraries. Few used this category, however. The phases for which it was checked by over 5% were taking action (6%), writing the planning document (9%), informing the public (9%), involving the public (11%), and reviewing results (11%). It should be noted also that the nonresponse rate (15%, 13%, 17%, 14%, and 15%, respectively) was higher for these phases than for the others.

Table 5.1 lists the percentages, followed by the numbers, of librarians marking "highly satisfied," "somewhat satisfied," "neutral," "somewhat dissatisfied," "highly dissatisfied," and "did not do" when asked to indicate their satisfaction with their libraries' use of the overall planning process and with its performance in each of the planning phases and aspects. The percentages and numbers of libraries not responding to each of these items are also provided. The percentages for the categories labeled "highly satisfied," "somewhat satisfied," "neutral," "somewhat dissatisfied," and "highly dis-

TABLE 5.1. Satisfaction with Planning Process and Its Various Phases

	Highly Satisfied	Somewhat Satisfied	Neutral	Somewhat Dissatisfied	Highly Dissatisfied	Did Not Do	No Response
Overall process	32% [76]	49% [116]	8% [18]	8% [20]	3% [7]	1% [3]	6% [15]
Planning to plan	19% [44]	38% [87]	29% [67]	12% [28]	2% [5]	3% [8]	6% [16]
Looking around	22% [50]	41% [94]	25% [56]	11% [24]	2% [4]	4% [9]	7% [18]
Developing roles & mission	39% [93]	45% [107]	8% [20]	6% [15]	1% [3]	0% [1]	6% [16]
Writing goals & objectives	33% [74]	52% [118]	7% [15]	6% [13]	2% [5]	2% [4]	10% [26]
Taking action	23% [46]	48% [97]	14% [28]	13% [26]	3% [5]	6% [15]	15% [38]
Writing document	24% [48]	45% [89]	20% [40]	10% [19]	1% [2]	9% [23]	13% [34]
Reviewing results	15% [28]	42% [77]	21% [39]	19% [35]	2% [4]	11% [28]	17% [44]
Staff involvement	24% [51]	38% [81]	18% [39]	18% [38]	3% [6]	4% [9]	12% [31]
Involving public	13% [25]	31% [59]	20% [39]	30% [57]	6% [11]	11% [27]	15% [37]
Informing public	10% [20]	32% [63]	22% [43]	29% [58]	7% [13]	9% [22]	14% [36]

satisfied" are based on the number of librarians who responded to each of the items; those for the "did not do" and "no response" categories are based on the total number of surveys returned.

Problems Experienced and Librarians' Ideas of What Should Have Been Done Differently

As reported previously, over three fourths of the responding librarians indicated satisfaction with their libraries' planning experiences, with almost a third being highly satisfied. When asked to relate the most significant problems they had experienced, 42 (16% of those returning surveys) responded that they had encountered "no problems." However, 114 (45%) listed a total of 161 specific problems experienced with various aspects of the process or manual (see Appendix D for a listing of many of these problems).

The librarians were also asked to describe what they wished had been done differently. Six replied that they would make no changes in their use of the process. Writing that they "would not do anything differently" and "would not fix something that worked fine," these librarians reported, "Everything went smoothly" and "I think the planning process was fine."

Many librarians supplied specific details of what they wished they had done differently, however. One hundred and eighty-six (73% of those returning surveys) responded with a total of 384 such comments (see Appendix E for a listing of the librarians' ideas of what they would do differently).

It is the author's hope that these librarians' comments will help current and future users of the public library planning process avoid or better deal with some of the problems experienced by its past users. Following a brief presentation of comments concerning their overall use of the process and its manual, the librarians' comments about problems they experienced and what they would do differently are arranged according to the following topics, many of which correspond to various steps or aspects of the planning process:

- Time and timing.
- Planning to plan.
- Levels of effort.
- Looking around.
- Selecting roles.
- Developing goals, objectives, and activities.
- Writing the planning document.
- Involvement of planning participants.

Overall Use of Process and Manual

Librarians wrote that they wished they had made more "specific use" of the planning process or had used the entire model rather than just the role-setting aspect. Others would have studied the manual more closely and encouraged planning participants to do likewise. One wished his library had used a "simpler" process.

Time and Timing

One difficulty reported was the amount of time required for the planning process. In fact, "time" was mentioned as a problem by 20 librarians. Several wrote that they did not have, or did not devote, sufficient time for the process. Others complained that the process took much too much time. Their responses were not surprising since 17% had indicated earlier that too little effort had been devoted to their planning process, while 10% felt their level of effort was too much. A few explained why their time for planning was limited (library moving, time limitation or deadline imposed by city, small library).

Several librarians wished they had apportioned the amount and length of time spent on the process differently. Twenty-two would have devoted more time and effort to the process; four would have "started sooner."

Eleven librarians explained that their process either took too much time or had been spread over too great a period of time. If they had it to do over, they would complete the process more quickly with steps closer together and fewer interruptions; set time limits for each phase; start with a one day 'mini' version limited to writing goals, objectives, and time lines followed the next year by a fuller version (library "bogged down" in the early phases and never finished); and try to develop roles, mission, and goals and objectives in an intense three day period. As for planning committee meetings, they felt these should be held separately from regular board meetings, be scheduled fairly close together, and should last for at least, but not more than two hours.

Librarians working in small libraries experienced particular difficulty with the amount of time and resources needed. Several objected that the process was geared to large and medium-sized libraries and that there was "never any real acknowledgment of problems of small libraries—with small overworked staff—trying to follow such time-consuming processes."

As mentioned earlier, many librarians had selected various aspects rather than using the whole process or they had "adapted" the process; this was especially true of those in small libraries and of library systems. One system director explained that since "there was not enough help for a system planning process... we were constantly adapting." Others wrote that they had problems adapting the process to meet their libraries' needs and limited resources.

Planning to Plan

Several librarians wrote that they wished they had devoted more time and effort to preparing for their libraries' use of the process. (Remember that one fourth had indicated that they felt too little effort was devoted to this aspect.) Two wished they had formed a task force to plan for the process, and one complained that he did not understand exactly what was expected at its beginning. Specifically mentioned were the need to create a "more hospitable planning culture," secure community support, and educate the board, staff, and planning committee members about the planning process. Librarians should provide participants with "extensive orientation so they feel more comfortable about contributing"; better inform committee members about the need for continued involvement, a written document, and follow-up activities; and ask each department to present a review of the library's existing services and programs.

Levels of Effort

Only 66% of the librarians had selected a level of effort for their overall process, and only 51% had chosen levels of effort for individual phases and steps. Some wrote that they found the discussion of levels of effort more confusing than helpful and described their definitions as vague and hard to use. One felt the minimal level was too complex and intensive; another reported that his planners found it difficult to select a level because they were uncomfortable not making an "all out effort" but recognized their limited capacity to do so.

Looking Around

Librarians experienced problems determining the amount of data to collect, developing useful and meaningful surveys, finding time to conduct surveys and compile data, and acquiring meaningful information from performance measures. Others reported having to go to another source (the 1980 planning manual) for guidance, being disgruntled over their committee's heavy reliance on survey data, devoting so much effort to data collection that there was less energy for planning, and finding it difficult to collect some of the internal statistics without automation.

Eight librarians wrote that they wished they had spent more time and effort on this step, while eleven specifically mentioned that they would conduct surveys of library users, citizens, and local government officials. (Twenty-seven percent had reported that they felt too little effort was expended.) Several others would have developed "better" surveys; these would have been professionally designed and conducted, more sophisticated, thorough and in-depth, with better worded, more specific, narrower questions offering fewer choices. Librarians also wished they had researched projected demographic changes, examined policies and long-range plans of other libraries, gathered more statistics, sampled for output measures and developed more valid ones, made more use of library measures and budget information, and paid more attention to regional and economic factors. Others wished they had gotten more input by increasing public awareness and interest in their surveys, using focus groups, and holding town meetings.

They explained, "We spent too much effort gathering data, not all of which proved useful"; and "We did a full community analysis. Such extensive work was not absolutely necessary to developing a plan supported by library board, staff and community." Seven librarians wrote that they wished they had devoted less time and effort to this step, while fifteen (only 6%) had previously reported that they felt too much effort was devoted to this purpose. They would combine surveys, develop shorter surveys aimed specifically at one or two items, and use fewer surveys spread over a longer time period.

Roles

Although 84% had reported satisfaction with this step, 29 librarians commented on problems experienced in choosing their libraries' roles. The librarians found the roles' titles confusing and misleading and their definitions unclear, too vague, or too rigid and narrow, with too much overlap among various roles. Some had trouble understanding the scope of certain roles; others were unable to articulate roles so that everyone had the same understanding or vision, making it difficult to bring staff and citizens to a common understanding. Several were concerned that there was no "children's role."

Librarians reported having difficulty limiting the number of roles chosen, making roles fit or adapting them to fit their libraries' specific needs, applying roles to library systems, seeing a relationship between roles and action, and linking role selection and resource allocation. Some found the concept of designating 2% of the points allotted the roles for "other" confusing.

Explaining that the manual's role definitions should be "much clearer," a librarian reported that "way too much time" was spent clarifying and defining what was meant by a certain role. One librarian felt his library's roles were based on "preconceived notions" because its role-setting exercise was done too early in the process. Others wished more time had been spent thinking about appropriate roles and adapting them to local communities, developing unique roles, and defining the roles for all persons involved.

One committee chose too many roles, while another found that limiting its library to two roles was not possible or appropriate. If they had it to do over, other librarians would pay more attention to library size and potential, involve staff and public in role setting, clarify the respective responsibilities of a central library and its branches, and give greater consideration to resource implications and funding.

Developing Goals, Objectives, and Activities

Even though 85 and 71%, respectively, had responded that they were satisfied with their efforts at writing goals and objectives and developing strategies (taking action), some librarians reported having trouble distinguishing between, writing, and developing time frames for goals and objectives, while others found it difficult to select activities, translate objectives into action, and develop adequate staffing and budgets to accomplish their libraries' objectives. One librarian wrote that his library did not attempt this step; another responded that his neglected to write objectives for their goals. Others wished their planners had been better prepared for their work on the library's mission, goals, and objectives and that they had used a "more expeditious method." Librarians would develop more focused and more precisely defined goals, spend more time writing objectives, involve their committees more, and have a more extensive review of their goals. One librarian wrote that he wished his planners "had discovered the key to setting goals about three meetings earlier. The whole committee had difficulties until we found the key statement 'The result will be that....'"

Ten librarians wrote that they wished they had devoted more time and effort to developing activities to accomplish their goals and objectives, while one whose planners spent six months on this step would have preferred a more structured attempt. Librarians would develop their activities more fully, select several alternatives for each objective, draw up a time line and assign staff responsibilities, and proceed immediately into the "taking action" phase after developing goals and objectives. Several would put more emphasis on developing financial strategies, while one wished they had raised funds to "test market" new services rather than using public funds. A librarian who wrote that he was "still shaky on creating the specific action plans to carry out our goals and objectives" would like to see more training in this area.

Planning Document

Some librarians found it difficult to write their libraries' planning documents. They complained that the manual neglected to suggest ways to incorporate management goals and objectives and offered very little help in writing and selling libraries' long-range plans.

Librarians wished they had had a better idea of the end product desired, and that they had allowed more time for writing the planning document, although one objected that writing his library's plan took far too long, resulting in lost momentum and interest. Explaining that "we had to prepare a plan; the effort seemed to be to just get it done," one librarian wrote that he wished their plan "would have been challenged more [and] generated more discussion." Some would make their planning documents "more appealing" or "self-explanatory" and capable of being used with the public and local government officials, while others would create a "more definitive," "more comprehensive and action-oriented" plan," a "working document" rather than a "PR piece."

Involvement of Planning Participants

Many of the librarians' explanations of problems encountered and what they would do differently concerned leadership of the process and/or participation (or the lack thereof) of directors, board members, staff, and citizens. A few mentioned the need for hiring consultants or for using them differently.

The matter of who should provide leadership or chair planning committees was addressed. One librarian wished he had used an "objective facilitator" to lead the committee through the process because "library staff, friends and board are too close to the issue to ask objective questions." Three other librarians stated explicitly that the committee should be led by someone other than the director. Six additional directors complained that they had had to play too strong a role. One wrote that "it was left up to the director to sort everything out and make a polished product"; and another who did "too much" questioned whether the trustees and staff "really agree with the final product or are they being too lazy to actively disagree."

A few librarians wished someone could have relieved them of their other duties during the process, or that they had been able to spend more of their time in planning. Others wrote that they wished they had hired consultants, used their consultants more, or worked more closely with them; assigned a staff member and provided adequate release time; and had a "stronger" leader or one with more skill in group process. One would "keep leadership within [the] staff and board [and] involve public in studies and task forces instead of steering the process."

Librarians reported that their boards lacked interest in the process, lacked time and inclination to study the manual, found the manual too technical and detailed and the process too complex to "leap into [the] middle of," and were too impatient to do what "the book says to do." Thirty-five wrote that they would like to have had greater cooperation, participation, support, and enthusiasm from their board members. One complained, "I wish my library commission members were more involved in writing the plan. They pretty much went with what I told or wrote for them"; another appreciated his board's confidence but "would have liked them to be more enthusiastic towards the future of the library." Others would provide more preparation and education for their board members.

Thirty-eight librarians wrote that they would have liked greater involvement of library staff members in the process. (Twenty-one percent had reported dissatisfaction, while 30% had reported too little effort expended for this step.) One librarian explained that "commitment to achieving goals and objectives was minimal because staff was not involved in all aspects of [the] process." Others complained that "it was hard to get involvement other than verbal opinions" or that "staff input was asked for. Usually they said 'you know best,' but did not always like the final decisions." Librarians would inform staff that not all ideas would be included in the written plan and that everything was not going to be implemented in the first one or two years; they also would provide more training for managerial staff unfamiliar with planning and making conceptual decisions.

Some librarians experienced lack of interest on the part of citizens and local government representatives and problems getting local government participation. They complained that the manual has limited references to techniques for involving the community and that its information is difficult to simplify for the public. In working with their planning committees, librarians found it difficult to educate uninformed citizens and to convey enough information about the library and process quickly enough for citizens to be confident and contributing members. One librarian felt his citizen group selected inappropriate roles, and another found it difficult to deal with the public when you "stop being what you've always been and move towards something new and different."

Ninety-five of the comments describing what librarians wish they had done differently concerned citizen involvement in the planning process, a finding that was not surprising since over a third (36%) had reported dissatisfaction with this step. Sixty-five of these librarians wrote that they would have liked "more" or "greater" involvement of citizens. (Forty-one percent had previously reported that they felt too little effort had been devoted to this important aspect.)

Six of the librarians reported that they would either form citizen planning committees or add citizens to their committees. One would have involved "a broader spectrum of the public" because "city council has a negative response when they see the same old names and faces involved with projects." Another wished his committee had been "less 'democratically' arrived at" and that members had been "very sharp" on the issues involved. Others would have involved the "general public," "ordinary citizens," and library non-users, as well as representatives from business, education, local agencies and clubs, and the media. Six specifically mentioned that they would have increased involvement of local government officials.

Librarians would have liked "more commitment," "better participation," and "more help" from their planning committees, with more time spent by individual committee members. One wrote, "The consultant used should have pushed the committee to *do* more, not just respond." Others would start out with a larger number because of "dropouts and erratic attendance" and would develop a mechanism to replace committee members who resigned.

Fifteen librarians wished they had done a better job of informing citizens of their libraries' planning efforts. Four of these specifically mentioned that they wished they had increased publicity aimed at local government officials.

TOWARD IMPROVED USE OF THE PLANNING PROCESS

What can be learned from the experiences and comments of librarians and others who have used and studied the use of *Planning and Role Setting for Public Libraries* (McClure et al., 1987)? As was true of the earlier planning manual, many libraries have benefited greatly from their use of the planning and role-setting manual. The many benefits reported in the literature and related in response to the author's survey were described at great length in the previous chapter. Readers will notice that many of these reported benefits closely match those attributed to use of the first planning manual (see Chapter 2).

As was also the case with the earlier manual, some librarians are, unfortunately, experiencing problems using the revised edition of the planning manual. To recap: Librarians expressed concern over the amount of time devoted to the process; some felt they spent far too much time, some felt they spent far too little time, and others felt they misapportioned the time spent on the process. Directors of small libraries had particular difficulty with the amount of time and resources needed.

Librarians used selected aspects and otherwise adapted the process. Some reported they wished they had used the entire process, whereas others experienced problems adapting it to fit their planning needs.

Several librarians wrote that they wished they had devoted more time and effort to studying the planning manual and preparing for their libraries' use of the process. They mentioned the need to create a hospitable planning culture, secure community support, and educate the board, staff, and planning committee members.

Less than half the survey respondents assigned levels of effort to individual phases of the process. Librarians found the discussion of the levels confusing and their definitions vague and hard to use. Some found the minimal level too complex and intensive; others were uncomfortable because they wanted to choose a higher level than their resources would allow.

The role-setting process proved difficult for quite a few librarians, who found the roles' titles and definitions unclear and confusing, had trouble understanding the scope of certain roles, and were unable to articulate roles so that everyone had the same understanding. Librarians also had difficulty limiting the number of roles and adapting them to fit their libraries, and linking role selection and resource allocation.

Despite the revised manual's deemphasis on data collection, several librarians still experienced problems with collecting planning information. They had trouble determining the amount of data to collect, developing useful and meaningful surveys, interpreting the data, and finding time for surveying. Some felt they devoted too much time and effort to this step; others felt they devoted too little.

Some librarians had trouble distinguishing between, writing, and developing time frames for goals and objectives. Others found it difficult to select activities, translate objectives into action, and develop adequate implementation plans.

Several librarians had difficulty writing their libraries' planning documents. Some indicated the need for an abbreviated document to distribute to local officials and citizens.

Many expressed disappointment with leadership of their committees and the extent of their involvement of library board and staff members and local area citizens. Several also expressed disappointment with the limited efforts made to publicize their use of the planning process.

With the exception of those related to choosing levels of effort and role setting, the problems experienced by many users of the revised planning manual seem oddly familiar. When the difficulties experienced by users of the first planning process manual, discussed in Chapter 2, are compared with those described here, it becomes apparent that many users of the current manual are encountering the same or similar problems as those who used the earlier manual. The analysis of the difficulties encountered by users of the first planning manual and the suggestions for improving its use outlined in Chapter 2 should, therefore, still be helpful to current and future users of the planning and role setting manual. These suggestions, along with ideas gleaned from the many librarians who shared the problems they experienced with the revised manual and their explanations of what they would do differently, have been compiled into the following list of guidelines for planners. It is the author's hope that the lessons learned from analysis of the earlier manual's use, the descriptions of problems experienced and suggestions made by users of the current manual, and the following recommendations will provide guidance for current and future users of the public library planning process.

- Ensure that the library's organizational climate is hospitable to planning and that a formal communication structure is in place.
- Create board and administrative support for the library's use of the process.
- Devote adequate time and effort to planning for the use of the process.
    - Make preliminary decisions about
        - who will have responsibility for planning,
        - whether to use a planning committee,
        - the amount and type of data needed,
        - how and by whom data will be collected, analyzed, and interpreted,
        - how the process will be funded, and
        - how board, staff, and citizens will be involved and kept informed about planning activities.
    - Secure additional funding and promises of volunteer assistance for

       the process, if needed.
     - Prepare board, staff, and the public for use of the process.
   - Try to involve library staff members in as many aspects of planning as possible.
     - Be sure that staff members' opinions are solicited.
     - Encourage staff attendance, presentations, and interaction at planning committee meetings.
   - Involve service area citizens in planning and consider involving citizens as planning committee members.
     - Provide citizen committee members with an adequate orientation period. Educate them
       - about the planning process and their roles and responsibilities,
       - about public library organization, services, and issues, and
       - about your specific library's background, services, and needs.
   - If using citizens as committee members is not feasible, use other methods such as town meetings, focus groups, visits to community organizations, etc. to involve citizens.
   - If a planning committee is used, conduct its work with as few meetings of the overall committee as feasible by using a data coordinator, library staff, and small subcommittees for much of the preliminary work.
   - Choose persons to lead the library's planning efforts who are
     - skilled in planning and group leadership, and
     - capable of being objective about the library and its strengths and weaknesses.
   - Give careful consideration to the amount and type of primary and secondary data that are collected.
     - Limit data collection to information that
       - is necessary for planning and decision making
       - can be collected, analyzed, interpreted, and understood by those involved.
   - If surveys are to be used, be sure they are conducted by someone competent in survey design and techniques of random sampling.
   - Try to secure funding for consulting assistance or to train a staff member who can be released from other duties to devote adequate time to data collection, especially if surveys are used.
   - Be sure that the meaning of the data and their implications are thoroughly explained to planners.
   - Make at least a tentative choice of roles and begin to develop a mission statement for the library before beginning to formulate goals and objectives.
     - Consider the appropriateness of the library's present roles (where such exist) and its current services.
     - Then begin choosing or developing a limited number of appropriate roles and services for the library's future.

- Develop service and management goals and objectives to enable the library to make progress on roles chosen by planners.
- Develop alternate strategies for accomplishing the goals and objectives; coordinate activities with budget cycles.
- Develop a plan designating how, when, and by whom the strategies will be implemented and how progress toward goals and objectives will be monitored.
- Create a detailed planning document and a shorter informational brochure for wide distribution to the public.
- Create a mechanism for reviewing both plans and planning process.
- Be sure staff members are kept informed of planning activities and decisions.
- Create and take advantage of all possible opportunities to publicize your library's planning efforts.
- Pay special attention to involving local government officials and keeping them informed of your library's planning activities.

LIBRARIANS' OPINIONS OF THE PLANNING MANUAL AND THEIR SUGGESTIONS FOR ITS IMPROVEMENT

Librarians' Opinions

The planning manual contains detailed information on how to use each of the various phases and aspects of the process. It also provides planners with specific tools such as workforms and other charts and figures. When asked to relate the most significant problems they encountered, over 40 of the librarians mentioned specific problems with the manual itself—its language, length, organization, or forms—as the most significant problems they encountered. Several complained that it was too "wordy"; others that the language was too "technical," "dull," and inaccessible to nonprofessionals and lay people who are not familiar with "library lingo." Many mentioned that the manual was "way too long," complex, cumbersome, complicated, and "overwhelming," and "not all that accessible as self-help." One person felt the manual was "too simplistic in its approach to planning," however, and another found it "too brief" and added that much more information on the "reality of working the process" was needed.

The organization of the manual was described as "repetitive" and "not always clear," making it difficult to know where to begin and how to start the process. Librarians felt it should be organized so that planners could "access the basic facts and see how the process is structured." Others found its illustrations and examples to be too intrusive, making it hard to follow the text, its charts rather difficult to comprehend, and its workforms too extensive, gathering more information than needed or used.

SATISFACTION AND RECOMMENDATIONS 129

Librarians were asked for their opinions on the extent to which information provided for using each of the process' various aspects was helpful. These included the following: the planning committee, the levels of effort, looking around outside, looking around inside, developing roles/mission, writing goals and objectives, selecting activities, writing the planning document, reviewing results, involving staff, and involving the public. They were also asked for their opinions on the helpfulness of workforms and other charts and figures. As before, because it was assumed that many libraries had not yet completed the process, librarians were given the opportunity to indicate that they had not used various aspects.

Despite the criticism of the manual reported above, a majority of those who responded rated information on using all but three aspects of the process (reviewing results, involving staff, and involving the public) as having been "extremely" or "very" helpful. With the exception of that on involving the public, fewer than 10% marked any of the information as being "not at all" helpful.

Aspects for which information provided was considered to be the most helpful were developing roles/mission and writing goals and objectives. Over three fourths (79%) of the librarians considered that the information on role setting was either extremely or very helpful, with almost one third (32%) reporting that it was extremely helpful. Nineteen percent found the information to be at least moderately helpful, whereas only 2% reported it as not at all helpful, and less than 1% reported it as not having been used.

Seventy percent of the librarians considered the information on goals and objectives writing to have been either extremely or very helpful, whereas just over one fourth (27%) found it to be at least moderately helpful. Only 3% of the librarians reported that this information was not at all helpful.

Information on using a planning committee was considered to have been either extremely or very helpful by 63% of those who rated it. Over one third (35%) found that this information was at least moderately helpful, and only 3% reported it as not at all helpful.

Sixty-two percent found information on assessing the library (looking around inside) to have been either extremely or very helpful. Well over one third of the librarians (37%) found it to have been at least moderately helpful, whereas only 2% indicated that it was not at all helpful. Information on analyzing the community (looking around outside) was considered to have been either extremely or very helpful by 57% of the librarians. Forty-one percent reported that this information was at least moderately helpful, and only 2% found that it was not at all helpful.

Information on both selecting activities and on writing the planning document was considered as having been either extremely or very helpful by 55%, and as at least moderately helpful by well over one third (38%) of the librarians. Six percent considered the former, and 7% considered the latter to have been not at all helpful. An additional 12% reported that they had not used the information on either of these steps, and 15% failed to respond to these items.

Information on using levels of effort was thought to have been either extremely or very helpful by 54% of the librarians. It was rated as at least moderately helpful by well over one third (39%), and not at all helpful by 7%. It is puzzling that only 19 librarians marked that they "did not use" the manual's information on levels of effort, since much larger numbers, 70 and 95, respectively, had indicated that they had not chosen levels of effort for either the planning process as a whole or for individual phases and steps. Perhaps some librarians used the information in a general sense but decided not to formally assign levels of effort.

Fewer than half the librarians reported information on involving library staff members, reviewing results, or involving the tax-paying public as having been either extremely or very helpful. The information on involving staff members was rated as extremely or very helpful by only 46% of the librarians. Just under half (47%) rated it as at least moderately helpful, and 7% rated it as not at all helpful. Twelve percent reported they had not used the information on this aspect of planning.

Only 41% of the respondents reported that they considered the manual's information on involving the public as having been either extremely or very helpful. Again, just under half (48%) considered this information to have been at least moderately helpful. Eleven percent rated it as being not at all helpful. Almost one fifth (17%) of the respondents reported that they had not used the information on this important aspect. Perhaps such a high rate of nonuse is not surprising when it is remembered that 60% of those reporting levels of effort reported that they had devoted a minimum level to involving the public, 58% had done the same in regard to informing the public, and that another 11 and 9%, respectively, had marked that they "did not do" either.

Information on reviewing results was thought of as having been either extremely or very helpful by 43% of the librarians. Almost half (49%) found it to be at least moderately helpful, while 8% considered that it was not at all helpful. An additional 15% reported that they had not used the information on this particular step, and 17% did not respond at all.

Sixty-six percent of the librarians reported that they had found the manual's workforms, and 57% that they had found its other charts and figures to have been either extremely or very helpful. Approximately one fifth, 21 and 17%, respectively, had found them to be extremely helpful. Almost one third (30%) rated the workforms as having been at least moderately helpful; only 4% rated them as having been not at all helpful. Forty-one percent rated the manual's other charts and figures as having been moderately helpful; only 3% found these to have been not at all helpful. Thirteen percent did not respond to the question about the workforms' helpfulness, and 15% did not respond to that about the helpfulness of the other charts and figures.

SATISFACTION AND RECOMMENDATIONS 131

Table 5.2. Helpfulness of Manual's Information on Various Planning Aspects

	Extremely Helpful	Very Helpful	Moderately Helpful	Not at all Helpful	Did Not Use	No Response
Planning committee	17% [36]	46% [98]	35% [74]	3% [6]	9% [23]	7% [18]
Levels of effort	13% [28]	41% [88]	39% [83]	7% [16]	7% [19]	8% [21]
Looking around outside	14% [29]	43% [92]	41% [87]	2% [4]	9% [23]	8% [20]
Looking around inside	15% [31]	47% [99]	37% [79]	2% [4]	7% [19]	9% [23]
Dev. Roles/ mission	32% [75]	47% [109]	19% [45]	2% [5]	1% [2]	7% [19]
Writing goals & objectives	25% [57]	45% [102]	27% [62]	3% [6]	4% [9]	7% [19]
Selecting activities	13% [25]	42% [79]	38% [72]	6% [12]	12% [30]	15% [37]
Writing document	16% [30]	39% [73]	38% [71]	7% [14]	12% [30]	15% [37]
Reviewing results	9% [16]	34% [59]	49% [84]	8% [13]	15% [39]	17% [44]
Involving staff	15% [28]	31% [59]	47% [88]	7% [14]	12% [30]	14% [36]
Involving public	13% [23]	28% [50]	48% [84]	11% [20]	17% [43]	14% [35]
Tools						
Workforms	21% [43]	45% [91]	30% [60]	4% [7]	9% [22]	13% [32]
Other charts & figures	17% [33]	40% [78]	41% [80]	3% [5]	8% [21]	15% [38]

Table 5.2 lists the percentages, followed by the numbers, of librarians who marked "extremely helpful," "very helpful," "moderately helpful," "not at all helpful," or "did not use" when asked to rate the helpfulness of the information and tools provided by the manual. The percentages and numbers of libraries not responding to each of these items are also provided. The percentages for the categories labeled "extremely helpful," "very helpful," "moderately helpful," and "not at all helpful" are based on the total number responding to each item; those for the categories labeled "did not use" and "no response" are based on the total number of surveys returned.

Librarians' Suggestions for Improving the Manual

As reported above, the majority of the librarians who responded to the author's survey rated most of the information provided by the planning manual as having been either extremely or very helpful. When asked to suggest improvements to the manual, six librarians responded by praising the manual, saying no improvements were needed, the manual should be left "the same," and that it was a "great improvement over the 'green peril' [1980 manual]."

Despite these positive comments offered by a small number of librarians, it will be remembered that when asked to relate significant problems encountered, 40 of the respondents had criticized various aspects of the manual. In addition to their comments, a total of 184 other ideas were gleaned from the author's request for suggestions for improving the manual, although one disgruntled librarian merely suggested the need to "start over."

Suggestions were made for improving almost every aspect of the manual, from its overall emphasis and arrangement to such concrete details as its typeface and index (see Appendix F for a listing of the suggestions offered). Many of these suggestions were very specific and quite appropriate; some contradicted others. The suggestions were grouped according to the following outline: First, general suggestions and suggestions for using the manual with small libraries and with library systems were reported, followed by those concerned with various aspects of using the process such as the planning committee, use of consultants and levels of effort, looking around, the mission statement and goals and objectives, the roles, and the planning document; suggestions concerning the manual's format, such as workforms, an index, and illustrations were presented last.

General Suggestions

One librarian who felt there should be more emphasis on the purpose of the plan and less on following the manual wrote, "We know the plan is intended to help us focus on where we are going, but we want to be able to use it as a road map on how to get there as well as a vehicle for estimating how much the trip will cost us and who will drive, navigate, entertain, etc." Another criticized that the planning process only focuses on public service when "all components of [the] library must be coordinated toward customer satisfaction to function effectively."

Describing the manual as a confusing "hybrid between strategic and tactical planning," a third librarian suggested that it be divided into two sections—the first strategic and the second tactical. A fourth pointed out the need for two additional publications, one on action planning and one on bud-

SATISFACTION AND RECOMMENDATIONS   133

get development for a long-range plan. Other suggestions for change included the need for more of a marketing orientation, a more realistic idea of how much time is involved, advice on why and to what extent libraries that have already completed a planning process should use the manual, suggestions for adapting the process, specific ideas for greater staff involvement, suggestions for helping planners identify values, and an explanation of the more detailed planning techniques mentioned on p. xix of the manual.

Many recommendations dealt with making the process easier to use, particularly for those working in small libraries. Flexibility should be encouraged, the language should be directed to laypersons rather than professionals, and the manual should be rewritten so that non professionals could understand and relate better to it. Sixteen librarians recommended that the manual be "simplified," "condensed," made "briefer" and more "concise," and that repetition be reduced. Summarizing each chapter at the beginning or end was suggested, as was a short pamphlet or reproducible "summary" to explain the process to board and planning committee members.

Several librarians expressed the need for the manual to be modified specifically for those working in small libraries. One requested "more emphasis on [the] effort of small libraries than saying, 'In very small libraries, the director will....' Even BASIC LEVEL is far above what is often possible." Others suggested that the manual be "rewritten for," "directed more towards," and easier to adapt to small libraries and mentioned the need for an abbreviated planning manual for smaller libraries or those unable to use the entire process or a pamphlet explaining and outlining the process directed to the small library with a staff of two or three.

A worthy example of just such an attempt to make the process outlined in *Planning and Role Setting* more useful (and less scary) to planners, especially those in smaller libraries, is Suzanne Bremer's *Long Range Planning: A How-To-Do-It Manual for Public Libraries* (1994). Bremer's recently published book offers many practical and helpful suggestions and workforms for use with various aspects of the process. A fictitious library serving a population of less than 10,000 is the example used throughout.

Several librarians pointed out the need for greater attention to planning for library systems, both those with a main library and branches and those consisting of a headquarters and individual member libraries. Librarians need assistance with collecting and analyzing data for multi-library systems; a work sheet designed for compiling looking-around statistics for systems with multiple outlets would be helpful.

Greater emphasis should be placed on making judgments within the context of a library system. Several librarians pointed out the need for more discussion of role setting for library systems, especially for cooperative systems with headquarters and member libraries. Better guidelines for developing different goals and roles for branch and central libraries and for member and headquarters libraries within library systems are needed, as is assistance with incorporating plans for these agencies' differing roles within the same planning document.

Several librarians requested that "real-life" examples of libraries' experiences with the process be included. One suggested having one "single concrete example per requirement," while another recommended a chapter describing the use of the process by a few libraries of varying size.

Planning Committee, Consultants, and Levels of Effort

Specific suggestions were offered for improving the manual's instructions on working with local planning committees, using consultants, and introducing the use of the levels of effort. Librarians requested more assistance with choosing and educating planning participants, understanding group dynamics, running meetings, and facilitating group decision making. Practical solutions to "political problems" such as the "role of hidden agendas and personal beliefs in blocking full discussion and/or reaching consensus" are needed, as is more discussion of methods to engage the community in decision making, with examples and citations to helpful resources. Librarians also requested information on when, where, how, and when not to utilize a consultant.

Changing the manner in which the levels of effort are presented in the manual was suggested by librarians who felt that it was "not completely clear how to progress from one level to the next and feel like you are accomplishing all that is possible for your library." These suggested changes included outlining the three levels (basic, moderate, extensive) in three separate sections, scaling down the extensive level, and presenting the levels as a checklist from which to choose committee activities. One librarian suggested that the minimum and moderate levels could be presented in a "scaled down" version for board members and citizens; this version would include all steps and workforms with references to chapters and examples in the original version.

Looking Around

Numerous suggestions were offered for improving the data collection or "looking-around" step. Librarians requested more help with surveying and interviewing patrons, using focus groups, and assessing other library services available in the area and expressed concern over the effectiveness of output measures.

Information on surveying should include more help with developing survey instruments, conducting surveys, using simple statistical measures, and sampling. One librarian recommended that the manual emphasize user surveys with detailed, open-ended questions because his library's user surveys "accounted for about one third of all our ultimate decisions regarding mission, roles, and specific short and long-term goals." It should include examples of community surveys, especially telephone surveys and surveys designed for rural, small, and medium-sized libraries; refer to the sample surveys in the first edition of the planning manual; and explain how to set up data electronically and manipulate it for various kinds of reports. The manual should also discuss the need to be responsive to constant change and should include more references to the census, local planning departments, and to the current management literature.

In addition to surveying, librarians requested that the manual provide sample interviews and describe and encourage the use of focus groups and panel interviews because "written surveys provide one type of information, but group discussions provide direct human contact—and that's very useful for staff and the public." Sample forms to use with suggestion boxes would be helpful, as would a summary of research most relevant to designing services, such as income, education, and library use—community profile-related data compared to library use. Sections on translating the results of data collection and on assessing other library services available in the area should be included.

Concern was expressed over the output measures. One librarian wrote that "an examination of output measures as effective tools is in order." Other comments included, "Data that is so difficult to collect and relies on staff hash marks is too prone to error—we should focus on information that is easily and accurately collected"; and "Revise data collection to increase validity." One librarian requested workable methods for libraries with little staff and money to use to collect statistics.

Roles

One librarian complained, "Brevity here harmed the product. I believe some people created alternative roles because they didn't understand some of the ones given." Several others stressed the need for modifying and expanding the section on role selection.

It was suggested that before choosing roles and missions, planners develop a list of assumptions about community growth or decline and the condition of the library's tax base, service areas, and state support during the planning period. Planners should also develop a list of the values agreed on by the group to avoid bickering over such value-based questions as whether the library will provide all formats, charge for services, or encourage input from the public.

Librarians complained that the roles as named and defined are "too rigid" or "set in concrete" and that the manual should encourage individual interpretation and clarification and provide either clearer definition of roles or a "looser" way to redefine them based on specific community needs along with discussion on how to modify or "blend" roles in a particular library. Conversely, one librarian felt the manual should stress the importance of using the roles as defined to enhance communication between libraries about use of the PLDP.

Other librarians suggested "rethinking" the roles, making role titles simpler and more self-explanatory, adding new roles, discussing changes in staffing and other costs and the size and type of collection needed to support various roles, and using "less jargon." Also requested were more examples of appropriate services to provide with each of the roles and statements from librarians explaining the philosophical basis for their choice (or nonchoice) of certain roles, with explanations of the tradeoffs involved in choosing certain roles rather than others; for example, which segment of users will "lose out" if certain roles are not chosen. Librarians asked for additional workforms such as a one- or two-page summary of the roles with more information than the block summary in Figure 11 (McClure et al., 1987, p. 28); a chart or graph to show the overlapping parts of some of the roles while emphasizing the major concepts differentiating the roles; and a worksheet on "Understanding Library Roles in the Local Setting," for listing current activities in each role, along with resources used, to prepare participants for Workform E. Specific roles for which suggestions were received were Preschooler's Door to Learning, Reference Library, Independent Learning Center, and Research Center. Varying ideas for the Preschooler's Door included broadening it to include children from kindergarten to second grade and from kindergarten to sixth grade, developing a role specifically for children's services rather than having all roles apply to children, and conversely, emphasizing that children and young adults are included in all of the roles rather than having a role that is age-specific.

Librarians suggested combining Reference Library with Research Center and with Independent Learning Center. Explaining that "Research Center and Independent Learning Center do not approach the scope of community libraries that try to balance some classics with newer fiction and nonfiction," one librarian suggested the need for a category that approaches the historical idea of "People's University."

Mission Statement, Goals, and Objectives

The manual should include more examples of mission statements and goals and objectives along with specific instructions on how to write them. One librarian wrote that "this was probably the hardest item to gain consensus on because committee members were not all familiar with mission statements." As discussed previously, better guidelines for writing mission statement and goals and objectives for different types of service outlets with their differing roles are especially needed.

Planning Document

More information was requested on writing, reviewing, and publicizing the planning document. The manual should include specific examples of what completed documents could look like and excerpts from actual planning documents, a section on reviewing former documents to evaluate past planning efforts and integrate what still needs addressing into a new planning process, and information on developing a budget for a long-range plan, as well as a discussion of how the plan evolves over a five-year period. Librarians would also appreciate more information on lobbying local government bodies and suggestions for presenting the plan, with "canned" public relations materials such as sample letters and speeches to present to commissioners, teachers, and businesses. Librarians should be strongly encouraged to continue the process once the planning document has been completed.

Format

Many recommendations had to do with the manual's format. Librarians suggested beginning with a recommended "timetable or outline" for conducting the various aspects or steps of the process, enlarging the typeface so it can be read more easily, making the manual "loose-leaf," and providing more reproducible pages for use as handouts or transparencies, such as outline summaries of each stage of planning, levels of effort for each stage, planning document guidelines, defining goals, objectives, and activities, and questions to consider in choosing and prioritizing roles. Some suggested condensing, reducing, or omitting the photographs; others found them "useful" but recommended having more up-to-date, color illustrations. A video and a computer software program to accompany the manual were suggested.

Although 66% had reported that they found them to be either extremely or very helpful, a few librarians criticized the manual's workforms as using "rather stilted language which we had to adapt" or being reduced to too small a size. Suggestions included consolidating and shortening the workforms, simplifying them for small libraries, and including examples of completed workforms with details of problems libraries might encounter. Additional workforms requested included job descriptions for planners, purposes of planning, an output measures summary, a publicity checklist, a community profile outline, a list of library strengths and weaknesses, action plans, and a time frame for a library's planning cycles. Librarians also recommended that a detailed index, index tabs for sections, and a more detailed glossary using nontechnical language be provided.

TOWARD A REVISED PLANNING MANUAL: THE AUTHOR'S RECOMMENDATIONS

The more than 200 suggestions for improving the planning manual included in the previous section should be considered very carefully by those planning its revision. Offered out of the frustrations and problems encountered by many librarians who worked with the manual in its present form, many are quite detailed, very specific, and concrete enough to guide its revisers; most are also quite appropriate. The following section contains additional recommendations for revising the manual offered by the author, many of which echo suggestions made by the manual's users.

Planning to Plan

The section on "planning to plan" should be greatly enlarged, and librarians and boards should be encouraged to devote more time and effort to preparing for use of the process. The basic and moderate levels call for far too little preparation for such an important undertaking; one fourth of the survey respondents indicated that too little effort was spent on this step. The extensive level's instructions to coordinate timing of planning recommendations with budget cycles, tie levels of effort chosen to a planning budget and schedule, and provide a detailed discussion of staff responsibilities and reporting patterns are good advice that would benefit all planners. Perhaps "planning to plan" should be recast as a preliminary step to precede steps for which planners choose varying levels of effort; this important aspect would then become a more fully developed prerequisite for all users.

The levels of effort themselves need to be rethought and reworded. Realistic estimates of how long it takes to complete various planning activities would be helpful.

Information on choosing, educating, and working with planning committee members needs to be enlarged to include much more specific advice, especially on understanding group dynamics, conducting meetings, and facilitating decision making. Leadership of the planning committee should be discussed more fully. The skills needed by the committee's chair and data coordinator should be specified, and the pros and cons of having the library's director or board chair lead the committee should be listed.

More attention should be devoted to securing funding for planning. Many libraries have secured small Library Services and Construction Act grants, and some have received larger amounts from foundations. Information on potential sources and on how to request funding should be included.

Looking Around

Although planners are encouraged to collect only those data considered necessary, many librarians feel the need to do some surveying or interviewing. Some indicated that they used the sample surveys in the 1980 manual. Perhaps sample user and community surveys similar to but simpler than these could be provided, along with basic instruction on sampling and using statistical measures. Advice on collating and analyzing data for multi-library systems is needed as is a worksheet for compiling "looking around" statistics for systems with multiple outlets. Sample interview schedules and instruction on selecting interviewees could be included.

Focus groups and town meetings are being used more and more by both small and large libraries. Librarians need information on how to choose participants and on the Nominal Group Process and other methods used with such groups. They also need more assistance in interpreting the results of data collection and on assessing services offered by other libraries and agencies in the area.

Workform C needs to be revised to match the current categories used in the *County and City Data Book* (U.S. Bureau of the Census, 1994). Several, such as those pertaining to the labor force, have changed. Use of management information systems should be introduced and encouraged. Librarians suggested that the manual explain how to manipulate data electronically and recommend (or be packaged with) appropriate software.

The D'Elia study (1993) cited previously would be useful as a preliminary to data collection. Librarians could be encouraged to use published records such as the census to draw up a demographic profile of their communities' residents and to consider the roles selected by libraries serving populations similar to theirs. They could use these as a starting point for their role-selection process by having focus group participants or planning committee members discuss their relevance.

Roles

The section on choosing roles should be rewritten and greatly expanded to include additional instruction on preparing for role selection and on selecting and creating appropriate roles. New roles should be added and the descriptions of the current roles should be revised. Particular attention should be paid to the brief annotations used in Figure 11 of *Planning and Role Setting for Public Libraries* (McClure et al., 1987, pg. 28).

Librarians' suggestions that planners prepare for role selection by developing lists of their assumptions about community growth or decline, various service areas, potential local tax revenues and state support, and their values regarding whether libraries should provide all formats, charge for services, or encourage public input are certainly worthy of consideration. More examples of services corresponding to particular roles, explanations of tradeoffs involved, and explanations of linking resource allocation to roles chosen are needed.

The manual's current roles have been criticized as "too traditional, somewhat out of date, and fail[ing] to include a range of service roles that are technologically oriented" (McClure, 1993, p. 199). Some roles do call for services (job and career information center, center for independent learning, information and referral services) that may be "traditional" in larger libraries, but that are virtually nonexistent in smaller communities. These roles and their examples should be retained so that they can be considered for adoption. The manual's descriptions may be the first opportunity many librarians have to find out about these important services.

Although many of the roles and their corresponding services would seem to include the use of technology, various uses of technology, particularly those more recently adopted, need to be described more fully and included in the examples of services rather than merely implied. A new role should be created for those libraries that provide Freenets and access to the Internet. A major purpose of the role descriptions, in this author's opinion, is to portray what is possible. The roles and their descriptions should together encompass all that public libraries are doing and all that they might do. They should provide planners with a menu from which to select, and to be realistic, they should include more detailed examples of services encompassed and a fuller explanation of the cost of each selection.

Many librarians still feel the need to create a separate "Children's Role" even though the roles' descriptions clearly specify that service to older children is included in most roles, particularly Formal Education Support Center, Independent Learning Center, and Popular Materials Center. Although their descriptions include the phrase "of all ages," the words "adults, teenagers, and children," may need to be substituted, and the manual may need to include specific instructions pointing out that children are included in each role. The necessity of the Preschoolers Door to Learning role should be questioned. The inclusion of this one specific role for children may create confusion, and it may, in fact, be considered redundant, as it was by one of the survey respondents who wrote, "We felt that Preschoolers Door to Learning was part of Reference and Popular Library."

The manual suggests that those planning at an extensive level may "identify or define roles unique to your library's circumstances," but it refers to those described in the manual as a "standard set" (McClure et al., 1987, p. 28) and provides no instruction for developing other roles. However, when respondents to the author's survey were asked to list roles chosen for their libraries, only 57% used role titles and descriptions exactly as they were listed in the manual whereas 28% used the manual's role titles but combined, reworded, or redefined them. Eight percent of the libraries used some of the manual's roles but also developed original roles, and another twelve libraries (7%) originated all of their roles rather than using or adapting those listed in the manual. In light of these findings, it is apparent that more help is needed for the many librarians who do wish to combine roles or to develop unique roles for their libraries.

Examples of role titles provided by the survey respondents are listed below to illustrate the great variety of roles chosen by planning librarians. Some were succinct descriptors modeled on the manual's; many were combinations; other "roles" read more like goals or explanations. One librarian wrote that the manual's roles were "only used as a starting point for development of... library specific role statements," another that "our main objective is to stay open and serve our community as best we can," and another, perhaps facetiously, gave his library's role as "To be a public library that serves the community—not save the world."

Examples of roles slightly different but similar to the manual's included Information Place, Hub of Community Activity, Gateway to Information, Community Education and Information Center, and To Enhance Learning for All Ages. Unique roles developed by librarians included the following:

- Local History Research Center, Genealogy/History Center.
- Community Spirited Local History of the Area.
- Cultural Center.
- Recreational Center.
- Partner in Economic Development (community and individual).
- Governing Body, Leader of the Community, Investigator.

The following read more like goals but were nevertheless provided by librarians in response to the author's request for library roles:

- Serve total community as a source of materials and activities for personal recreation, intellectual growth and cultural enlightenment.
- Improve the informational, cultural, and recreational needs of all ages.
- Providing all different types of media needed for the community.
- Outreach service for disabled and elderly people in the community.
- Search out new patrons.

- Work with local organizations to develop methods to make library more useful.
- Construction of new library.
- To have a year-round children's program.
- To acquire a book-leasing program.
- To provide an atmosphere that encourages personal, individual growth.
- To provide appropriate technologies that will benefit users.
- Expand into new soft and hardware as new media become a reality.
- Function as administrative unit of town government.
- Maintain, expand, and promote materials and services in the areas of business and economics.
- Continue to develop programs for children and adults which complement those offered by other organizations in the community.
- Service, programming (children especially) and education.
- Monitor growth and needs of minority groups within the district.

System librarians asked that the manual provide help with developing roles for systems. Guidelines for developing different roles for central libraries and individual branches and for headquarters and member libraries within cooperative systems should be included as well. As presently written, the roles describe public services as provided to patrons by libraries or branches. None describe services offered to branch or member libraries by a system's central or headquarters library.

Several librarians listed roles they developed for their systems. These included:

- Resource point for contact to State Library and Interlibrary Loan Services.
- Regional Resource Center, Lifelong Learning, Reference/Information, Children's Programs.
- Facilitator of Communication, Enablers of Economies of Scale, Conduit for State and Federal Aid, Consultant and Educator, Advocate, Coordinator of Resource Sharing, Planner and Manager.
- Promotion, Development, Implementation, and Maintenance of Interlibrary Networks, Support and Training Services for Member Libraries, Access to Library Services for Individuals in Areas Belonging to the System.

The following model roles were developed for use with library systems by a committee within PLA's Systems Section:

- Regional Library Planning Office.
- Resource and Financial Development Office.
- Consultation and Staff Training Center.

- Centralized Technical Services and Automation.
- Centralized Reference Service and Interlibrary Loan.
- Library Administration Center.
- Outreach Services Center.
- Library Advocacy and Communications Center.

These roles are accompanied by a set of full descriptions ("Make a Choice," 1990). Inclusion of these or other similar roles specifically oriented to services provided to branch or member libraries should be encouraged.

The role titles and the brief role descriptions in Figure 11 (see McClure et al., 1987, pg. 28) appear to be causing great confusion. This is especially apparent for those roles that are closely related such as Reference Library, Community Information Center, Formal Education Support Center, Independent Learning Center, and Research Center.

A large proportion of what librarians are accustomed to thinking of as "reference work" or "research" is helping students find materials and factual information for research papers, retrieving materials (periodical articles and books) on lists provided by teachers, and recommending books for book reports. This is probably the main type of reference work done in many libraries. It may be difficult for librarians used to thinking in such terms to make the transition to thinking of "reference" as the provision of "timely, accurate, and useful information for community residents" and to understand that the Formal Education Support Center's description, "assists students of all ages in meeting educational objectives established during their formal courses of study" (McClure et al., 1987, p. 34), means helping students find materials for papers. Part of the description of the Research Center role, "the library assists scholars and researchers to conduct in-depth studies" (McClure et al., 1987, p. 39), may add to the confusion for librarians (and even more so for others) who think of students as "scholars."

The fuller descriptions of the current roles (McClure et al., 1987, pp. 32–39) help clarify distinctions among the roles, although these still include some overlap and may not describe actual experience accurately, leading to perhaps even greater confusion. "Offers tours for classes and instructs students on using library tools"; "may sponsor a homework service using qualified volunteers to assist students with assignments"; "may reserve special materials to meet classroom assignment needs"; "may develop a clearinghouse to identify providers of formal education and training or may support a literacy program"; and "may supply supplementary print and audiovisual material for classroom use" (Formal Education Support Center, McClure et al., 1987, p. 34) by no means constitutes a full or exact description of librarians' interactions with elementary and high school students after school and on weekends. "The library promotes on-site and telephone reference/information services to aid users in locating needed information" (Reference

Library, McClure et al., 1987, p. 38), or "Scholars intensively pursue intellectual and professional interests using locally owned materials" (Research Center, McClure et al., 1987, p. 39) may seem to some to be a closer fit.

Which role does recommending books for children to read for fun fall under, Independent Learning Center or Popular Materials Center? The descriptions indicate that recreational reading about pets, rocks, stamps, or dinosaurs would fall under the former; would fiction reading fall under Popular Materials Center, or only if the books are award winners or best sellers?

In fact, where does the readers' advisory function for adults fall? It would seem to fit the Popular Materials Library role, but its description makes this role sound more like that of a self-service book or video store. Or does "special booklists may be distributed or materials gathered together to encourage circulation in connection with a library program, such as a children's story hour, summer reading program, or a young adult program" (McClure et al., 1987, p. 36) mean that programming for older children and teenagers belongs to the Popular Materials role? What if the programming is for educational purposes? Which role does a literacy program sponsored in the library by a community group belong to, Community Activities Center, or Formal Education Support Center (if formally registered) and Independent Learning Center (if not)?

The fuller descriptions do provide a much clearer picture of what is intended for each of the current roles. They are a good beginning and may just need to be rethought and fine-tuned to more accurately describe actual services provided by libraries. The role descriptions do need to be carefully read to be fully understood, however. This author's concern is that librarians, board members, planning committee members, government officials, and community group members may not spend sufficient time studying these more complete descriptions, may not fully understand or remember their implications, or may merely depend on the role titles or brief descriptions when choosing or prioritizing roles.

An even greater concern is that some librarians may not use the longer descriptions at all but may merely use the role titles and perhaps the brief descriptions for their own selection and prioritizing process and that board members, planning committee members, local government officials and community group members may be given only the titles with (or without) brief descriptions. The author's findings that several libraries whose roles were included in the PLDS *Statistical Report* had not used the planning manual supports these concerns, as does the fact that many librarians still feel the need to create a separate "Children's Role" even though the full descriptions clearly specify that service to older children is included in most of the roles.

Although unfortunate, librarians and community groups may be making decisions based on only these skeletal descriptions. This use should perhaps be warned against, but it should also be acknowledged and carefully considered when revising the annotations. They should be rewritten to include more than just the first paragraph from the fuller descriptions, or those first paragraphs need to be expanded, or both. Examples of actual services provided by libraries choosing particular roles could be included; the descriptions used in the D'Elia study (1993) might serve as a model. Any new annotations developed should certainly be reviewed as if they, alone, might be used for role selection. One should ask whether they accurately describe *what* is provided for *whom*: For example, does the Formal Education Support Center's revised description state how "the library assists students" and define what is meant by "students of all ages"?

An alternative to merely revising the manual's present roles might be to downplay the emphasis placed on these roles and to instead concentrate on teaching planners to develop unique service roles for their libraries. New technology-based roles and revised versions of the present roles could still be included as examples, but planners would be encouraged to create their own roles and role descriptions. The author's survey findings revealed that many librarians chose to combine roles or to develop unique roles. This alternative would provide greater assistance for such librarians; it might also alleviate some of the current confusion, encourage greater diversity among libraries, and promote stronger feelings of ownership by planners.

If this suggestion were followed, greater emphasis would then need to be placed on actual services provided to patrons by libraries. Lists of services offered by public libraries to patrons and by headquarters to member libraries would need to be developed. These arrays of services would be included as a menu from which to select those most appropriate for individual communities and library systems. Services chosen would then be grouped into roles, which would be described and given titles that planners felt were most descriptive of their intent. Instead of comparing roles that might or might not mean the same thing in different libraries, researchers could determine what services were chosen by planners and then provide their own groupings to provide a more accurate portrayal of the roles libraries are fulfilling.

Mission Statement, Goals, Objectives, and Activities

The manual should include more detailed instruction on how to write mission statements, and goals and objectives, accompanied by several examples of each. The concept of a vision statement, an expression of the contribution the library hopes to make to society, should be considered. If included, detailed information on creating a vision statement such as that available in *Evaluating Library Programs & Services: Tell It!* (Zweizig, Johnson, Robbins, & Owens, 1993, pp. 25–30), should be provided.

Better guidelines are needed for incorporating management goals and for writing goals and objectives for different types of service outlets with their differing roles, both for library systems with a central library and branches and for those with headquarters and member libraries. Inclusion of library staff members should be encouraged in each of the levels of effort.

There is also a need for additional, more specific instruction on creating activities to carry out goals and objectives, again particularly for library systems. The importance of coordinating a library's activities with its budget cycle should be stressed.

Planning Document/Review of Plan and Process

More information is needed on writing, reviewing, and especially on publicizing the planning document. Librarians indicated the need to use their documents both for internal use by staff planners and for distribution to government officials and patrons, so more consideration should be given to designing a document (or documents) that would achieve both purposes. Information on developing a budget for a long-range plan would be helpful as would inclusion of excerpts from actual planning documents.

The manual's information on reviewing results was thought of as having been extremely or very helpful by only 43% of the librarians surveyed, and almost one fourth (21%) were dissatisfied with this aspect of their planning. Obviously, more help is needed in evaluating both progress made toward achieving libraries' goals, objectives, and activities and the planning process by which these were developed. Instruction on evaluating past planning efforts to integrate those not yet accomplished into a new planning process was specifically requested.

Two books published during 1993 offer excellent information on evaluating library services and programs: *What's Good? Describing Your Public Library's Effectiveness* (Childers & Van House, 1993) and *Evaluating Library Programs and Services: Tell It* (Zweizig et al., 1993). Their suggestions should be incorporated or at least cited. A checklist or list of guidelines for using the planning process such as those found in this chapter could be included in the discussion of reviewing the planning process itself.

Involvement of Staff and Public

The manual's discussion of involving library staff and community members is woefully inadequate; 54% of the responding librarians rated the information on staff involvement, and 59% rated that on citizen involvement as only moderately helpful or as not helpful at all. Perhaps a lack of knowing

SATISFACTION AND RECOMMENDATIONS 147

how to include staff and citizens in the planning process partially explains why almost one third (30%) of the libraries placed too little effort on staff involvement and over half (51%) placed too little effort on involvement of citizens, aspects that are crucial to the immediate and long-term success of the planning process. Additional discussion of the potential benefits and concrete, detailed suggestions on when, how, and how not to use staff and citizens should be included. Instruction for using volunteers for data collection, report writing, and other aspects of planning should be provided.

Publicizing planning activities and especially the decisions made as a result of planning deserve much more discussion. Less than half (42%) of the libraries reported being satisfied with their efforts to keep the public informed; in fact, 29% were "somewhat," and 7% were "highly" dissatisfied. Perhaps the 57% who made "too little" effort and the 9% who "did not do" this at all would have expended greater efforts if the manual had provided more direction. Generic news releases and a publicity checklist were requested by librarians.

What's Good? Describing Your Public Library's Effectiveness (Childers & Van House, 1993) and *Evaluating Library Programs and Services: Tell It* (Zweizig et al., 1993) contain many practical and helpful suggestions for publicizing the library to community leaders and groups. The planning manual (McClure et al., 1987) could incorporate some of their examples or at least refer users to these and other books on public relations and publicity for librarians.

Format

The manual's format is perhaps the most difficult aspect for which to offer recommendations. Several librarians requested a simplified version or pamphlet; many others made quite helpful suggestions that would of necessity result in a much longer, more inclusive, more complicated document. There is no doubt that additional space needs to be devoted to more detailed instruction on planning for smaller libraries, for libraries in systems, and for public libraries as they relate to other libraries and agencies in their communities. Actual examples of planning documents, surveys, interview schedules, publicity materials, and transcripts of focus group and planning committee meetings and hearings would benefit the manual's users, as would discussions of problems encountered and case studies of libraries that used the process successfully. The librarians surveyed by the author recommended several additional workforms that would facilitate the use of the manual.

It is hard to imagine that one volume could contain all the additional information and supporting documents needed to help planners proceed through the process. Even if possible, that one volume would obviously not meet the need of some librarians for a shorter, less complex, less overwhelming document. Perhaps what is needed is a basic volume outlining specific detailed steps to complete the process in very clear, nontechnical language, written for board members and librarians with less than a graduate education. A second volume could supply far greater detail on all aspects of using the planning manual and could include samples and examples of all kinds of helpful forms and data collection instruments, as well as transcripts, case materials, and publicity materials. The second volume could be sold separately from the first and would be intended for planners in larger libraries and for county and regional directors and consultants and state library agency consultants to use with smaller libraries. A video or videos explaining and demonstrating the use of the process and software for use in data collection and presentation could be produced and sold separately or packaged with the second volume. An alternative approach would be a series of pamphlet-sized documents similar to those written for ALA's Small Libraries Publications Series; these could be written for different audiences and could be sold separately or packaged together.

SUMMARY

This chapter continued the assessment of the revised planning process begun in Chapter 4. The few problems and suggestions reported by planning librarians in the professional literature were presented, followed by the remainder of the results of the author's survey.

Over three fourths of the librarians reported being from somewhat to highly satisfied with their libraries' overall use of the planning process. Almost one third (32%) were highly satisfied. A clear majority also reported being satisfied with their libraries' use of five out of seven individual aspects: setting roles, writing goals and objectives, planning strategies, staff involvement, planning to plan, and reviewing results. Less than half were satisfied with their libraries' attempts to involve or inform their communities' taxpayers, which was not surprising, as a majority had also indicated that they felt too little effort had been devoted to these important public relations aspects.

Although 16% of those returning surveys responded that they had had "no problems," 114 (45%) reported a total of 161 specific problems experienced during their planning processes, and 186 (73%) responded with a total of 384 comments describing what they wished they had done differently.

The librarians' opinions of how helpful they found the revised planning manual to be were reported also. Over three fourths (79%) of the respondents had found the information on role setting, and 70% the information on goals and objectives writing to have been either extremely or very helpful. In fact, a majority regarded information on using all but three aspects of the process (reviewing results, involvement of staff, and involvement of public) as having been either extremely or very helpful.

Although fewer than 10% rated any of the information except that on involving the public as "not at all helpful," 40 of the librarians criticized various aspects of the manual when asked to relate significant problems. These criticisms were listed, followed by 184 other suggestions (for a total of over 200) the librarians made for improving almost every aspect of the planning manual. The author's recommendations for improved use of the planning process and for revision of the planning manual were also offered for the use of future planners and those responsible for further revision of the planning manual.

Conclusion

In assessing PLA's planning process for public libraries, the author had five objectives: to provide a historical record of the background and use of this radical and revolutionary development in public library planning, to examine whether revisions included in the 1987 manual were accomplishing the desired changes in its use, to encourage librarians and trustees to consider using the process by relating the many benefits received by its users, to offer suggestions for improving librarians' use of the process, and to make recommendations for revising the current planning manual. This book examines two versions of the planning process, the first planning manual published in 1980 and the second published in 1987.

The first two chapters were devoted to comprehensive planning processes used by libraries and to the first of the two planning manuals developed for use by public libraries. Chapter 1 presented the rationale and status of comprehensive planning in libraries and provided background and a description of the first PLA manual and its use. Chapter 2 discussed the lessons learned from libraries' experiences and the recommendations made for revising the 1980 manual.

The remaining chapters concentrated on the second planning manual, published in 1987. Chapter 3 traced the development, provided a description of the manual's content and revisions, and began to describe its use. Chapters 4 and 5 attempted to assess the manual's value by reporting its impact and the satisfaction of its users.

Both the professional literature and the author's 1991 study indicated that *Planning and Role Setting for Public Libraries* has had a most beneficial impact on the majority of its users. Change definitely has occurred as a result of its adoption. Libraries have added new formats, chosen new services, and developed new policies and procedures. Many libraries experienced gains in circulation, numbers of reference questions, and registered borrowers; increased community awareness of library services; better communication between administration and staff; and improved staff morale. Some librarians reported that their local officials were easier to work with and cited increased budgets. In addition to improving planning and evaluation of services and programs, librarians found the process helpful in working with trustees and library staff members, and in facilities and automation planning.

Over three fourths of the librarians surveyed by the author were satisfied with their libraries' overall use of the planning process. The vast majority of comments about the impact of the process were very positive, although a fourth of those who offered comments either indicated that the process had little impact, included negative comments along with their more positive ones, or offered nothing but negative comments. A majority of librarians rated most of the planning manual's information as either extremely or very helpful.

Almost half the librarians surveyed shared specific problems they had experienced, however, and over 200 suggestions were made for improving almost every aspect of the current planning manual. A few of the reports in the professional literature also described librarians' difficulties and made additional suggestions. These problems and suggestions were described fully, and were accompanied by the author's recommendations for making better use of the planning process and for revising the planning manual.

Because so many librarians who had never engaged in comprehensive planning have been inspired to do so and because so many of its users have benefited so greatly, the author concludes her assessment by recommending that librarians continue to adopt the public library planning process. A further recommendation is that those who do so adapt the process to their own resources and needs, and that they benefit by paying close attention to the planning experiences and suggestions shared by its previous users.

Further research should be conducted on the use of the planning process and its manual. While the author certainly agrees with a survey respondent's description of the 1987 version as "a great improvement over [the] 'green manual' [1980 version]," there is obviously still a need for much additional improvement.

Finally, it is the author's hope that the evidence of the process' impact presented in this assessment will be considered carefully, that the 1987 manual will be revised rather than abandoned, and that the recommendations for revision offered herein will be of assistance to the manual's revisers. That hope is well illustrated by the following quote from yet another survey respondent, whose words contain excellent advice for future users of the manual and for those considering its revision: "*Planning and Role Setting* was a great help. I will always be better off adapting a tool that has been carefully drafted by thoughtful professionals than I will be trying to reinvent the wheel." The respondent's expression of appreciation and praise for PLA's planning tool, accompanied by an acknowledgment of its need for adaptation, also provides a most fitting ending for this author's assessment of the public library's planning process.

References

The academic library program: Self-improvement process for academic libraries. (1978). Washington, DC: Office of Management Studies, Association of Research Libraries.

Adams, J. E. (1982). Developing data collection instruments for the planning process. *Public Libraries, 21,* 60–61.

American Association of School Librarians. (1988). *Information power: Guidelines for school library media programs.* Chicago: American Library Association.

American Library Association Committee on Post-war Planning. (1943). *Post-war standards for public libraries.* Chicago: American Library Association.

American Library Association Coordinating Committee on Revision of Public Library Standards. (1956). *Public library service: A guide to evaluation with minimum standards.* Chicago: American Library Association.

American Library Directory (47th ed.). (1994–95). New Providence, New Jersey: Bowker.

Ang, J. S., & Chua, J. H. (1979). Long range planning in large United States corporations—A survey. *Long Range Planning, 12,* 99–102.

Anthony, C. A. (1987). The public library development program: Options and opportunities. Public Libraries, 26, 55–57.

Association of College and Research Libraries. (1994). *Formal planning in college libraries, clip note 19.* Chicago: Author.

Association of Research Libraries. Office Management Studies. (1980). *Academic library program brochure.* Washington, DC: Author.

Baker, J. (1987). Rural library focus on mission. *Public Libraries,* 26, 58–59.

Balcom, K. M. (1986). "To concentrate and strengthen": The promise of the Public Library Development Project. *Library Journal, 111,* 36–40.

Barrish, A., & Carrigan, D. (1991). Strategic planning and the small public library: A case study. *Public Libraries, 30,* 283–287.

Beasley, K. E. (1970). *Measurement of effectiveness of public library service.* Proposal for research submitted to the U.S. Commissioner of Education.

Bellassai, M. C. (1982). Public library planning and the ALA/PLA process: What's in it for your library? *Journal of Library Administration, 2,* 81–96.

Betz-Zall, J. (1985). Is the planning process worthwhile? *Public Libraries, 24,* 18–19.

Blasingame, R., & Lynch, M. J. (1974). Design for diversity: Alternatives to standards for public libraries. *PLA Newsletter, 13,* 4–22.

Bloss, M. (1976). Standards for public libraries—Quo vadis? *Library Journal, 101,* 1259–1260.

Bone, L. (1975). The public library goals and objectives movement: Death gasp or renaissance? *Library Journal, 100,* 1283–1286.

Bremer, S. (1994). *Long range planning: A how-to-do-it manual for public libraries.* New York: Neal-Schuman.

Carr, M., & Wiese, J. (1987). Long-range planning—a learning process. *Show-Me Libraries, 38,* 9–12.

Childers, T., & Van House, N. (1993). *What's good? Describing your public library's effectiveness.* Chicago: American Library Association.

Chislett, P. & Soltys, A. (1984). Planning process—Grande Prairie. *Public Libraries, 23,* 19–20.

Community Library Services—Working papers on goals and guidelines. (1973). *School Library Journal, 98,* 21–27.

Conroy, B. (1982). Public libraries using the planning process: Is that the question—or the answer? *Public Libraries, 21,* 99–101.

County and City Data Book. (1994). Washington, DC: U.S. Department of Commerce, Bureau of the Census.

Cronin, M. J. (1985). *Performance measurement for public services in academic and research libraries.* Washington, DC: Office of Management Studies, Association of Research Libraries.

Crum, N. (1973). *Library goals and objectives: Literature review.* Santa Barbara, CA: Technical Information Center, TEMPO Center for Advanced Studies. (ERIC Document Reproduction Service No. ED 082 794)

Davoren, D. (1983). A planning process for public libraries: One library's experience. *Arkansas Libraries, 40,* 19–24.

D'Elia, G., Rodger, E. J, & Williams, C. (1991). Involving patrons in the role-setting process. *Public Libraries, 30,* 338–345.

D'Elia, G. (1993). *The roles of the public library in society: The results of a national survey: Final report.* Evanston, IL: The Urban Libraries Council.

DeProspo, E., Altman, E., & Beasley, K. E. (1980). *Performance measures for public libraries.* Chicago: American Library Association.

Detweiler, M. J. (1981). What difference does planning make? — The Prince William Public Library field test. In C. Muller (Ed.), *Small public libraries and the planning process. Proceedings of the Public Library Association Small and Medium Sized Libraries Section, American Library Association Annual Conference* (pp. 27–40). Chicago: American Library Association.

Detweiler, M. J. (1983). Planning—more than process. *Library Journal, 108,* 23–26.

Drucker, P. F. (1974). *Management: Tasks, responsibilities, practices.* New York: Harper and Row.

Drucker, P. F. (1980). *Managing in turbulent times.* New York: Harper and Row.

Duquette, D. (1982). Planning at Steamboat. *Colorado Libraries, 8,* 11–24.

Durrance, J. C., & Allen, C. (1991). WHCLIS goals vs. PLA roles. *Library Journal, 116,* 43.

Evans, G. E. (1976). *Management techniques for librarians.* New York: Academic Press.

Friedman, A. (1983). From objectives to strategies: Completing the first cycle. *Public Libraries, 22,* 64–67.

Garrison, G. (Ed.). (1973). *Total community library service: Report of the Joint Committee sponsored by the American Library Association and the National Education Association.* Chicago: American Library Association.

Gault, R. (1986). Planning for children's services in public libraries. *Public Libraries, 25,* 60–62.
Goals and Guidelines for Community Library Services. (1975). *PLA Newsletter, 14,* 9–13.
Halliday, J. (1985). A process for ~~planning~~ getting: The real value of PLA's planning process is not in goal-setting. *American Libraries, 16,* 177.
Harris, R. B. (1983). A survey of the use being made of the planning process. *Public Libraries, 22,* 144–146.
Hawgood, J. (1981). You too can be a library planner (parts 1 and 2). *Public Libraries, 20,* 19–22, 53–57.
Heidrick and Struggles, Inc. (1977). *Profile of a chief executive officer.* New York: Author.
Heim, K. M., & Wallace, D. P. (Eds.). (1990). *Adult services: An enduring focus for public libraries.* Chicago: American Library Association.
Hiatt, P. (1967). Traditional standards. *Library Journal, 92,* 4387–4388.
Hopper, L. (1991). Planning pays for the small, the poor, and the busy: An exhortation and a bibliography. *Public Libraries, 30,* 21–24.
Hunt, S. (1982). The participation problem in planning. *Public Libraries, 21,* 151–152.
Johnson, D. W., & Rossiter, M. D. (1986). Planning library services for special needs populations. *Public Libraries, 25,* 94–98.
Johnson, E. R., & Mann, S. H. (1977). *An assessment of the impact of the Management Review and Analysis Program (MRAP).* University Park: The Pennsylvania State University.
Kemper, R. (1970). Library planning: The challenge of change. In M. Voight (Ed.), *Advances in librarianship* (pp. 207–239). New York: Academic Press.
Liesener, J. W. (1976). *A systematic process for planning media programs.* Chicago: American Library Association.
Lynch, M. J. (1980). Public library planning: A new approach. *Library Journal, 105,* 1131–1134.
McClure, C. R. (1978). The planning process: Strategies for action. *College and Research Libraries, 39,* 456–466.
McClure, C. R. (1986). Library planning: A status report. In *The ALA yearbook of library and information services* (pp. 7–16). Chicago: American Library Association.
McClure, C. R. (1993). Updating *Planning and Role Setting for Public Libraries: A Manual of Options and Procedures. Public Libraries, 32,* 198–199.
McClure, C. R., Owen, A., Zweizig, D. L., Lynch, M. J., & Van House, N. A. (1987). *Planning and role setting for public libraries: A manual of options and procedures.* Chicago: American Library Association.
McKay, D. (1980). A state agency view of PLA's new planning process. *Public Libraries, 19,* 115–117.
Make a choice: Defining systems and their roles. (June 1990). Hand-out presented at a meeting of the PLA Public Library Systems Section.
Martin, A. B. (1972). *A strategy for public library change: Proposed public library goals-feasibility study.* Chicago: American Library Association.
Martin, A. B. (1976). Studying the community: An overview. *Library Trends, 24,* 425–439.

Martin, L. (1972). Standards for public libraries. *Library Trends, 21,* 164–177.
Martin, L. (1976). User studies and library planning. *Library Trends, 24,* 483–484.
Martin, L. (1981). Library planning and library standards. *The Bookmark, 39,* 253–260.
Metz, R. F., Van House, N. A., & Scarborough, K. T. A. (1989). A new twist for the PLDP: Simultaneous planning amidst a cooperative library system. *Public Libraries, 28,* 216–221.
Miller, L. R. (1987). The use of public library roles in planning at the Tucson Public Library. *Public Libraries, 26,* 69–71.
Morein, P.G., Boykin, J.F., Jr., Wells, H., & Givens, J. (1976). *Academic library development program: A self-study.* Charlotte: J. Murrey Atkins Library, University of North Carolina at Charlotte.
Morein, P.G., Sitts, M.K., & Webster, D.E. (1980). *Planning program for small academic libraries: An assisted self-study manual.* Washington, DC: Office of Management Studies, Association of Research Libraries.
Morey, G. (1970). *The identification of common library goals, objectives, and activities relative to a planning, programming, budgeting system.* Kalamazoo: Western Michigan University. (ERIC Document Reproduction Service No. ED 048 876).
Oklahoma State Department of Libraries. (1982). *Performance measures for Oklahoma public libraries.* Rockville, MD: King Research, Inc.
An odd euphoria. (1980). *Library Journal, 105,* 1575–1598.
Palmour, V. E. (1977). Planning in public libraries: Role of citizens and library staff. *Drexel Library Quarterly, 13,* 33–43.
Palmour, V., Bellassai, M., & DeWath, N. (1980). *A planning process for public libraries.* Chicago: American Library Association.
Public Library Association. (1967). *Minimum standards for public library systems, 1966.* Chicago: American Library Association.
Public Library Association. Goals, Guidelines and Standards Committee. (1979). *The public library mission statement and its imperatives for service.* Chicago: American Library Association.
Public Library Association. Goals, Guidelines and Standards Committee. (1985). [Survey of state, territorial, and provincial library agencies: use of the planning process]. Unpublished raw data.
Public Library Association. (1988–1994). *Public library data service statistical report* (7 volumes). Chicago: American Library Association.
Pungitore, V. (1991). *The public library planning process. Case studies of its implementation in smaller libraries* (Final Report). Bloomington: Indiana University, School of Library and Information Science.
Quinn, J., & Rogers, M. (1991). Free Library of Philadelphia unveils five-year plan. *Library Journal, 116,* 14–15.
Richmond, E. (1988). Planning and role setting: Alone or together? *Wilson Library Bulletin, 63,* 28–34.
Riggs, D. E. (1982). *Strategic planning for library managers.* Phoenix: Oryx Press.
Rohlf, R. (1981). The New PLA Planning Process. *Public Libraries, 20,* 3–5.
Ruccio, N. C. (1980). The planning process—is it for me? *Rural Libraries, 1,* 45–87.
Sager, D. (1986). Planning factors in large and small public libraries. *Public Libraries, 25,* 26–29.

Schremser, D. B. (1984). [Summary of comments made in response to survey on use of planning process conducted for the PLA Goals, Guidelines, and Standards Committee]. Unpublished raw data.
Sertic, K. (1982). Rural public libraries and the planning process. *Public Libraries, 21,* 19–20.
Shearer, K. (1993). Confusing what is most wanted with what is most used: A crisis in public library priorities today. *Public Libraries, 32,* 193–197.
Sheldon, B. E. (1989). Strategic planning for public library services in the 21st century. *Public Library Quarterly, 11,* 199–208.
Sinclair, D. (1981). Reviews. *Library Quarterly, 51,* 211–213.
Smith, C. (1989). *Role setting in public libraries: The choices selected, the planning involved, and the impact on resource allocation.* Unpublished master's thesis, University of North Carolina, Chapel Hill.
Smith, N. (1994). State agency use of *Planning and Role Setting for Public Libraries* and *Output Measures for Public Libraries. Public Libraries, 33,* 211–212.
Speer, R. (1983). Guidelines for pre-planning. *Public Libraries, 22,* 26–27.
Standards for public libraries. (1933). *Bulletin of the American Library Association, 27,* 513–514.
Stephens, A. K. (1988). *A Planning Process for Public Libraries:* Its use in three selected libraries. *Dissertation Abstracts International, 49,* 2852-A, (University Microfilms No. 8827655).
Stephens, A. K. (1989). Staff involvement and the public library planning process. *Public Libraries, 28,* 175–181.
Stephens, A. K. (1990). Three libraries' use of the public library planning process, an analysis accompanied by recommendations for future users. In *Advances in library administration and organization.* (Vol. 9, pp. 57–82). Greenwich, CT: JAI Press.
Stephens, A. K. (1991). Citizen involvement in public library planning. *Public Libraries, 30,* 150–155.
Sutton, B. (1991). *Project on long range planning in public libraries* (Preliminary Report). Urbana-Champaign: University of Illinois, Graduate School of Library and Information Science.
Tooker, B. (1982). Community analysis. *Colorado Libraries, 8,* 11–24.
Turock, B. (1981). The planning process: Progress not panacea. *The Bookmark, 40,* 56–61.
Utah State Library. (1985). *The upgrade process: Planning, evaluating, and measuring for excellence in public library service.* Salt Lake City: Utah State Library.
Van House, N. A., Lynch, M. J., McClure, C. R., Zweizig, D. L., & Rodger, E. J. (1987). *Output measures for public libraries: A manual of standardized procedures* (2nd ed.). Chicago: American Library Association.
Van House, N.A., Weil, B.T., & McClure, C.R. (1990). *Measuring academic library performance: A practical approach.* Chicago: American Library Association.
Webster, D.E. (1973). *Library management review and analysis program: Handbook for guiding changes and improvement in research library management.* Washington, DC: Office of University Library Management Studies, Association of Research Libraries.
Welles, G. (March 1983). Public relations and *A Planning Process. Illinois Libraries, 65,* 194–196.

White, B. (1985). Planning and performance in public libraries—the U.S. and the U.K. experience. *Public Libraries, 24,* 156–159.

White, L. (1981). What parts of *A Planning Process for Public Libraries* are essential? In C. Muller (Ed.), *Small public libraries and the planning process. Proceedings of the Public Library Association Small and Medium Sized Libraries Section, American Library Association Annual Conference* (pp. 51–58). Chicago: American Library Association.

Whittaker, J. (1978). *Strategic planning in a rapidly changing environment.* Lexington, MA: Lexington Books.

Wight, E. A. (1968). The contributions of the library survey. *Library Quarterly, 38,* 297–298.

Williams, P. (1983). Double fault: A critique of *A Planning Process for Public Libraries. Library Quarterly, 53,* 448–455.

Yesner, B.L., & Jay, H. (1987). *The school administrator's guide to evaluating library media programs.* Hamden, CT: Library Professional Publications.

Zweizig, D. L., Johnson, D. W., Robbins, J., & Owen, A. (1993). *Evaluating library programs and services: Tell it!* Madison: University of Wisconsin School of Library and Information Studies.

Zweizig, D. L., & McClure, C. R. (1982). Issues in training practitioners for library planning. *Journal of Library Administration, 2,* 235–250.

Appendix A

All Public Libraries with Roles Included in the Public Library Data Service *Statistical Report,* 1988–1994

Abbeville–Greenwood Regional Library
(Greenwood, SC)

Abilene Public Library
(Abilene, TX)

Abington Free Library
(Abington, PA)

Adams County Public Library
(Thornton, CO)

Aiken–Bamberg–Barnwell–Edgefield
 Regional Library System
(Aiken, SC)

Alameda County Library
(Fremont, CA)

Alexandria Library
(Alexandria, VA)

Allen Memorial Public Library
(Hawkins, TX)

Allen Public Library
(Allen, TX)

Allentown Public Library
(Allentown, PA)

Amarillo Public Library
(Amarillo, TX)

Ames Public Library
(Ames, IA)

Amherst Public Library
(West Amherst, NY)

Anchorage Municipal Libraries
(Anchorage, AK)

Anderson County Library System
(Anderson, SC)

Anderson Public Library
(Anderson, IN)

Ann Arbor Public Library
(Ann Arbor, MI)

Anne Arundel County Public Library
(Annapolis, MD)

Anoka County Library
(Blaine, MN)

Appalachian Regional Library
(North Wilkesboro, NC)

Appleton Public Library
(Appleton, WI)

Appomattox Regional Library
(Hopewell, VA)

Arapahoe Library District
(Littleton, CO)

Arlington County Department of
    Libraries
(Arlington, VA)

Arlington Heights Memorial Library
(Arlington Heights, IL)

Ascension Parish Library
(Donaldsonville, LA)

Asheville–Buncombe Library System
(Asheville, NC)

Ashtabula County District
(Ashtabula, OH)

Athens Regional Library System
(Athens, GA)

Atlanta–Fulton Public Library
(Atlanta, GA)

Atlantic County Library
(Mays Landing, NJ)

Auburn–Placer County Library
(Auburn, CA)

Aurora Public Library
(Aurora, CO)

Aurora Public Library
(Aurora, IL)

Austin Public Library
(Austin, TX)

Babbitt Public Library
(Babbitt, MN)

Babylon Public Library
(Babylon, NY)

Baltimore County Public Library
(Towson, MD)

Bangor Public Library
(Bangor, ME)

Barnesville Hutton Memorial Library
(Barnesville, OH)

Bay County Library System
(Bay City, MI)

Bayonne Free Public Library
(Bayonne, NJ)

Beaver Dam Community Library
(Beaver Dam, WI)

Benicia Public Library
(Benecia, CA)

Berkeley County Library
(Moncks-Corner, SC)

Berkeley Public Library
(Berkeley, CA)

Berkshire Athenaeum
(Pittsfield, MA)

Bibliotheque de Quebec
(Quebec, QU)

Blair County Library System
(Altoona, PA)

Blanchester Public Library
(Blanchester, OH)

Bloomfield Township Public Library
(Bloomfield Hills, MI)

Bloomingdale Public Library
(Bloomingdale, IL)

Boise Public Library
(Boise, ID)

Bosler Free Library
(Carlisle, PA)

Boulder Public Library
(Boulder, CO)

Bowling Green Public Library
(Bowling Green, KY)

Boyd County Public Library
(Ashland, KY)

Bradford Memorial Library
(El Dorado, KS)

Brazoria County Library System
(Angleton, TX)

Brentwood Public Library
(Brentwood, NY)

Bridgeport Public Library
(Bridgeport, CT)

Broome County Public Library
(Binghamton, NY)

Broward County Library System
(Ft. Lauderdale, FL)

Brown County Library
(Green Bay, WI)

Bryan/College Station Public Library System
(Bryan, TX)

Bucks County Free Library
(Doylestown, PA)

Buena Park Library District
(Buena Park, CA)

Buffalo & Erie County Public Library
(Buffalo, NY)

Burlington Public Library
(Burlington, ON)

Burnham Library
(Bridgewater, CT)

Cabell County Public Library
(Huntington, WV)

Calcasieu Parish Public Library
(Lake Charles, LA)

Cambridge Public Library
(Cambridge MA)

Camden County Library
(Voorhees, NJ)

Campbell County Public Library
(Cold Spring, KY)

Carmel Clay Public Library
(Carmel, IN)

Carnegie Library of Pittsburgh
(Pittsburg, PA)

Carnegie–Stout Public Library
(Dubuque, IA)

Carrolton Public Library
(Carrolton, TX)

Carver County Library
(Chaska, MN)

Cass County Public Library
(Harrisonville, MO)

Cecil County Public Library
(Elkton, MD)

Central Arkansas Library System
(Little Rock, AR)

Central Rappahannock Regional Library
(Fredericksburg, VA)

Chandler Public Library
(Chandler, AZ)

Charles County Public Library
(La Plata, MD)

Charleston County Library System
(Charleston, SC)

Charlotte–Glades Library System
(Port Charlotte, FL)

Chattanooga–Hamilton County Bicentennial Library
(Chattanooga, TN)

Cherokee County Public Library
(Gaffney, SC)

Chesapeake Public Library System
(Chesapeake, VA)

Chestatee Regional Library
(Gainesville, GA)

Chester County Library & District Center
(Exton, PA)

Chicago Public Library
(Chicago, IL)

Choctawhatchie Regional Library System
(Ozark, AL)

Chula Vista Public Library
(Chula Vista, CA)

Churchill County Library
(Fallon, NV)

Citrus County Library System
(Crystal River, FL)

City County Public Library
(Moundsville, WV)

Clackamas County Public Library
(Oak Grove, OR)

Clark County Public Library
(Springfield, OH)

Clayton County Library System
(Jonesboro, GA)

Clearwater Public Library System
(Clearwater, FL)

Clermont Public Library
(Batavia, OH)

Cleveland Public Library
(Cleveland, OH)

Coleman Public Library
(Coleman, TX)

Collier County Public Library
(Naples, FL)

Concord Public Library
(Concord, NH)

Contra Costa County Library System
(Pleasant Hill, CA)

Corpus Christi Public Libraries
(Corpus Christi, TX)

Corunna Public Library
(Corunna, MI)

Corvallis–Benton County Public Library
(Cornvallis, OR)

Council Bluffs Public Library
(Council Bluffs, IA)

County of Henrico Public Library
(Richmond, VA)

Coventry Public Library
(Coventry, RI)

Coyle Free Library
(Chambersburg, PA)

Cranberry Public Library
(Mars, PA)

Cresco Public Library
(Cresco, IA)

Crystal Lake Public Library
(Crystal Lake, IL)

Cullman County Public Library
(Cullman, AL)

Cumberland County Public Library & Information Center
(Fayetteville, NC)

Cuyahoga County Public Library
(Cleveland, OH)

Dakota County Library
(Eagan, MN)

Dalton Regional Library
(Dalton, GA)

Daniel Boone Regional Library
(Columbia, MO)

Darlington County Library
(Darlington, SC)

Dauphin County Library System
(Harrisburg, PA)

Davenport Public Library
(Davenport, IA)

Davidson County Public Library
(Lexington, NC)

Davis County Library
(Farmington, UT)

Dayton & Montgomery County Public Library
(Dayton, OH)

Dayton Public Library
(Dayton, IA)

Dearborn Public Library
(Dearborn, MI)

Decatur Public Library
(Decatur, IL)

Dekalb–Rockdale–Newton Library System
(Decatur, GA)

Delaware County Library System
(Media, PA)

Denison Public Library
(Denison, TX)

Denton Public Library
(Denton, TX)

Des Moines, Public Library of
(Des Moines, IA)

Des Plaines Public Library
(Des Plaines, IL)

Deschutes County Library System
(Bend, OR)

Douglas County Library System
(Roseburg, OR)

Dover Public Library
(Dover, NH)

Downers Grove Public Library
(Downers Grove, IL)

Driftwood Library Of Lincoln City
(Lincoln City, OR)

Duluth Public Library
(Duluth, MN)

Durham County Library
(Durham, NC)

East Brunswick Public Library
(East Brunswick, NJ)

East Central Regional Library
(Cambridge, MN)

East Chicago Public Library
(East Chicago, IN)

East Islip Public Library
(East Islip, NY)

East Meadow Public Library
(East Meadow, NY)

East Providence Public Library
(East Providence, RI)

East York Public Library
(Toronto, ON)

Edmonton Public Library
(Edmonton, AB)

El Dorado County Library
(Placerville, CA)

El Paso Public Library
(El Paso, TX)

Elizabeth Public Library
(Elizabeth, NJ)

Elizabethton–Carter County Public Library
(Elizabethton, TN)

Elyria Public Library
(Elyria, OH)

Englewood Public Library
(Englewood, CO)

Enid & Garfield County, Public
  Library of
(Enid, OK)

Ennis Public Library
(Ennis, TX)

Escondido Public Library
(Escondido, CA)

Etobicoke Public Libraries
(Etobicoke, ON)

Euclid Public Library
(Euclid, OH)

Eugene Public Library
(Eugene, OR)

Evanston Public Library
(Evanston, IL)

Everette Public Library
(Everette, WA)

Fairbanks North Star Borough Public
  Library
(Fairbanks, AK)

Fairfield Public Library
(Faifield, CT)

Farmers Branch Manskee Library
(Farmers Branch, TX)

Farmington Community Library
(Farmington Hills, MI)

Ferguson Library, The
(Stamford, CT)

Findlay Hancock County Public Library
(Findlay, OH)

Fitchburg Public Library
(Fitchburg, MA)

Florence County Public Library
(Florence, SC)

Forsyth County Public Library
(Winston-Salem, NC)

Fort Bend County Libraries
(Richmond, TX)

Fort Colins Public Library
(Fort Collins, CO)

Fort Worth Public Library
(Fort Worth, TX)

Framingham Public Library
(Framingham, MA)

Frankston Depot Library
(Frankston, TX)

Frederick County Public Libraries
(Frederick, MD)

Free Library of Philadelphia
(Philadelphia, PA)

Free Public Library of Monroe
  Township
(Williamstown, NJ)

Fresno County Library
(Fresno, CA)

Gadsden Public Library
(Gadsden, AL)

Gail Borden Public Library District
(Elgin, IL)

Garfield County Public Library
(New Castle, CO)

Gary Public Library
(Gary, IN)

Gaston-Lincoln Regional Library
(Gastonia, NC)

Geauga County Public Library
(Chardon, OH)

Glendale Public Libraries
(Glendale, AR)

Glendale Public Library
(Glendale, CA)

Glendora Public Library
(Glendora, CA)

Glenview Public Library
(Glenview, IL)

APPENDIX A

Grafton Midview Public Library
(Grafton, OH)

Grand Forks Public City–County
Library
(Grand Forks, ND)

Grand Prairie Memorial Library
(Grand Prairie, TX)

Grande Prairie Public Library District
(Hazel Crest, IL)

Grand Rapids Public Library
(Grand Rapids, MI)

Granite City Public Library
(Granite City, IL)

Greece Public Library
(Rochester, NY)

Greensboro Public Library
(Greensboro, NC)

Greenville County Library
(Greenville, SC)

Grosse Pointe Public Library
(Grosse Pointe, MI)

Guthrie Public Library
(Guthrie, OK)

Hailey Public Library
(Hailey, ID)

Half Hollow Hills Community Library
(Dix Hills, NY)

Halifax City Regional Library
(Halifax, NS)

Halifax County Regional Library
(Lower Sackville, NS)

Hamilton Public Library
(Hamilton, ON)

Hammond Public Library
(Hammond, IN)

Hampton Library in Bridgehampton
(Bridgehampton, NY)

Hampton Public Library
(Hampton, VA)

Handley Library
(Winchester, VA)

Harford County Library
(Belcamp, MD)

Harvey Public Library District
(Harvey, IL)

Haverhill Public Library
(Haverhill, MA)

Hayward Public Library
(Hayward, CA)

Helen Matthes Library
(Effingham, IL)

Hialeah Public Library
(Hialeah, FL)

High Point Public Library
(High Point, NC)

Highland Park Library
(Dallas, TX)

Hildebrand Memorial Library
(Boscobel, WI)

Hills Memorial Library
(Hudson, NH)

Hillsboro Public Library
(Hillsboro, OR)

Holyoke Public Library Corporation
(Holyoke, MA)

Horry County Memorial Library
(Conway, SC)

Houston Public Library
(Houston, TX)

Howard County Library
(Columbia, MD)

Howard County Library
(Big Spring, TX)

Howe Community Library
(Howe, TX)

Humboldt County Library
(Eureka, CA)

Huntington Woods Public Library
(Huntington Woods, MI)

Huntsville–Madison County Public Library
(Huntsville, AL)

Hutchinson Public Library
(Hutchinson, KS)

Idaho Falls Public Library
(Idaho Falls, ID)

Indian River County Library
(Vero Beach, FL)

Indian Trails Public Library District
(Wheeling, IL)

Indianapolis–Marion County Public Library
(Indianapolis, IN)

Iowa City Public Library
(Iowa City, IO)

Irving Public Library System
(Irving, TX)

Islip Public Library
(Islip, NY)

Itasca Community Library
(Itasca, IL)

J. F. Kennedy Memorial Library
(Hialeah, FL)

Jackson District Library
(Jackson, MI)

Jackson–Madison County Library
(Jackson, TN)

Jackson/Hinds Library System
(Jackson, MS)

Jackson–George Regional Library System
(Pascagoula, MS)

Jacksonville Public Libraries
(Jacksonville, FL)

Jacob Edwards Library
(Southbridge, MA)

James V. Brown Library
(Williamsport, PA)

Janesville Public Library
(Janesville, WI)

Jefferson County Library, Central Services
(High Ridge, MO)

Jefferson County Public Library
(Lakewood, CO)

Jefferson–Madison Regional Library
(Charlottesville, VA)

Jersey City Free Public Library
(Jersey City, NJ)

John Graham Public Library
(Newville, PA)

John Jermain Memorial Library
(Sag Harbor, NY)

John Tomay Memorial Library
(Georgetown, CO)

Johnson City Public Library
(Johnson City, TN)

Johnson County Library
(Shawnee Mission, KS)

Johnson County Public Library
(Franklin, IN)

Joliet Public Library
(Joliet, IL)

Kalamazoo Public Library
(Kalamazoo, MI)

Kanawha County Public Library
(Charleston, WV)

APPENDIX A

Kansas City Missouri Public Library
(Kansas City, MO)

Kellogg-Hubbard Library
(Montpelier, VT)

Kemp Public Library of Wichita Falls
(Wichita Falls, TX)

Kemper-Newton Regional Library System
(Union, MS)

Kenosha Public Library
(Kenosha, WS)

Kern County Library
(Bakersfield, CA)

King County Library System
(Seattle, WA)

Kitchener Public Library
(Kitchener, ON)

Kitsap Regional Library
(Bremerton, WA)

Klamath County Library
(Klamath Falls, OR)

Klyte Burt Memorial Library
(Curtis, NE)

Knox County Public Library System
(Knoxville, TN)

L.E. Phillips Memorial Public Library
(Eau Claire, WI)

Lake Agassiz Regional Library
(Moorhead, MN)

Lake Lanier Regional Library
(Lawrenceville, GA)

Lake Oswego Public Library
(Lake Oswego, OR)

Lakeland Public Library
(Lakeland, FL)

Lancaster County Library
(Lancaster, PA)

Lane Public Library
(Hamilton, OH)

Laramie County Library System
(Cheyenne, WY)

Laredo Public Library
(Laredo, TX)

Las Vegas-Clark County Library District
(Las Vegas, NV)

Lawrence County Public Library
(Louisa, KY)

Lawrence Public Library
(Lawrence, MA)

Lawton Public Library
(Lawton, OK)

Lebanon Community Library
(Lebanon, PA)

Lee County Library System
(Fort Myers, FL)

Leon County Public Library
(Tallahassee, FL)

Lewiston Public Library
(Lewiston, MA)

Lexington County Public Library System
(Batesburg, SC)

Lexington Public Library
(Lexington, KY)

Lincoln City Libraries
(Lincoln, NE)

Lincoln Library
(Springfield, IL)

Lindenhurst Memorial Library
(Lindenhurst, NY)

Linebaugh Public Library
(Murfreesboro, TN)

Lisle Library District
(Lisle, IL)

Livermore Public Library
(Livermore, CA)

Livonia Public Library
(Livonia, MI)

Lockport Public Library
(Lockport, NY)

Logan Library
(Logan, UT)

London Public Libraries
(London, ON)

Long Beach Public Library & Information Center
(Long Beach, CA)

Longview Public Library
(Longview, WA)

Longwood Public Library
(Middle Island, NY)

Lordsburg–Hedalgo Public Library
(Lordsburg, NM)

Los Angeles Public Library
(Los Angeles, CA)

Louisville Free Public Library
(Louisville, KY)

Lower Merion Library Association
(Ardmore, PA)

Lubbock City–County Library
(Lubbock, TX)

Lucius Beebe Memorial Library
(Wakefield, MA)

Macomb County Library
(Clinton Township, MI)

Madison Public Library
(Madison, WI)

Madison–Jefferson County Public Library
(Madison, IN)

Manatee County Public Library System
(Bradenton, FL)

Mansfield Library
(Temple, NH)

Maplewood Memorial Library
(Maplewood, NJ)

Marathon County Public Library
(Wausau, WI)

Maricopa County Library District
(Phoenix, AR)

Marin County Free Library
(San Rafael, CA)

Marrowbone Public Library District
(Bethany, IL)

Mastics–Moriches–Shirley Community Library
(Shirley, NY)

McKinney Memorial Public Library
(McKinney, TX)

Mead Public Library
(Mead, WI)

Medina County District Library
(Medina, OH)

Memphis/Shelby County Public Library
(Memphis, TN)

Menomonie Public Library
(Menomonie, WI)

Mentor Public Library
(Mentor, OH)

Merced County Library
(Merced, CA)

Mercer County Library System
(Lawrenceville, NJ)

Meriden Public Library
(Meriden, CT)

Meridian–Lauderdale County Public Library
(Meridian, MS)

Mesa Public Library
(Mesa, AZ)

APPENDIX A 169

Mesquite Public Library
(Mesquite, TX)

Metropolitan Library System
(Oklahoma City, OK)

Miami Dade Public Library System
(Miami, FL)

Mid Columbia Library
(West Richland, WA)

Mid–Continent Public Library
(Independence, MO)

Middle Country Public Library
(Centereach, NY)

Middle Georgia Regional Library
(Macon, GA)

Midland County Public Library
(Midland, TX)

Milwaukee Public Library
(Milwaukee, WI)

Minnesota Valley Regional Library
(Mankato, MN)

Mishawaka–Penn Public Library
(Mishawaka, IN)

Missoula Public Library
(Missoula, MT)

Mobile Public Library
(Mobile, AL)

Mohave County Library District
(Kingman, AZ)

Monroe County Public Library
(Bloomington, IN)

Montauk Library
(Montauk, NY)

Montclair Public Library
(Montclair, NJ)

Monterey County Library
(Salinas, CA)

Montgomery County Department of Public Libraries
(Rockville, MD)

Montgomery County Library
(Conroe, TX)

Montgomery–Floyd Regional Library
(Christiansburg, VA)

Mount Prospect Public Library
(Mount Prospect, IL)

Mt. Pleasant Public Library
(Mt. Pleasant, TX)

Multnomah County Library
(Portland, OR)

Muskegon County Library
(Muskegon, MI)

Naperville Public Libraries
(Naperville, IL)

Nevada County Library
(Nevada City, CA)

New Canaan Library
(New Canaan, CT)

New Castle County Public Library System
(New Castle, DE)

New Hanover County Library
(Wilmington, NC)

New Orleans Public Library
(New Orleans, LA)

New Rochelle Public Library
(New Rochelle, NY)

Newark Free Library
(Newark, DE)

Newark Public Library
(Newark, NJ)

Newport News Public Library System
(Newport News, VA)

Newton Free Library
(Newton, MA)

Nichols Library
(Naperville, IL)

Nicholson Memorial Library System
(Garland, TX)

Niles Public Library
(Niles, IL)

Nippersink District Library
(Richmond, IL)

Nobles County Library and
    Information Center
(Worthington, OH)

North Olympic Library System
(Port Angeles, WA)

Norfolk Public Library
(Norfolk, VA)

North Arkansas Regional Library
(Harrison, AR)

North Central Regional Library
(Wenatchee, WA)

North Richland Hills Public Library
(North Richland Hills, TX)

Northbrook Public Library
(Northbrook, IL)

Northland Public Library
(Pittsburg, PA)

Northport–East Northport Public
    Library
(Northport, NY)

Norwalk Public Library
(Norwalk, CT)

Oak Lawn Public Library
(Oak Lawn, IL)

Oak Park Public Library
(Oak Park, IL)

Oakland Public Library
(Oakland, CA)

Oakville Public Library
(Oakville, ON)

Ocean County Library
(Toms River, NJ)

Oceanside Free Library
(Oceanside, NY)

Okanagan Regional Library
(Kelowna, BC)

Olathe Public Library
(Olathe, KS)

Oldham County Public Library
(LaGrange, KY)

Omaha Public Library
(Omaha, NE)

Onandaga County Public Library
    System
(Syracuse, NY)

Onslow County Public Library
(Jacksonville, NC)

Ontario City Library
(Ontario, CA)

Orange Public Library
(Orange, CA)

Oshkosh Public Library
(Oshkosh, WI)

Osterhout Free Library
(Wilkes–Barre, PA)

Ottawa Public Library
(Ottawa, ON)

Otterbein Public Library
(Otterbein, IN)

Oxnard Public Library
(Oxnard, CA)

Palatine Public Library District
(Palatine, IL)

Palm Springs Public Library
(Palm Springs, CA)

Palo Alto City Library
(Palo Alto, CA)

Palos Verdes Library District
(Rolling Hills Estates, CA)

Pamunkey Regional Library
(Hanover, VA)

Paris Public Library
(Paris, TX)

Parkland Community Library
(Allentown, PA)

Parmly Billings Library
(Billings, MT)

Pasco County Library System
(Hudson, FL)

Pawtucket Public Library
(Pawtucket, RI)

Peoria Public Library
(Peoria, IL)

Peterborough Town Library
(Peterborough, NH)

Philip Read Memorial Library
(Plainfield, NH)

Phoenix Public Library
(Phoenix, AR)

Pickens County Library System
(Easley, SC)

Pierce County Library District
(Tacoma, WA)

Pioneer Library System
(Norman, OK)

Pittsburg–Camp County Library
(Pittsburg, TX)

Plano Public Library System
(Plano, TX)

Polk Public Library
(Polk, NE)

Pollard Memorial Library
(Lowell, MA)

Portage Public Library
(Portage, WI)

Porter County Public Library
(Valparaiso, IN)

Portland Library
(Portland, CT)

Prince William Public Library System
(Prince William, VA)

Providence Public Library
(Providence, RI)

Provincetown Public Library
(Provincetown, MA)

Public Libraries of Saginaw
(Saginaw, MI)

Pueblo Library District
(Pueblo, CO)

Puyallup Public Library
(Puyallup, WA)

Racine Public Library
(Racine, WI)

Ramsey County Public Library
(Shoreview, MN)

Randolph Free Library
(Randolph, NY)

Randolph County Public Library
(Asheboro, NC)

Rapid City Public Library
(Rapid City, SD)

Rapides Parish Library
(Alexandria, LA)

Redondo Beach Public Library
(Redondo Beach, CA)

Redwood City Public Library
(Redwood City, CA)

Richland County Public Library
(Columbia, SC)

Richmond Public Library
(Richmond, VA)

River Bluffs Regional Library
(St. Joseph, MO)

Riverhead Free Library
(Riverhead, NY)

Roanoke City Public Library System
(Roanoke, VA)

Rochester Hills Public Library
(Rochester, MI)

Rochester Public Library
(Rochester, MN)

Rochester Public Library
(Rochester, NH)

Rockaway Borough Free Public Library
(Rockaway, NJ)

Rockaway Township Free Public Library
(Rockaway, NJ)

Rockbridge Regional Library
(Lexington, VA)

Rockford Public Library
(Rockford, IL)

Rockingham County Public Library
(Eden, NC)

Rockingham Public Library
(Harrisonburg, VA)

Rosenberg Library
(Galveston, TX)

Roswell P. Flower Memorial Library
(Watertown, NY)

Rowan Public Library
(Salisbury, NC)

S.W. Smith Memorial Library
(Port Allegany, PA)

Sachem Public Library
(Holbrook, NY)

Sacramento Public Library
(Sacramento, CA)

Saginaw Public Libraries
(Saginaw, MI)

Saint Clair County Library System
(Port Huron, MI)

Saint Johns County Public Library
(Saint Augustine, FL)

Saint Paul Public Library
(St. Paul, MN)

Salamanca Public Library
(Salamanca, NY)

Salem Public Library
(Salem, OR)

Salmon River Public Library
(Riggins, ID)

Salt Lake City Public Library
(Salt Lake City, UT)

Salt Lake County Library System
(Salt Lake City, UT)

San Bernandino County Library
(San Bernandino, CA)

San Bernandino Public Library
(San Bernandino, CA)

San Diego Public Library
(San Diego, CA)

San Francisco Public Library
(San Francisco, CA)

San Luis Obispo City–County Library
(San Luis Obispo, CA)

Sandusky Library
(Sandusky, OH)

Santa Barbara Public Library
(Santa Barbara, CA)

APPENDIX A 173

Santa Cruz City–County Library System
(Santa Cruz, CA)

Sara Hightower Regional Library
(Rome, GA)

Sarasota County Library System
(Sarasota, FL)

Saskatoon Public Library
(Saskatoon, SK)

Saugus Public Library
(Saugus, MA)

Scarborough Public Library
(Scarborough, ME)

Schaumburg Township District Library
(Schaumburg, IL)

Scott County Library System
(Shakopee, MN)

Scranton Public Library
(Scranton, PA)

Seattle Public Library
(Seattle, WA)

Selby Public Library
(Sarasota, FL)

Service de la Bibliotheque, Ville de Laval
(Chomedey, PQ)

Shaler North Hills Library
(Glenshaw, PA)

Shasta County Library
(Redding, CA)

Sheppard Memorial Library
(Greenville, NC)

Sherman Public Library
(Sherman, TX)

Shorewood Public Library
(Shorewood, WI)

Sidney Public Library
(Sidney, MT)

Silas Bronson Library
(Waterbury, CT)

Sioux City Public Library
(Sioux City, IA)

Sioux Falls Public Library
(Sioux Falls, SD)

Skokie Public Library
(Skokie, IL)

Smithtown Library, The
(Smithtown, NY)

Sno-Isle Regional Library
(Marysville, WA)

Snowflake Public Library
(Snowflake, AZ)

Somerset County Library
(Somerset, PA)

Somerset County Library System
(Bridgewater, NJ)

Somerville, Public Library of the City of
(Somerville, MA)

Sonoma County Library
(Santa Rosa, CA)

South Country Library
(Bellport, NY)

South Huntington Public Library
(Huntington Station, NY)

Southfield Public Library
(Southfield, MI)

Southwest Arkansas Regional Library
(Hope, AR)

Southwest Public Library
(Grove City, OH)

Spartanburg County Public Library
(Spartanburg, SC)

Spokane County Library District
(Spokane, WA)

Springfield City Library
(Springfield, MA)

St. Catharines Public Library
(St. Catharines, ON)

St. Charles City–County Library
    District
(St. Peters, MO)

St. Johnsbury Athenaeum
(St. Johnsbury, VT)

St. Joseph County Public Library
(South Bend, IN)

St. Lucie County Library
(Fort Pierce, FL)

St. Mary's County Memorial Library
(Leonardtown, MD)

St. Tammany Parish Library
(Covington, LA)

Stanislaus County Free Library
(Modesto, CA)

Steele Memorial Library
(Elmira, NY)

Sterling Heights Public Library
(Sterling Heights, MI)

Stockton–San Joaquin County Public
    Library
(Stockton, CA)

Stoughton Public Library
(Stoughton, MA)

Stratford Library Association
(Stratford, CT)

Sunnyvale Public Library
(Sunnyvale, CA)

Surrey Public Library
(Surrey, BC)

Tacoma Public Library
(Tacoma, WA)

Tangipahoa Parish Library
(Amite, LA)

Tauton Public Library
(Taunton, MA)

Tempe Public Library
(Tempe, AZ)

Terrebonne Parish Library
(Houma, LA)

Texarkana Public Library
(Texarkana, TX)

Thomas Crane Public Library
(Quincy, MA)

Timberland Regional Library
(Olympia, WA)

Tippecanoe County Public Library
(Lafayette, IN)

Tipton County Public Library
(Tipton, IN)

Tomahawk Public Library
(Tomahawk, WI)

Topeka Public Library
(Topeka, KS)

Toronto Public Library
(Toronto, ON)

Torrance Public Library
(Torrance, CA)

Trenton Public Library
(Trenton, NJ)

Troup–Harris–Coweta Regional
    Library
(LaGrange, GA)

Tucson–Pima Library
(Tuscon, AZ)

Tulsa City–County Library
(Tulsa, OK)

Tuscaloosa Public Library
(Tuscaloosa, AL)

Twin Falls Public Library
(Twin Falls, ID)

Twin Mountain Public Library
(Twin Mountain, NH)

Union County Public Library
(Monroe, NC)

Upper Arlington Public Library
(Upper Arlington, OH)

Upshur County Library
(Gilmer, TX)

Vancouver Island Regional Library
(Nanaimo, BC)

Ventura County Library Services
    Agency
(Ventura, CA)

Vespacian Warner Public Library
    District
(Clinton, IL)

Victoria Public Library
(Victoria, TX)

Vienna Public Library
(Vienna, WV)

Virginia Beach Public Library
(Virginia Beach, VA)

Volusia County Public Library
(Daytona Beach, FL)

Waco–McLennan County Library
(Waco, TX)

Wake County Public Libraries
(Raleigh, NC)

Warren Public Library
(Warren, MI)

Warren Trumbull County Public
    Library
(Warren, OH)

Warwick Public Library
(Warwick, RI)

Washoe County Library
(Reno, NV)

Waterford Township Public Library
(Waterford, MI)

Waterloo Public Library
(Waterloo, IA)

Watertown Free Public Library
(Watertown, MA)

Waukegan Public Library
(Waukegan, IL)

Waukesha Public Library
(Waukesha, WI)

Wauseon Public Library
(Wauseon, OH)

Wauwatosa Public Library
(Wauwatosa, WI)

Way Public Library
(Perrysburg, OH)

Weber County Library
(Ogden, UT)

Webster Parish Library
(Minden, LA)

Weld Library District
(Greeley, CO)

Wellesley Free Library
(Wellesley, MA)

Wenham Public Library
(Wenham, MA)

West Babylon Public Library
(West Babylon, NY)

West Bend Public Library
(West Bend, IA)

West Bloomfield Township Public
    Library
(West Bloomfield, MI)

West Georgia Regional Library
(Carrollton, GA)

West Hartford Public Library
(West Hartford, CT)

West Islip Public Library
(West Islip, NY)

West Palm Beach Public Library
(West Palm Beach, FL)

West Shore Public Library
(Camp Hill, PA)

Westhampton Free Library
(Westhampton, NY)

Westminster Public Library
(Westminster, CO)

Westmont Public Library
(Westmont, IL)

Westerville Public Library
(Westerville, OH)

Whatcom County Library System
(Bellingham, WA)

Wheeler Basin Regional Library
(Decatur, AL)

Whitehouse Community Library
(Whitehouse, TX)

Wichita Public Library
(Wichita, KS)

Wicomico County Free Library
(Salisbury, MD)

Willard Library of Evansville, Indiana
(Evansville, IN)

Williamsburg Regional Library
(Williamsburg, VA)

Wilmington Library
(Wilmington, DE)

Wilton Library Association Inc.
(Wilton, CT)

Winfield Public Library
(Winfield, IL)

Worcester Public Library
(Worcester, MA)

Worthington Public Library
(Worthington, OH)

Yakima Valley Regional Library
(Yakima, WA)

Yolo County Library
(Woodland, CA)

Yonkers Public Library
(Yonkers, NY)

Youngstown and Mahoney County, Public Library of
(Youngstown, OH)

Yuma County Library District
(Yuma, AZ)

Appendix B

Planning and Role Setting for Public Libraries: Its Use and Impact

1. Please check all individuals involved with your current/recent use of *Planning and Role Setting*. (If your library formed a planning committee, please use both columns. If it did not, please use the right-hand column only and circle the person who directed the process.)

These served on our
Planning Committee:

These did not serve as
Planning Committee members
but were directly involved (other
than only filling out surveys)

Please	☐ director of library or system	☐
circle	☐ associate or assitant director	☐
Planning	☐ heads of member libraries (Systems only)	☐
Committee	☐ branch and/or departement heads	☐
chair	☐ professionals other than the above	☐
	☐ paraprofessional and clerical staff	☐
	☐ chair of Board of Trustees	☐
	☐ members of Board of Trustees	☐
	☐ members of Friends of the Library	☐
	☐ officials of local governments	☐
	☐ citizens other than Board members/ Friends/local government officials	☐
☐	consultant	☐
☐	others (Please list)	☐

2. Libraries may use different aspects of the planning manual. To describe your library's use, please check the appropriate box for all of the statements listed below. (Please check only one box.)

YES NO PLAN TO

☐ ☐ ☐ We formed a Planning Committee.
☐ ☐ ☐ We chose a level of effort for the planning process as a whole.
☐ ☐ ☐ We chose levels of efforts for individual phases and steps.
☐ ☐ ☐ We used printed sources and library statistics for "Looking Around."
☐ ☐ ☐ We conducted interviews and/or surveys for "Looking Around." [Please list] _____

☐ ☐ ☐ We calculated output measures. [Please list] _____

☐ ☐ ☐ We selected roles from those in *Planning and Role Setting...*
☐ ☐ ☐ We adapted its roles or chose other roles. [Please explain] _____

☐ ☐ ☐ We wrote a mission statement.
☐ ☐ ☐ We developed goals and objectives.
☐ ☐ ☐ We selected activities and tasks to accomplish objectives.
☐ ☐ ☐ We assigned responsibility for implementing activities/tasks.
☐ ☐ ☐ We prepared a planning document.
☐ ☐ ☐ We have reviewed our plan (mission, goals & objectives, activities)
☐ ☐ ☐ We have reviewed our planning process.

3. Please circle the level of effort (extensive, moderate, minimum) spent on the Planning Process as a whole and on each of the planning phases aspects and then check your opinion of these amounts of effort.

				FAR TOO MUCH	TOO MUCH	ABOUT RIGHT	TOO LITTLE	FAR TOO LITTLE
ext.	mod.	min.	Process as a whole	☐	☐	☐	☐	☐
ext.	mod.	min.	Planning to Plan	☐	☐	☐	☐	☐
ext.	mod.	min.	Looking Around	☐	☐	☐	☐	☐
ext.	mod.	min.	Dev. Roles/Mission	☐	☐	☐	☐	☐
ext.	mod.	min.	Writing Goals and Objectives	☐	☐	☐	☐	☐
ext.	mod.	min.	Taking Action	☐	☐	☐	☐	☐
ext.	mod.	min.	Writing the Planning Document	☐	☐	☐	☐	☐
ext.	mod.	min.	Reviewing Results	☐	☐	☐	☐	☐
ext.	mod.	min.	Staff Involvement	☐	☐	☐	☐	☐
ext.	mod.	min.	Informing Public	☐	☐	☐	☐	☐
ext.	mod.	min.	Involving Public	☐	☐	☐	☐	☐

4. How satisfied are you with your library's use of the Planning Process and with its performance in each of the planning phases and aspects?

	HIGHLY SATIS- FIED	SOMEWHAT SATIS- FIED	NEUTRAL	SOMEWHAT DIS- SATIS- FIED	HIGHLY DIS- SATIS- FIED	DID NOT DO
Planning Process as a whole	❏	❏	❏	❏	❏	❏
Planning to Plan	❏	❏	❏	❏	❏	❏
Looking Around	❏	❏	❏	❏	❏	❏
Dev. Roles/Mission	❏	❏	❏	❏	❏	❏
Writing Goals and Objectives	❏	❏	❏	❏	❏	❏
Taking Action	❏	❏	❏	❏	❏	❏
Writing the Planning Document	❏	❏	❏	❏	❏	❏
Reviewing Results	❏	❏	❏	❏	❏	❏
Staff Involvement	❏	❏	❏	❏	❏	❏
Informing Public	❏	❏	❏	❏	❏	❏
Involving Public	❏	❏	❏	❏	❏	❏

5. What are the three major things you wish had been done differently during the use of the planning process?

   a) _____

   b) _____

   c) _____

6. Please describe the impact of the planning process on your library by checking "yes" or "no" for all of the statements listed below.

As a result of our use of the planning process:

Yes No
❏ ❏ our overall budget has been increased.
❏ ❏ our budget has been reallocated. [Please explain]

_____

❏ ❏ our local officials are easier to work with.
❏ ❏ our community seems more aware of our services.
❏ ❏ our registered borrowers have increased.
❏ ❏ our circulation has increased.
❏ ❏ our reference questions have increased.

180 STEPHENS

☐ ☐ our program attendance has increased.
☐ ☐ our staffs' morale has improved.
☐ ☐ communication has improved between our admin. and staff.
☐ ☐ we have added/dropped/changed emphasis on certain types of materials.
     [Please explain] _____

☐ ☐ we have added/dropped/changed emphasis on certain services.
     [Please explain] _____

☐ ☐ we have changed our policies and/or procedures.
     [Please explain] _____

7. In what other ways (both positive and negative) has using this planning process affected your library?
_____
_____

8. How helpful were the information and tools provided by the manual?

	EXTREMELY HELPFUL	VERY HELPFUL	MODERATELY HELPFUL	NOT AT ALL HELPFUL	DID NOT USE
INFORMATION ON					
Planning committee	☐	☐	☐	☐	☐
Levels of effort	☐	☐	☐	☐	☐
Looking around outside	☐	☐	☐	☐	☐
Looking around inside	☐	☐	☐	☐	☐
Dev. roles/mission	☐	☐	☐	☐	☐
Writing goals and objectives	☐	☐	☐	☐	☐
Selec. activities	☐	☐	☐	☐	☐
Writing the planning document	☐	☐	☐	☐	☐
Reviewing results	☐	☐	☐	☐	☐
Involving staff	☐	☐	☐	☐	☐
Involving public	☐	☐	☐	☐	☐
TOOLS					
Workforms	☐	☐	☐	☐	☐
Other charts and figures	☐	☐	☐	☐	☐

9. What were the two most significant problems encountered in using the manual? [The next question will ask you to suggest improvements.]

a) _____

b) _____

10. What are four specific improvements that should be made to the manual?
 a) _____

 b) _____

 c) _____

 d) _____

11. Please list all roles chosen for your library.
_____
_____
_____

12. Please check all manuals used for your library's current/recent planning efforts.
 ❑ *Planning and Role Setting for Public Libraries*
 ❑ *A Planning Process for Public Libraries* ("green manual")
 ❑ *Output Measures for Public Libraries*
 ❑ Others [Please list] _____
 _____

13. What is the population of your library's legal service area? _____

14. Please check the description that fits your library best.
 ❑ single library without branches
 ❑ library system with branches (One board governs entire system)
 ❑ library system with member libraries (Members have own legal Boards)

15. For systems with branches/member libraries only. Please check purpose for which *Planning and Role Setting for Public Libraries* was used.
 ❑ used to plan for system as a whole (no specific planning for individual branches or member libraries)
 ❑ used to plan for individual branches/member libraries only (no planning for overall system)
 ❑ used to plan for individual branches/member libraries *and* for system as a whole (could include planning for services to be offered to branches/member libraries by headquarters library)
 ❑ used *only* to plan services to be offered to branches/member libraries by headquarters library
 ❑ other [Please explain] _____

Name _____
Title _____
Library _____

Appendix C

Inclusion of Study Libraries in Public Library Data Service's *Statistical Report*, 1988–1991

ALL STUDY LIBRARIES THAT HAD LISTED ROLES IN THE PUBLIC LIBRARY DATA SERVICE'S *STATISTICAL REPORT* BY THE TIME OF THE AUTHOR'S 1991 STUDY

Alexandria Library
(Alexandria, VA)

Athens Regional Library System
(Athens, GA)

Auburn-Placer County Library
(Auburn, CA)

Baltimore County Public Library
(Towson, MD)

Barnesville Hutton Memorial Library
(Barnesville, OH)

Benecia Public Library
(Benicia, CA)

Bloomfield Township Public Library
(Bloomfield Hills, MI)

Bradford Memorial Library
(El Dorado, KS)

Brazoria County Library System
(Angleton, TX)

Buffalo & Erie County Public Library
(Buffalo, NY)

Calcasieu Parish Public Library
(Lake Charles, LA)

Clearwater Public Library System
(Clearwater, FL)

Clermont County Public Library
(Batavia, OH)

Corvallis Public Library
(Corvallis, OR)

Cresco Public Library
(Cresco, IA)

Cumberland County Public Library
and Information Center
(Fayetteville, NC)

Davis County Public Library
(Farmington, UT)

Dayton Public Library
(Dayton, IA)

Decatur Public Library
(Decatur, IL)

Dekalb County Public Library
(Decatur, GA)

Durham County Library
(Durham, NC)

Findlay–Hancock County Public Library
(Findlay, OH)

Finkelstein Memorial Library
(Spring Valley, NY)

Florence County Library
(Florence, SC)

Free Library of Philadelphia
(Philadelphia, PA)

Gail Borden Public Library District
(Elgin, IL)

Garfield County Public Library
(New Castle, CO)

Granite City Public Library
(Granite City, IL)

Harford County Public Library
(Belcamp, MD)

Helen Matthes Library
(Effingham, IL)

Hildebrand Memorial Library
(Boscobel, WI)

Houston Public Library
(Houston, TX)

Howe Community Library
(Howe, TX)

Iowa City Public Library
(Iowa City, IA)

Jefferson–Madison County Library
(Charlottesville, VA)

Kalamazoo Public Library
(Kalamazoo, MI)

Lakeland Public Library
(Lakeland, FL)

Lancaster County Library
(Lancaster, PA)

Leon County Public Library
(Tallahassee, FL)

Lincoln Library
(Springfield, IL)

Mead Public Library
(Mead, WI)

Menomonie Public Library
(Menomonie, WI)

Metropolitan Library System
(Oklahoma City, OK)

Monterey County Free Libraries
(Salinas, CA)

Nippersink Public Library
(Richmond, IL)

Oak Lawn Public Library
(Oak Lawn, IL)

Okanagan Regional Library
(Kelowna, BC)

Peterborough Town Library
(Peterborough, NH)

Portage Public Library
(Portage, WI)

Puyallup Public Library
(Puyallup, WA)

APPENDIX C 185

Redwood City Public Library
(Redwood City, CA)

Rockbridge Regional Library
(Lexington, VA)

Rockford Public Library
(Rockford, IL)

Salt Lake City Public Library
(Salt Lake City, UT)

Salt Lake County Library System
(Salt Lake City, UT)

San Bernardino Public Library
(San Bernardino, CA)

Santa Cruz City–County Library System
(Santa Cruz, CA)

Sno-Isle Regional Library
(Marysville, WA)

Somerset County Library
(Bridgewater, CT)

Spartanburg County Public Library
(Spartanburg, SC)

Springfield City Library
(Springfield, MA)

St. Joseph County Public Library
(South Bend, IN)

Sterling Heights Public Library
(Sterling Heights, MI)

Stockton–San Joaquin County Public Library
(Stockton, CA)

Sunnyvale Public Library
(Sunnyvale, CA)

Tempe Public Library
(Tempe, AZ)

Tomahawk Public Library
(Tomahawk, WI)

Topeka Public Library
(Topeka, KS)

Torrance Public Library
(Torrance, CA)

Tulsa City–County Public Library
(Tulsa, OK)

Waco–McLennon County Library
(Waco, TX)

Warren–Trumbull County Public Library
(Warren, OH)

Wenham Public Library
(Wenham, MA)

West Bend Public Library
(West Bend, IA)

Westerville Public Library
(Westerville, OH)

Wichita Public Library
(Wichita, KS)

Wicomico County Free Library
(Salisbury, MD)

Williamsburg Public Library
(Williamsburg, VA)

The Wilmington Library
(Wilmington, Delaware

Worcester Public Library
(Worcester, MA)

Worthington Public Library
(Worthington, OH)

LIBRARIES THAT DID NOT HAVE ROLES LISTED IN THE PUBLIC LIBRARY DATA SERVICE'S *STATISTICAL REPORT* BY THE TIME OF THE AUTHOR'S 1991 STUDY

Alexandria Public Library
(Alexandria, IN)

Allerton Public Library
(Monticello, IL)

Andrews Dallas Township Public Library
(Andrews, IN)

Arcade Free library
(Arcade, NY)

Arcola Public Library
(Arcola, IL)

Argos Public Library
(Argos, IN)

Arthur Public Library
(Arthur, IL)

Baldwinsville Public Library
(Baldwinsville, NY)

Barclay Public Library District
(Warrensburg, IL)

Bell Memorial Public Library
(Mentone, IN)

Bloomfield Eastern Hills Greene County Public Library
(Bloomfield, IN)

Blount County Library
(Maryville, TN)

Booth & Dimock Memorial Library
(Coventry, CT)

Bristol TN–VA Public Library
(Bristol, VA)

Brownsburg Public Library
(Brownsburg, IN)

Bud Werner Memorial Library
(Steamboat Springs, CO)

Burke Public Library
(Burke, SD)

Canandaigua–Wood Library Association
(Canandaigua, NY)

Chattanooga–Hamilton County Library
(Chattanooga, TN)

Cheatham County Public Library
(Ashland City, TN)

Chesapeake Public Library
(Chesapeake, VA)

Chester County Library
(Chester, SC)

Chrisman Public Library
(Chrisman, IL)

City of San Marino
(San Marino, CA)

Clarendon County Library
(Chester, SC)

Cleveland Public Library
(Cleveland, TN)

Clinton Public Library
(Clinton, TN)

Coffee County Lannom Memorial Library
(Tullahoma, TN)

Corning Area Public Library
(Corning, NY)

Cortez Public Library
(Cortez, CO)

Cragin Memorial Library
(Colchester, CT)

Custer County Public Library
(Chambersburg, PA)

Danville Center Township Public Library
(Danville, IN)

Darlington County Library
(Darlington, SC)

Decatur Public Library
(Decatur, TN)

Derby Public Library
(Derby, CT)

Douglas County Public Library System
(Roseburg, OR)

Douglas County Public Library
(Castle Rock, CO)

Elm Grove Public Library
(Elm Grove, WI)

Elma Public Library
(Elma, NY)

Flora Monroe Township Public Library
(Flora, IN)

Forsyth Public Library
(Forsyth, IL)

Fred A. Vaught Memorial Library
(Hartsville, TN)

Freeman Public Library
(Freeman, SD)

Gilpin County Public Library
(Black Hawk, CO)

Goshen Public Library
(Goshen, IN)

Grand Island Memorial Library
(Grand Island, NY)

Greenup Township Carnegie Library
(Greenup Township, IL)

Greece Public Library
(Rochester, NY)

Gregory Public Library
(Gregory, SD)

Hammond Public Library
(Hammond, IN)

Handley Library
(Winchester, VA)

Havre Hill County Library
(Havre, MT)

Hickman County Public Library
(Centerville, TN)

Hoopeston Public Library
(Hoopeston, IL)

Horry County Memorial Library
(Conway, SC)

Illiopolis Public Library
(Illiopolis, IL)

Jack McConnico Memorial Library
(Selmer, TN)

Jackson/Madison County Library
(Jackson, TN)

Jordanville Public Library
(Jordanville, NY)

Junction City Public Library
(Junction City, OR)

Kent County Public Library
(Chestertown, MD)

Kershaw County Library
(Camden, SC)

Kingston City Library
(Kingston, TN)

Lackawana Public Library
(Lackawana, NY)

LaFollette Public Library
(LaFollette, TN)

Livermore Public Library
(Livermore, CA)

Loda Township Public Library
(Loda, IL)

Louisville Public Library
(Louisville, CO)

Lubbock City–County Library
(Lubbock, TX)

Madisonville Public Library
(Madisonville, TN)

Margaret Cooper Public Library
(Linton, IN)

Marigold Library System
(Strathmore, AB)

Marrowbone Public Library District
(Bethany, IL)

Marshall Public Library
(Marshall, IL)

Mattoon Public Library
(Mattoon, IL)

Maynardville Public Library
(Maynardville, TN)

Memphis/Shelby County Library
(Memphis, TN)

Milford Public Library
(Milford, CT)

Mishawaka Penn Public Library
(Mishawaka, IN)

Mohave County Library District
(Kingman, AZ)

Morrison–Reaves Public Library
(Richmond, IN)

Morristown Centenniel Library
(Morrisville, VT)

Moyer Library
(Gibson City, IL)

Mt. Zion District Library
(Mt. Zion, IL)

Muncie Center Township Public
    Library
(Muncie, IN)

Ncoga Public Library District
(Ncoga, IL)

Newton Free Library
(Newton, MA)

North Manchester Public Library
(North Manchester, IN)

Northeast Texas Library System
(Garland, TX)

Norwich Public Library
(Norwich, VT)

Okefenokee Regional Library
(Waycross, GA)

Oneida Public Library
(Oneida, TN)

Ontario Public Library
(Ontario, NY)

Orange Public Library
(Orange, CT)

Oshkosh Public Library
(Oshkosh, WI)

Oshwood Public Library District
(Oshwood, IL)

Otis Library
(Norwich, CT)

Palestine Public Library
(Palestine, TX)

Paris Public Library
(Paris, IL)

Peabody Institute Library
(Peabody, MA)

Pendleton Public Library
(Pendleton, OR)

Penn Yan Public Library
(Penn Yan, NY)

Petersburg Public Library
(Petersburg, IL)

APPENDIX C

Petros Public Library
(Petros, TN)

Phoenix Public Library
(Phoenix, AZ)

Pike County Public Library
(Petersburg, IN)

Plainville Public Library
(Plainville, CT)

Pleasant Valley Free Library
(Pleasant Valley, NY)

Port Ewan Public Library
(Port Ewan, NY)

Portland Public Library
(Portland, CT)

Potomac Public Library
(Potomac, IL)

Rapid City Public Library
(Rapid City, SD)

Richmond Memorial Library
(Batavia, NY)

Ridgefield Library & Historical Association
(Ridgefield, CT)

Roddenberry Public Library
(Cairo, GA)

Salem Public Library
(Salem, OR)

Scott County Public Library
(Oneida, TN)

Seekonk Public Library
(Seekonk, MA)

Seminole Public Library
(Seminole, OK)

Shelbyville Shelby County Public Library
(Shelbyville, IN)

Sherburne Memorial Library
(Killington, VT)

Simsbury Public Library
(Simsbury, CT)

Smithtown Library
(Smithtown, NY)

Somerville–Fayette County Library
(Somerville, TN)

South Burlington Community Library
(South Burlington, VT)

Southbury Public Library
(Southbury, CT)

Southeast Arkansas Regional Library
(Monticello, AR)

Springfield Town Library
(Springfield, VT)

Sumter County Library
(Sumter, SC)

Tellico Plains Public Library
(Tellico Plains, TN)

Thetford Town Library
(Thetford, VT)

Thomas Crane Public Library
(Quincy, MA)

Tolland Public Library
(Tolland, CT)

Venice Public Library
(Venice, FL)

Ventura County Library Service Agency
(Ventura, CA)

Vespasian Warner Public Library
(Clinton, IL)

Viborg Public Library
(Viborg, SD)

Victoria Public Library
(Victoria, TX)

Vigo County Public Library
(Terre Haute, IN)

Vonore Public Library
(Vonore, TN)

Wakarusa Public Library
(Wakarusa, IN)

Washington Township Public Library
(Lynn, IN)

Webster Public Library
(Webster, SD)

West Lebanon Pike Township Public Library
(West Lebanon, IN)

West Texas Library System
(Lubbock, TX)

Westchester Public Library
(Chesterton, IN)

Westfield Public Library
(Westfield, IN)

Westville Public Library
(Westville, IL)

White Pine Public Library
(White Pine, TN)

Willard Library
(Evansville, IN)

Appendix D

Problems Encountered During Use of Planning and Role-Setting Manual

The following problems experienced by librarians during their use of the planning and role-setting manual were either published in the literature or supplied by the librarians in answer to the author's request to relate the most significant problems they encountered:

General

- Did not understand exactly what was expected at beginning.
- Had problems adapting the process to meet their libraries' needs and limited resources.
- Discussion of levels of effort more confusing than helpful.
- Difficult to select a level because uncomfortable not making all-out effort, but recognized limited capacity to do so.
- Minimal level was too complex and intensive.
- Difficulty of keeping to basic level of effort.

Time and Timing

- Amount of time required.
- Did not devote sufficient time for the process.
- Either took too much time or spread process over too great a period of time.

Data Collection

- Conducting surveys prior to forming a planning committee was a mistake.
- Data collection phase took too long.
- Amount of data suggested for comprehensive level not needed.

192 STEPHENS

- Determining amount of data to collect.
- Developing useful and meaningful surveys.
- Finding time to conduct surveys and compile data.
- Acquiring meaningful information from performance measures.
- Having to go to another source for guidance.
- Being disgruntled over committee's heavy reliance on survey data.
- Devoting so much effort to data collection that there was less energy for planning.
- Finding it difficult to collect some of the internal statistics without automation.

Roles and Mission Statement

- Roles' titles confusing and misleading and their definitions unclear, too vague, or too rigid and narrow, with too much overlap among various roles.
- Trouble understanding the scope of certain roles.
- Unable to articulate roles so that everyone had the same understanding or vision, making it difficult to bring staff and citizens to a common understanding.
- Concerned that there was no "children's role."
- Making roles fit, or adapting them to fit, library's specific needs.
- Applying roles to library systems.
- Seeing a relationship between roles and action.
- Linking role selection and resource allocation.
- Concept of designating two percent of points allotted for roles not chosen as primary or secondary confusing.
- Felt library's roles were based on preconceived notions because role-setting exercise done too early.
- Limiting the number of roles chosen.
- Chose too many roles.
- Limiting library to two roles not possible or appropriate.
- Roles often needed to be adapted to local priorities.

Goals, Objectives, and Activities

- Underestimating time and effort required for goals and objectives setting.
- Distinguishing between, writing, and developing time frames for goals and objectives.
- Difficult to select activities, translate objectives into action, and develop adequate staffing and budgets to accomplish objectives.
- Neglected to write objectives for goals.
- Plans and completion dates established with no regard to the budgeting cycle.

Planning Document

- Difficult to write planning document.
- Manual offered very little help in writing and selling library's long-range plan.
- Writing library's plan took far too long.

Leadership

- Director played too passive a role, turning leadership over to committee chair (plans were made without considering his recommendations).

- Director had to play too strong a role in process.

Staff Involvement

- Needed greater involvement of library staff members in the process; commitment to achieving goals and objectives was minimal because staff was not involved in all aspects.
- Hard to get involvment other than verbal opinions from staff.
- High levels of staff involvement time-consuming.

Citizen Involvement

- Boards lacked interest in process, lacked time and inclination to study manual, found manual too technical and detailed and process too complex, and were too impatient to do what 'the book' says.
- Needed greater cooperation, participation, support, and enthusiasm from board members.
- Needed more preparation and education for board members.
- Lack of interest of citizens and local government representatives and problems getting local government participation.
- Manual has limited references to techniques for involving community and its information is difficult to simplify for the public.
- Difficult to educate uninformed citizens and to convey enough information about library and process quickly enough for citizens to be confident and contributing members.
- Citizen group selected inappropriate roles.
- Difficulty of dealing with the public when you stop being what you've always been and move towards something new and different.

Appendix E

Librarians' Suggestions for Improved Use of the Planning Process

The following suggestions were either published in the literature or provided by the librarians surveyed by the author when asked what they wished they had done differently:

General

- Must have the following to be successful:
  - support by management and supervision by a planning coordinator.
  - a process tailored to the local environment.
  - a solid foundation and an orderly structure (events clearly scheduled, meetings at appropriate times, follow-through, staff receipt of planning information).
  - appropriate involvement of staff at all levels.
  - a means of overcoming resistance to long-range thinking (good organization, balanced attention to both immediate and long term problems, and good communication).
  - specific, implementable goals.

Timing

- Complete the process more quickly with steps close together and few interruptions.
- Set time limits for each phase (start with one-day 'mini' version limited to writing goals, objectives, and time lines followed the next year by a fuller version).
- Try to develop roles, mission, and goals and objectives in an intense three-day period.
- Planning committee meetings should be held separately from regular board meetings, scheduled fairly close together, and last at least, but not more than two hours.

Preplanning

- Carefully consider amount of time required.

- Be realistic about whether the results of working at a basic level will be satisfactory.
- Obtain funding for consultants' and specialists' services.
- Form a task force to plan for the process.
- Create a "more hospitable planning culture."
- Secure community support.
- Educate the board, staff, and planning committee members about the planning process.
- Study the manual closely and have planning participants do likewise.
- Provide participants with extensive orientation so they feel more comfortable about contributing.
- Inform committee members about the need for continued involvement, a written document, and follow-up activities.

Data Collection

- Conduct surveys of library users, citizens, and local government officials.
- Develop professionally designed and conducted surveys.
- Research projected demographic changes.
- Examine policies and long-range plans of other libraries.
- Gather more statistics.
- Sample for output measures and develop valid ones.
- Make use of library measures and budget information.
- Pay attention to regional and economic factors.
- Get more input by increasing public awareness and interest by surveys, using focus groups, and holding town meetings.
- Devote less time and effort to data collection.
- Combine surveys.
- Develop shorter surveys aimed specifically at one or two items.
- Use fewer surveys spread over a longer time period.

Roles and Mission Statement

- Devote adequate time and effort to discussing roles.
- Spend time thinking about appropriate roles and adapting them to local communities, developing unique roles, and defining the roles for all persons involved.
- Pay more attention to library size and potential.
- Involve staff and public in role setting.
- Clarify the respective responsibilities of a central library and its branches.
- Give greater consideration to resource implications and funding.
- Development of mission statements should be saved until late in the process.

Goals, Objectives, Activities

- Develop more focused and more precisely defined goals.
- Spend more time writing objectives.
- Involve planning committees more.
- Have a more extensive review of goals.
- Devote more time and effort to developing activities to accomplish goals and objectives.

- Develop activities more fully.
- Select several alternatives for each objective.
- Draw up a time line and assign staff responsibilites.
- Proceed immediately into the "taking action" phase after developing goals and objectives.
- Emphasize developing financial strategies more.
- Give more training in creating specific action plans to carry out goals and objectives.
- Plans should be tied to yearly budget cycles.

Planning Document

- Have an idea of the end product desired.
- Allow more time for writing the planning document.
- Prepare brief, professionally prepared planning documents for commumnicating with libraries' external environments.
- Make planning documents more appealing or self-explanatory and capable of being used with the public and local government officials.
- Create a more definitive, more comprehensive and action-oriented plan, a working document rather than a PR piece.

Leadership

- Use an objective facilitator to lead the committee through the process (library staff, Friends, and board are too close to the issue to ask objective questions).
- Committee should be led by someone other than the director.
- Directors should assume responsibility for the process.
- Use a facilitator.
- Hire consultants, use consultants more, and work more closely with consultants.
- Assign a staff member and provide adequate release time.
- Have a strong leader, one with skill in group process.
- Keep leadership within the staff and board; involve public in studies and task forces instead of steering of process.

Staff Involvement

- Staff and citizen input is crucial.
- Ask each department to present a review of the library's existing services and programs.
- Educate staff that not all ideas will be included in the written plan and that everything is not going to be implemented in the first one or two years.
- Provide more training for managerial staff unfamiliar with planning and making conceptual decisions.

Citizen Involvement

- Have greater involvement of citizens.
- Staff and citizen input is crucial.
- Form citizen planning committees or add citizens to staff committees.
- Involve a broad spectrum of the public.

- Involve the "general public," "ordinary citizens," and library non-users, as well as representatives from business, education, local agencies and clubs, and the media.
- Increase involvement of local government officials.
- Start out with a larger number on planning committee because of "dropouts and erratic attendance."
- Develop a mechanism to replace committee members who resign.
- Inform citizens of their libraries' planning efforts.
- Increase publicity aimed at local government officials.

Appendix F

Suggestions for Improving *Planning and Role Setting for Public Libraries*

The following suggestions for improving the planning and role-setting manual were either published in the literature or supplied by the librarians in answer to the author's request:

Levels of Effort
- Present the three levels separately.
- Scale down the intensive level.
- Present the levels as a checklist from which to choose committee activities.

Looking Around (Data Collection)
- More help with development of surveys.
- More information on surveying, simple statistical measures, sampling, and data collection.
- Emphasize surveys of library users with detailed questions and open-ended questions.
- Examples of surveys designed for rural small and medium-sized libraries.
- Sample community surveys, especially telephone surveys.
- Suggestions on how to set up data electronically and manipulate data for various kind of reports.
- Samples of interviews for a process that is trying to get as much public input as possible.
- Help with an open-ended user opinion survey.
- Focus on information that is easily and accurately collected.
- Revise data collection to increase validity.
- Give workable methods for libraries with little staff and money to use to collect

statistics.
- Include ditto forms to use with suggestion boxes.
- Recommend the use of focus groups and panel interviews.
- Offer help dealing with multi-library systems such as a work sheet for looking-around statistics.
- Emphasize the possibility of making judgments in the context of a library cooperative (highlight in the looking around section).
- Include section on assessing other library services available in area.
- In a separate publication summarize research most relevant to design of services (income, education, library use, community profile-related data compared to library use).

Mission Statement, Goals and Objectives
- Include more examples of mission statements and how to write them.
- Offer more help with writing goals and objectives, including examples.

Planning Document
- Give specific examples of what completed documents could look like; samples of actual planning documents.
- Give ideas of ways of presenting the plan with hints on how to sell it including public relations materials such as sample letters and speeches to commissioners, teachers, and businesses to present along with plan.
- Include more information on how to lobby government bodies such as city councils.
- Include section on reviewing former planning documents to evaluate what was done in the past and integrate what still needs addressing into a new planning process.
- Information on budget development from long-range plan.

Citizen Involvement/Planning Committee
- Offer more help with use of a planning committee, such as selection of citizen members and information on group dynamics, facilitating group decision making, how to run meetings.
- Expand the information on educating planning participants, including how to structure a workshop for citizen members.
- Acknowledge the role of hidden agendas and personal beliefs in blocking full discussion and/or reaching consensus and practical solutions to such political problems.
- Discuss methods to engage the community in decision making, with examples or citations to helpful resources.

Roles
- Be more explicit in the ideas for roles.
- Take another look at the roles (labels and content).
- Rethink roles a bit—for small libraries the concept of Gateway to Information is very useful (Inter Library Loan).
- Use less jargon (make names of roles simpler and more self-explanatory).

- Discuss how libraries handle choice of roles.
- Expand information about the roles (some people created alternate roles because they didn't understand some of the ones given).
- Provide more information on what selecting a particular role will cost vis a vis other roles (how staffing needs will change etc.).
- Include more examples of services relating to specific roles.
- A detailing of pro & con arguments could be included as a spur to thinking. Also, a view of the tradeoffs that might be involved in choosing one role and forgoing another, e.g., what segment of users stand, theoretically, to lose out if "scholar's resource" is not chosen.
- Include statements from libraries that have chosen certain roles explaining the philosophical basis for their choice (or non-choice).
- More advice or discussion or explanation on collections (size, types) would be beneficial.
- Perhaps more roles might be provided.
- Have a one or two page summary of the public library roles so committee members can study them more thoroughly than the block summary in Figure 11 (McClure et al., 1987, p. 28), without having to jump back and forth among the eight pages that describe the roles.
- Use a chart or graph or other means to show the overlapping parts of some of the roles while emphasizing the major concepts that differentiate roles.
- There need to be some added steps at the beginning—before developing roles and missions. 1) Develop a list of assumptions about your community/library for period covered—what the committee expects the community to do (grow, decrease), the tax base, the service areas, state support, etc. 2) Develop a list of values that group agrees on. This helps later on so that you are not bickering over value-based questions—Does library provide all formats? Will all services remain free? Will you encourage input from public?
- To better prepare committee members for Workform E, have a worksheet on Understanding Library Roles in the Local Setting, where current activities in each role could be listed and relative concentration of resources discussed. This might facilitate the assignment of point values and provide helpful perspective for later goal/objective preparation.
- Roles should be library-specific.
- Make roles less rigid.
- Some libraries seemed to feel the roles were set in concrete or "ordained" by PLA. Allow libraries to create their own roles.
- Encourage individual interpretation and clarification.
- Have either clearer "role" definition or a looser way to redefine based on specific community needs.
- Include more discussion on how roles might be modified or blended in your particular library.
- Stress the importance of using the roles as defined, if possible, to enhance communication between libraries.
- Need better guidelines to develop different goals and roles for branches and main library.
- Need better guidelines when writing mission statement to cover roles for different

types of service outlets.
- Have more content for system role setting and mission statements.
- Have planning roles for larger systems and different roles for smaller libraries.
- Because branches play roles different from the central library, roles differ. Cannot be writing several documents. This must be addressed.

Preschoolers Door to Learning
- Need broader definition of Preschoolers Door to Learning.
- Amend role to include children K–6.
- Revise to include primary-age (K–2nd grade) children.
- Clarify a concept for children—it is not enough to say all roles (i.e., popular materials library equals Sweet Valley High) apply to children.
- Perhaps emphasize more the fact that young adults and children can fit into most roles.

Reference Library/Independent Learning Center
- Need a category that approaches the historical idea of "People's University," which is practical for smaller, isolated communities (Research Center and Independent Learning Center do not approach the scope of community libraries that try to balance some classics with newer fiction and nonfiction).
- Reference library seems to be a relative term for smaller libraries, often confused with Research Center. Perhaps combine the two.

Author Index

A
Adams, J.E., 14, 47, *153*
Allen, C., 74, 75, *154*
Altman, E., 8, *154*
Ang, J.S., 2, *153*
Anthony, C.A., 62, *153*

B
Baker, J., 71, 88, *153*
Balcom, K.M., 60, *153*
Barrish, C., 72, 88, *153*
Beasley, K.E., 8, *153, 154*
Bellassai, M.C., 7, 10, 12, 23, 26, 51, 53, 57, 58, 69, *153, 156*
Betz-Zall, J., 15, 16, 48, *153*
Blasingame, R., 9, *153*
Bloss, M., 8, *153*
Bone, L., 8, *153*
Boyhin, J.F., Jr., 5, *156*
Bremer, S., 133, *154*

C
Carr, M., 16, *154*
Carrigan, D., 72, 88, *153*
Childers, T., 146, 147, *154*
Chislett, P., 16, *154*
Chua, J.H., 2, *153*
Conroy, B., 52, *154*
Cronin, M.J., 6, *154*
Crum, N., 8, *154*

D
Davoren, D., 15, 47, *154*
D'Elia, G., 72, 75, 89, 139, 145, *154*
DeProspo, E., *154*
Detweiller, M.J., 13, 46, 52, *154*
DeWath, H., 7, 10, 12, 23, 26, 53, 57, 58, 69, *156*
Drucker, P., 1, 2, *154*
Duquette, D., 14, *154*
Durrance, J.C., 74, 75, *154*

E
Evans, G.E., 3, *154*

F
Friedman, N., 15, *154*

G
Garrison, G., 8, *154*
Gault, R., 52, *155*
Givens, J., 5, *156*

H
Halliday, J., 16, 48, *155*
Harris, R.B., 14, 47, *155*
Hawgood, J., 50, *155*
Heim, K.M., 13, *155*
Hiatt, P., 8, *155*
Hopper, L., 71, 88, *155*
Hunt, S.P., 14, 47, *155*

J
Jay, H., 7, *158*
Johnson, D.W., 2, 145, 146, *155, 158*

K
Kemper, R., 3, *155*

L
Liesner, W., 6, *155*
Lynch, M.J., 4, 9, 10, 12, 49, 52, 57, 58, 61, 62, 64, 65, 66, 67, 68, 69, 76, 85, 86, 125, 136, 140, 141, 143, 144, 147, 153, *155, 157*

M
Mann, S.H., 5, *155*
Martin, A.B., 7, 8, *155*
Martin, L., 8, *156*
McClure, C.R., 3, 4, 5, 6, 57, 58, 61, 62, 64, 65, 66, 67, 68, 69, 76, 85, 86, 125, 136, 140, 141, 143, 144, 147, *155, 157, 158*
McKay, D., 50, *155*

Metz, R.F., 71, 88, 114, *156*
Miller, L.R., 71, 88, *156*
Morein, P.G., 5, *156*
Morey, G., 8, *156*

O
Owen, A., 4, 57, 58, 61, 62, 64, 65, 66, 67, 68, 69, 76, 85, 86, 125, 136, 140, 141, 143, 144, 145, 147, *155*

P
Palmour, V., 7, 10, 12, 23, 26, 49, 53, 57, 58, 69, *156*
Pungitore, V., 13, 58, 62, 68, 69, 72, 89, 114, *156*

Q
Quinn, J., 72, 88, *156*

R
Richmond, E., 73, *156*
Riggs, D.E., *156*
Robbins, J., 145, 146, 147, *158*
Rodger, E.J., 4, 72, 89, *154*
Rogers, 72, 88, *156, 157*
Rohlf, R., 50, *156*
Rossiter, M.D., *155*
Ruccio, N.C., 50, *156*

S
Sager, D., 53, *156*
Scarborough, K.I.A., 71, 88, 114, *156*
Schremser, D.B., 15, 47, *157*
Sertic, K., 14, 47, *157*
Shearer, K., 75, 76, *157*
Sheldon, B.E., 73, *157*
Sinclair, D., 50, *157*
Sitts, M.R., 5, *156*

Smith, C., 74, *157*
Smith, N., 4, 68, 69, *157*
Soltys, A., 16, *154*
Speer, R., 14, 47, *157*
Stephens, A.K., *157*
Sutton, B., 72, 115, *157*

T
Tooker, B., *157*
Turock, B., 51, *157*

V
Van House, N., 4, 6, 57, 58, 61, 62, 64, 65, 66, 67, 68, 69, 71, 76, 85, 86, 88, 114, 125, 136, 140, 141, 143, 144, 146, 147, *154, 155, 156, 157*

W
Wallace, D.P., 13, *155*
Webster, D.E., 5, *156, 157*
Weil, B.T., 6, 58, *157*
Welles, G., 47, *157*
Wells, H., 5, *156*
White, B., 16, *158*
White, L., 47, *158*
Whittaker, J., 2, *158*
Wiese, J., *154*
Wight, E.A., 7, *158*
Williams, P., 52, 72, 89, *154, 158*

Y
Yesner, B.L., 7, *158*

Z
Zweizig, D.L., 4, 57, 58, 61, 62, 64, 64, 66, 67, 68, 69, 76, 85, 86, 125, 136, 140, 141, 143, 144, 145, 146, 147, *155, 157, 158*

Subject Index

A

Academic Library Development Program (Morein et al.), 5
Academic Library Program, 5
Activities, *see* Strategies (actions/activities)
Adapting PRS, 66, 76, 79, 114, 115, 119, 121, 125, 133, 137, 141, 152, 191, 195, *see also* Flexibility
A Planning Process for Public Libraries (APP); *see* Articles about manuals; Benefits of using manuals; Budget increases and reallocations; Citizen involvement; Comparison of APP and PRS; Criticisms of manuals; Data collection (looking around); Description; Development of process and manuals; Directors; Dissemination; Evaluation (review) of process and plan; Flexibility; Friends of the Library; Goals and objectives; Government officials; Funding; Implementation, assigned responsibility for; Leadership; Lessons Learned from use of APP; Libraries studied by author; Participants; Planning committee; Preplanning (planning to plan); Problems experienced in using manuals; Publicity about process and plan; Revising manuals, recommendations for; Roles and mission; Satisfaction with use of planning processes; Staff involvement; Strategies (actions/activities); Time and timing; Trustee development; Trustee involvement; Use of manuals, extent of
Articles about manuals
   APP, 12–17, 46–53
   PRS, 60, 62, 68, 69, 71–76, 88, 89, 114, 115
Aspects of PRS, extent used by libraries, 78–81
   aspect used least, 78, 80
   aspect used most, 78
   citizen involvement, 78, 116, 117
   data collection (looking around), 79, 80, 117
   evaluation (review) of process and plan, 80, 116, 117
   goals and objectives, 79, 80, 117
   implementation, assigned responsibility for, 80
   level of effort, 78–80
   output measures, 79, 80
   planning committee, 77, 80
   planning document, writing 80, 116, 117
   preplanning (planning to plan), 117
   publicity about process and plan, 116, 117
   roles and mission, 79, 80, 117
   staff involvement, 117
   strategies (actions/activities), 79, 80, 116, 117
Automation, 14, 20, 93, 96, 108, 151

B

Benefits of using manuals, *see also* Satisfaction with use of planning processes
   APP, 13–17, 18, 21–23, 28–30, 40, 44–46, 53, 54, 56
   PRS, 71–73, 88–108, 112, 151
      automation, 93, 96, 108, 151
      budget increases and reallocations, 88, 90, 91, 94, 100–102
      buildings, 88, 89, 107, 108
      changes in collections, 88, 89, 91, 93–95
      changes in policies and procedures, 88–91
      changes in services, 88–91, 95–97
      communication between administration and staff, 88, 90, 91, 97, 151
      community awareness about library, 90, 91, 97
      community involvement with library, 88, 98, 99

205

direction and focus, 88, 89, 104
increased circulation, 90, 91, 151
increased number of registered borrowers, 90, 91, 151
increased program attendance, 90, 91
increased reference questions, 90, 91, 151
new directors, 102
planning and evaluation, 73, 88, 89, 92, 99, 102–105, 151
relationship with local officials, 89–91, 100
staff development, 89, 94, 106, 107
staff morale, 88–91, 99
trustee development, 105, 106
Board members, *see* Trustee development; Trustee involvement
Budget increases and reallocations, 13, 17, 22, 88, 90, 91, 94, 100–102, 107–109
Buildings, 13, 14, 16, 20, 21, 88, 89, 107, 108

C

Changes, *see* Benefits of using manuals
Charts and figures, *see* Workforms and other charts and figures
Circulation, 90, 91, 151
Citizen involvement, *see also* Participants; Planning committee
  APP, 10–14, 18–22, 28–30, 43–48, 51, 54–56
  PRS, 99
    extent used, 78, 116, 117
    level of effort, 84
    manual's helpfulness, 124, 130–131, 146
    problems with, 110, 124–126, 193
    rec. for revising, 134, 147, 200
    rec. for using, 110, 114, 119–121, 124–128, 197, 198
    satisfaction with, 88, 116, 117
Collections, *see* Materials
Communication between administration and staff, 88, 90, 91, 97, 151
Community analysis, *see* Data collection (looking around)
Community awareness and involvement with library, 14, 22, 23, 48, 88, 90, 91, 97, 98, 99
Comparison of APP and PRS, 60, 64–68
Components, *see* Aspects of PRS, extent of use by libraries
Comprehensive planning, *see* Long-range planning

Consultants, 34, 47, 49, 53, 54, 78, 114, 123, 127, 134, 196, 197
Criticisms of manuals, *see also* Articles about manuals; Information in PRS, helpfulness of; Problems experienced in using manuals
  APP, 15, 16, 46, 50–52
  PRS, 73, 76, 109–111, 128, 132, 136, 137, 149, 152
Cutbacks, *see* Budget increases and reallocations; Funding, for plan

D

Data collection (looking around)
  APP, 10, 11, 13–16, 18–23, 33, 34, 46–49, 51, 52, 55
  PRS, 63, 67, 72, 82, 99
    extent used, 79, 80, 117
    level of effort, 82, 84
    manual's helpfulness, 129, 131
    problems with, 111, 114, 120, 121, 125, 191, 192
    rec. for revising, 76, 134, 135, 139, 199, 200
    rec. for using, 73, 114, 120, 121, 126, 127, 196
    satisfaction with, 88, 103, 116, 117
Description, *see also* Comparison of APP and PRS
  APP, 10–12, 50, 51, 53
  PRS, 62–64
Development of process and manuals
  APP, 7–10
  PRS, 60–62
Developing roles and mission, *see* Roles and mission
Developing strategies, *see* Strategies (actions/activities)
Difficulties in using manuals, *see* Problems experienced in using manuals
Direction and focus, 13, 17, 22, 88, 89, 104, *see also* Vision
Directors, 21, 22, 55, 77, 114, 123, 138, 192, 193, 197
  new, 102
Dissemination
  APP, 12, 68
  PRS, 68–69

E

Evaluating Library Programs and Services: Tell It (Zweizig et al.), 145–147

SUBJECT INDEX 207

Evaluation (review) of process and plan
  APP, 11, 12, 18, 20, 49
  PRS, 63
    extent used, 80, 116, 117
    level of effort, 83, 84
    manual's helpfulness, 130, 131
    rec. for using, 128
    rec. for revising, 146
    satisfaction with, 116, 117
Extent of use by libraries, *see* Use of manuals, extent of

F
Flexibility,
  APP, 56
  PRS, 66, 78, 81, 133, *see also* Adapting PRS
Format and language, 62–64
  problems with, 111, 128
  rec. for revising, 111, 128, 132–134, 137–139, 147, 148, 199–201
Friends of the Library, 16, 18–20, 78, 98
Funding
  APP, 27, 28, 34, 54
  PRS, 61, *see also* Budget increases and reallocations
    for plan, 101, 102, 111, 114, 121, 122, 138, 146, 200
    for process, 54, 67, 114, 126, 127, 139, 196

G
Goals and Guidelines for Community Library Services, 9
Goals and objectives
  APP, 10, 11, 15, 16, 18–22, 47, 35, 36
  PRS, 63, 66, 68
    extent used, 79, 80
    level of effort expended, 82, 84
    manual's helpfulness, 129, 131
    problems with, 111, 114, 121, 122, 126, 192
    rec. for using, 115, 122, 128, 195, 196
    rec. for revising, 133, 136, 137, 145, 146, 200
    satisfaction with, 105, 115, 117
Goals, Guidelines and Standards Committee, *see* PLA Goals, Guidelines and Standards Committee
Government officials, *see also* Budget increases and reallocations; Funding, for plan
  APP, 14, 16, 18–20, 22, 23, 27, 28,
    43–47, 54–56
  PRS, 78, 88, 89–91, 100, 101, 108, 109, 120, 122, 124, 128, 137, 198
Grant-writing, *see* Budget increases and reallocations
Guidelines for planners, *see* Use of PRS, recommendations for improving

H
History, *see* Development of process and manuals

I
Impact, negative, *see* Problems experienced in using manuals
Impact, positive, *see* Benefits of using manuals
Implementation, assigned responsibility for, 11, 18, 20, 80, 126, 128, 197
Information in PRS, helpfulness of, 129–132, 148, 149
  citizen involvement, 124, 130–131, 146
  data collection (looking around), 120, 129, 131
  evaluation (review) of process and plan, 130, 131
  goals and objectives, 122, 129, 131
  level of effort, 114, 120, 125, 130, 131, 134
  planning committee, 124, 129, 131
  planning document, writing, 122, 129, 131
  publicity about process and plan, 147
  roles and mission, 121, 129, 131
  strategies (actions/activities), 129, 130
  staff involvement, 130, 131, 137
  workforms and other charts and figures, 130, 131, 197
Information Power: Guidelines for School Library Media Programs (American Association of School Librarians), 6
Informing public, *see* Publicity about process and plan
Interviews and surveys, *see* Data collection (looking around)
Involving public, *see* Citizen Involvement
Involving staff, *see* Staff Involvement

K
King Research, 9

L
Leadership
  APP, 18, 27, 31–33, 55

PRS, 78
  problems with, 114, 123, 126, 192, 193
  rec. for using, 114, 115, 123, 126, 127, 195, 197
  rec. for revising, 134, 138
Lessons learned from use of APP, 26–56
Levels of effort, 66, 81–85
  expended for overall process, 81, 84
  expended for each step, 81–85
  extent used, 78–80
  manual's helpfulness, 114, 120, 125, 130, 131, 134
  problems with, 114, 120, 125, 134, 191
  rec. for using, 114, 138, 146
  rec. for revising, 134, 137, 138, 199
  satisfaction with, 81–84
Libraries studied by author
  APP
    Library A, 17, 18–19, 21–22, 27–38, 41–44
    Library B, 17, 19–20, 22, 27–36, 38–46
    Library C, 17, 20–23, 28, 32, 33
  PRS, 76, 77–85, 89–112, 115–126, 128–138, 183–202
Library systems, *see* Systems
Local government officials, *see* Government officials
Long-range planning
  academic libraries, 5, 6
    criticisms of, 5
    tools for planning, 5, 6
  business planning, 1, 2
  public libraries (pre APP), 7, 8
  rationale for, 1–3
  school library media centers, 6, 7
    tools for planning, 6, 7
  special libraries, 3
  statewide, 3, 4,
Long Range Planning: A How to Do It Manual for Public Libraries (Bremer), 133
Looking around, *see* Data collection (looking around)

M
Management Review Analysis Program (Webster), 5
Manuals, extent of use, *see* Use of manuals, extent of
Materials, 20, 22, 88, 89–91, 93–95
Measurement of Effectiveness of Public Library Service (Beasley), 8

Measuring Academic Library Performance (Van House et al.), 6
Mission statement, *see* Roles and mission
Morale, *see* Staff morale

N
New Standards Task Force, 60, 61

O
Output measures, 15, 16, 19, 63, 64, 68, 120, 135
  extent used, 79, 80
  problems with, 110, 120,
  rec. for using, 120
  rec. for revising, 134, 135, 137
Output Measures for Public Libraries (Van House et al.), 59

P
Participants, *see also* Citizen involvement; Leadership; Planning committee; Staff involvement
  APP, 10, 12, 28–46, 55, 56
  PRS, 67, 77, 78, 119, 123–128, 134, 146, 147, 192, 193, 197, 198, 200
Performance Measurement for Public Services in Academic and Research Libraries (Cronin), 6
Performance measures, *see* Output measures
PLA Goals, Guidelines and Standards Committee, 8, 9, 60, 62
Plan, review of, *see* Evaluation (review) of process and plan
Planners, *see* Participants
Planning and evaluation, 73, 76, 88, 89, 92, 99, 102–105, 151
Planning and Role Setting for Public Libraries (PRS), *see* Adapting PRS; Articles about manuals; Aspects of PRS, extent used by libraries; Benefits of using manuals; Citizen involvement; Comparison of APP and PRS; Consultants; Criticisms of manuals; Data collection (looking around); Description; Development of process and manual; Directors; Dissemination; Evaluation (review) of process and plan; Flexibility; Format; Friends of the Library; Funding; Goals and objectives; Government officials; Implementation, assigned responsibility for; Information in

PRS, helpfulness of; Leadership;
Levels of effort; Libraries studied by
author; Output measures;
Participants; Planning committee;
Planning document, writing;
Preplanning (planning to plan);
Problems experienced in using manuals; Publicity about process and plan;
Revising manuals, recommendations
for; Roles and mission; Satisfaction
with use of manuals; Staff involvement; Strategies (actions/activities);
Time and timing; Trustee development; Trustee involvement; Use of
manuals, extent of; Use of PRS, recommendations for improving;
Vision; Workforms and other charts
and figures
Planning Committee, see also Leadership;
Participants
APP, 10–12, 28–32, 46, 47, 48, 49, 51, 53–54
PRS, 64, 67, 77–78
  extent used, 77, 80
  manual's helpfulness, 129, 131
  problems with, 124, 193
  rec. for using, 119, 122–125, 127, 197, 198
  rec. for revising, 134, 146, 147, 200
Planning components, see Aspects of PRS, extent used by libraries
Planning document, writing, 63, 99
  extent used, 80, 116, 117
  level of effort, 82–84
  manual's helpfulness, 122, 129, 131, 192
  problems with, 122, 126, 192
  rec. for using, 114, 122, 128, 197
  rec. for revising, 137, 146, 200
  satisfaction with, 99, 115–117
Planning manuals, extent of use, see Use of manuals, extent of
Planning Participants, see Participants
Planning Program for Small Academic Libraries (Morein et al.), 5
Planning steps, see Aspects of PRS, extent used by libraries; Description (PRS)
Planning to plan, see Preplanning (planning to plan)
Policies and procedures, 88, 90, 91, 93, 94
Population studied by author, see Libraries studied by author
Preplanning (planning to plan)
  APP, 10, 14, 18–20, 26–28, 47–49, 54, 55

PRS, 62, 67
  extent used, 81, 117
  level of effort expended, 81, 84
  problems with, 119, 125
  rec. for using, 119, 126, 127, 196
  rec. for revising, 138, 139
  satisfaction with, 116, 117
Printed sources and statistics, see Data collection (looking around)
Problems experienced in using manuals, see also Criticisms
  APP, 13–15, 18, 19, 21, 22, 27, 28, 31–37, 41, 46, 49, 51, 54, 60
  PRS 108–112, 115, 117–126, 148, 149, 152, 191, 193
    citizen involvement, 110, 124–126, 193
    data collection (looking around), 111, 114, 120, 121, 125, 191, 192
    format, 111, 128
    goals and objectives, 111, 114, 121, 122, 126, 192
    leadership, 114, 123, 126, 192, 193
    level of effort, 114, 120, 125, 191, 194
    planning committee, 124, 193
    planning document, 122, 126, 192
    preplanning, 119, 125
    publicity about process and plan, 126, 192
    roles and mission, 114, 121, 125, 192
    staff involvement, 109, 110, 114, 123, 193
    strategies (actions/activities), 122, 126, 192
Programs, 90, 91
Public Library Data Service *Statistical Report*, 59, 69, 70, 74, 75, 77, 144, 159–176, 183–185
Public Library Development Program, 59, 60, 62
Public relations, see Citizen involvement; Community awareness and involvement;
Publications, see Articles about manuals; Criticisms of manuals
Publicity about process and plan
  APP, 14, 15, 20, 21, 43–46, 48, 56
  PRS
    extent used, 116, 117
    level of effort, 84
    manual's helpfulness, 192
    problems with, 126, 192
    rec. for using, 124, 126–128, 197, 198

rec. for revising, 137, 146, 147, 200
  satisfaction with, 116, 117
Published reports, see Articles about manuals; Criticisms of manuals

R

Recommendations for improving, see Revising manuals, recommendations for; Use of PRS, recommendations for improving
Recommendations for revising, see Revising manuals, recommendations for
Reduced funding, see Budget increases and reallocations; Funding, for plan
Reference questions, 90, 91, 151
Registration, 90, 91, 151
Reports of planning by libraries, see Articles about manuals; Criticisms of manuals
Review, see Evaluation (review) of process and plan
Revising manuals, recommendations for
  APP, 47, 48, 50, 56, 57, 65
  PRS, 74–76, 132–148, 152, 199–202
    citizen involvement, 134, 147, 200
    data collection (looking around), 76, 134, 135, 139, 199, 200
    evaluation (review) of process and plan, 146
    format and language, 111, 128, 132–134, 137–139, 147, 148, 199–201
    goals and objectives, 133, 136, 137, 145, 146, 200
    leadership, 134, 138
    level of effort, 134, 137, 138, 199
    planning committee, 134, 146, 147, 200
    planning document, writing, 137, 146, 200
    preplanning (planning to plan), 138, 139
    publicity about process and plan, 137, 146, 147, 200
    roles and mission, 76, 121, 133–137, 139–146, 200–202
    staff involvement, 133, 138, 146, 147
    strategies (actions/activities), 146
Revision, recommendations for, see Revising manuals, recommendations for
Roles and mission
  APP, 11, 16, 18, 19, 22, 35, 36, 50, 52, 56
  PRS, 63, 67, 68, 71, 74–76, 79, 82, 94–98
    extent used, 79, 80
    level of effort expended, 82, 84, 117
    manual's helpfulness, 121, 129, 131, 196

problems with, 114, 121, 125, 192
rec. for using, 114, 119, 121, 127, 196
rec. for revising, 76, 121, 133–137, 139–146, 200–202
satisfaction with, 104, 105, 115, 117

S

Satisfaction with use of planning processes, see also Benefits of using manuals
  APP, 13–17, 22, 41, 46
  PRS, 114–118, 148, 152
    citizen involvement, 88, 116, 117
    data collection (looking around), 103, 116, 117
    evaluation (review) of process and plan, 116, 117
    goals and objectives, 105, 115, 117
    level of effort, 81–84
    overall process, 115, 117
    planning document, 99, 115, 117
    preplanning (planning to plan), 116, 117
    publicity about process and plan, 116, 117
    roles and mission, 104, 105, 115, 117
    staff involvement 106, 107, 116, 117
    strategies (actions/activities), 115–117
School Administrators' Guide to Evaluating School Media Programs (Yesner & Jay), 6, 7
Selecting activities, see Strategies (actions/activities)
Services, 16, 18–23, 47, 51, 88, 89, 91, 95–97, 99, 127, 128, 140, 145, 201
Small libraries, 53, 60, 72, 111, 119, 125, 133, 147
Staff development, 13, 14, 22, 23, 40, 56, 89, 92, 94, 106, 107
Staff involvement, see also Participants; Planning committee
  APP, 14, 18–21, 36–43, 46–49, 51, 52, 56
  PRS, 77, 78, 106, 107
    extent used, 77, 78, 117
    level of effort, 83, 84
    manual's helpfulness, 130, 131
    problems with, 109, 110, 114, 123, 193
    rec. for using, 106, 107, 114, 115, 119, 123, 124, 126–128, 195, 197
    rec. for revising, 133, 138, 146, 147
    satisfaction with, 106, 107, 116, 117
Staff morale, 13, 88, 90, 91, 99, 110
Standards, 4, 7–9, 61, 69
Standards Committee, see PLA Goals,

SUBJECT INDEX 211

Guidelines and Standards Committee
State library agencies, *see* Dissemination; Extent of use by libraries; Long-range planning, statewide
Steps, *see* Aspects of PRS, extent used by libraries; Description (PRS)
Strategic planning, *see* Long-range planning
Strategies (actions/activities)
  APP, 11, 15, 18–20, 56
  PRS, 63, 68, 82
    extent used, 79, 80, 116, 117
    level of effort, 82, 84
    manual's helpfulness, 129, 130
    problems with, 122, 126, 192
    rec. for using, 122, 128, 196, 197
    rec. for revising, 146
    satisfaction with, 115–117
Strategy for Public Library Change: Proposed Library Goals Feasibility Study (Martin), 8
Suggestions for improving, *see* Revising manuals, recommendations for; Use of PRS, recommendations for improving
Survey population, *see* Libraries studied by author
Surveys, *see* Data collection (looking around)
Systematic Process for Planning Media Programs (Liesener), 6
Systems, 73, 77, 119, 121, 133, 142, 143, 146, 147, 192, 202

T

Taking action, *see* Strategies (actions/activites)
Time and timing
  APP, 13, 14, 16, 18, 20, 46, 56
  PRS, 110, 114, 115, 118–122, 125, 127, 133, 138, 191, 195, 196
Total Community Library Service (Garrison), 8
Trustee development, 22, 30, 47, 105, 106
Trustee involvement
  APP, 20, 30, 46, 47, 55
  PRS, 77, 78, 105, 106, 109, 110, 119, 123, 126, 127, 138, 193, 197

U

Use of PRS, recommendations for improving, 73, 126–128, *see also* Articles about manuals; Lessons learned from use of APP

citizen involvement, 111, 114, 119–121, 124–128, 197, 198
data collection (looking around), 73, 74, 120, 121, 126, 127, 196
evaluation (review of process and plan), 128
goals and objectives, 115, 122, 128, 195, 196
leadership, 114, 115, 123, 126, 127, 195, 197
level of effort, 114
planning committee, 119, 122–125, 127, 197, 198
planning document, 114, 122, 128, 197
preplanning (planning to plan), 119, 126, 127, 196
publicity about process and plan, 124, 126–128, 197, 198
roles and mission, 75, 114, 119, 121, 127, 196
staff involvement, 107, 114, 115, 119, 123, 124, 126–128, 195, 197
strategies (actions/activities), 122, 128, 196, 197
Use of manuals, extent of
  APP, 12, 13
  PRS, 68–70
Use, recommendations for, *see* Use of PRS, recommendations for improving

V

Vision, 92, 103, 106, 111, 121
  statement, 145

W

What's Good? Describing Your Public Library's Effectiveness (Childers & Van House), 146, 147
Workforms and other charts and figures, 63–65
  manual's helpfulness, 128, 130, 131, 137
  rec. for revising, 133, 136, 137, 138, 148
Writing goals and objectives, *see* Goals and objectives
Writing the planning document *see* Planning document, writing

www.ingramcontent.com/pod-product-compliance
Lightning Source LLC
Chambersburg PA
CBHW052108300426
44116CB00010B/1585